HARVEY SACKS

HARVEY SACKS

Social Science and Conversation Analysis

David Silverman

Polity Press

First published in 1998 by Polity Press
in association with Blackwell Publishers Ltd.

Editorial office:
Polity Press
65 Bridge Street
Cambridge CB2 1UR, UK

Marketing and production:
Blackwell Publishers Ltd
108 Cowley Road
Oxford OX4 1JF, UK

ISBN 0–7456–1710–7
ISBN 0–7456–1711–5 (pbk)

A catalogue record for this book is available from the British Library.

Typeset in 10½ on 12pt Palatino
by Wearset, Boldon, Tyne and Wear.
Printed in Great Britain by MPG Books, Bodmin, Cornwall

The book is printed on acid-free paper.

Key Contempory Thinkers

Published

Jeremy Ahearne, *Michel de Certeau: Interpretation and its Other*
Peter Burke, *The French Historical Revolution: The Annales School 1929–1989*
Colin Davis, *Levinas: An Introduction*
Simon Evnine, *Donald Davidson*
Edward Fullbrook and Kate Fullbrook, *Simone de Beauvoir: A Critical
    Introduction*
Andrew Gamble, *Hayek: The Iron Cage of Liberty*
Phillip Hansen, *Hannah Arendt: Politics, History and Citizenship*
Sean Homer, *Fredric Jameson: Marxism, Hermeneutics, Postmodernism*
Christopher Hookway, *Quine: Language, Experience and Reality*
Simon Jarvis, *Adorno: A Critical Introduction*
Douglas Kellner, *Jean Baudrillard: From Marxism to Post-Modernism and Beyond*
Chandran Kukathas and Phillip Pettit, *Rawls: A Theory of Justice and its Critics*
Lois McNay, *Foucault: A Critical Introduction*
Philip Manning, *Erving Goffman and Modern Sociology*
Michael Moriarty, *Roland Barthes*
William Outhwaite, *Habermas: A Critical Introduction*
John Preston, *Feyerabend: Philosophy, Science and Society*
Susan Sellers, *Hélène Cixous: Authorship, Autobiography and Love*
David Silverman, *Harvey Sacks: Social Science and Conversation Analysis*
Georgia Warnke, *Gadamer: Hermeneutics, Tradition and Reason*
Jonathan Wolff, *Robert Nozick: Property, Justice and Minimal State*

Forthcoming

Alison Ainley, *Irigaray*
Maria Baghramian, *Hilary Putnam*
Sara Beardsworth, *Kristeva*
Michael Caesar, *Umberto Eco*
James Carey, *Innis and McLuhan*
Thomas D'Andrea, *Alasdair MacIntyre*
Eric Dunning, *Norbert Elias*
Jocelyn Dunphy, *Paul Ricoeur*
Graeme Gilloch, *Walter Benjamin*
Christina Howells, *Derrida: Deconstruction from Phenomenology to Ethics*
Paul Kelly, *Ronald Dworkin*
Valerie Kennedy, *Edward Said*
Carl Levy, *Antonio Gramsci*
Harold Noonan, *Frege*
Wes Sharrock and Rupert Read, *Kuhn*
Nick Smith, *Charles Taylor*
Geoffrey Stokes, *Popper: Philosophy, Politics and Scientific Method*
Nicholas Walker, *Heidegger*
James Williams, *Lyotard: Towards a Postmodern Philosophy*

Contents

Preface

In September 1964, after a first degree at the London School of Economics, I enrolled as a graduate student and Teaching Assistant in the Department of Sociology at the University of California, Los Angeles. By chance this coincided with Harvey Sacks's first set of lectures in this very department.

This might have offered an entirely new direction to my thought. Unfortunately, like nearly everybody else at the time, I had never heard about Sacks or his ideas. Moreover, given my background in the 'conflict' sociology then fashionable in the UK, I probably would not have been interested anyway.

A few years later, back in London, I started to read Alfred Schutz's phenomenology of the everyday world. Then, in 1971–2, I was introduced to ethnomethodology by Aaron Cicourel who was a visitor at Goldsmiths' College. Ultimately, this led to a book, *New Directions in Sociological Theory* (Filmer et al. 1972) which had a short-lived fame as an early British text sympathetic to ethnomethodology.

Shortly after, in June 1972, I met Harvey Sacks at the celebrated Edinburgh 'Ethnomethodology and Symbolic Interactionism' conference. I remember the originality of what Sacks had to say (his lecture on dreams at that conference is not unlike the one reprinted in his published *Lectures on Conversation* (LC 2: 512–20). I can also recall my ex-tutor at LSE, Ernest Gellner, noisily walking out in disgust from the hall during Sacks's talk. This culminated in a paper (Gellner 1975) which Sacks's colleague, Emanuel Schegloff, fairly dismisses in his introduction to volume 2 of the *Lectures on Conversation* as 'intellectually evasive' (p. x, n. 2).

My contact with Sacks's work was deepened by reading the photocopied versions of his lectures which circulated in the early 1970s. After a period immersed in organization theory and philosophy, by the mid–1980s I had moved first into ethnomethodologically inspired ethnography and then into conversation analysis. The publication in 1992 of Sacks's lectures was a wonderful opportunity to reflect further on what I and others could learn from Sacks's example.

In writing this introduction to Sacks's work, I am conscious of Schegloff's reminder in introducing volume 1 of the *Lectures* that 'the extraordinary richness and multifacetedness of Sacks' corpus' offers a 'variety, depth and freshness of vision [which] defies domestication into convenient guidelines to a reader' (p. lviii). Certainly, there is nothing that I could write that would replace what is available from the experience of reading Sacks for oneself. Indeed, such 'domestication' as I offer is intended to encourage readers to enjoy that direct experience for themselves.

As we shall see, Sacks recommended his method as a method anyone could use. In this sense, his lectures and other writings offer a toolbox rather than a museum exhibition. It is that toolbox which I hope to help make more widely known. To help in its assimilation, the appendices at the end of this book offer page references to key passages in Sacks's lectures as well as summaries of most of his published papers.

This book is based, then, on the assumption that people doing conversation analysis (CA) do not need to be told about the significance of Sacks's work. Instead, I have written it for a wider audience of scholars and students, particularly for those who have never read Sacks, perhaps because they have assumed him to be 'one of those ethnos'.

To such an audience, I want to show that there is no sectarianism or petty-mindedness in Sacks's work. Instead, there is intellectual breadth and rigour. Whether or not we follow the path that Sacks sets out is perhaps less important than whether we respond to the questions that Sacks poses about social science. After more than twenty years, they are, I believe, still vitally important and still largely unanswered.

Of course, no one familiar with Sacks's lectures could be unaware of the risks involved in writing an introduction to his work. As Sacks once told his students: 'I can tell you something, but you have to be careful what you make of it.' Sacks implies that too frequently we assume that, in science, unlike poetry, paraphrasing will do. We do this: 'rather than having to stick to what was heard to find out what it might be about. What I'm saying is, if anyone wants to paraphrase, that's their business' (*LC*1: 621).

In Sacks's case, we must never fail 'to stick to what was heard'. Here is a mind at work. Like only Wittgenstein before him, and nobody since, Sacks had the ability to turn the apparently trivial into the gripping and insightful.

I gratefully acknowledge the kind permission of Professor Emanuel Schegloff and Blackwell Publishers to quote at length from Harvey Sacks, *Lectures on Conversation*, edited by Gail Jefferson, with an introduction by Emanuel Schegloff (Oxford and Cambridge, Mass., 1992). I am most grateful to Andrew Winnard, lately editor at Polity Press, who gave me the idea for this book. I must also thank the colleagues and friends who have commented on earlier drafts: Susan Ableson, Jay Gubrium, Tony Hak, Christian Heath, John Heritage, Ian Hutchby, Georgia Lepper and Gillian Silverman. Of course, I remain responsible for any errors or omissions that remain.

David Silverman

1

Beginnings

On first encounter, Sacks's work presents something of a paradox. On the one hand, it deals with everyday events, like a telephone conversation or a newspaper story, with which we are all familiar. On the other, Sacks's analysis of these events derives from a highly complex way of reasoning, leading to a level of detail which even his peers can find challenging.

For the moment, I want to postpone both this detail and the form of reasoning that lay behind it. Instead, I will introduce Sacks's work to new readers in the way that he often did himself.

In his introduction to the second volume of Sacks's published *Lectures on Conversation* (1992), his colleague Emanuel Schegloff notes that in the late 1960s Sacks liked to 'have "bits" with which to tell lay people ... what "the work" consisted in [bits with] a kind of transparent appeal and interest ... graspable in a relatively non-technical way, capturing "experiences" virtually anyone would have had access to more or less directly' (*LC2*: xiv–xv).

In this chapter, I will offer some examples of these 'bits' which I hope will serve to whet the appetite of readers unfamiliar with Sacks's work. A more technical account of Sacks's position will appear in subsequent chapters. In the meantime, I hope you enjoy the following examples.

Suicide, Laughter and Rationality

An old Lancashire saying is that 'There's nowt so queer as folk.' The assumption that ordinary people often behave in crazy or unintelligible ways provides endless material for the tabloid media. But is such behaviour always crazy? And is it unintelligible?

Sacks shows us how some apparently bizarre behaviour is not crazy or random but skilful and often routinized. Take his example of people reporting that their suicide threats had not been treated seriously (*LC1*: 13). Sacks asks: why are statements like 'I'm going to kill myself' often met with laughter?

Sacks suggests that possible suicide threats work in two opposed ways. First, assume someone actually takes their own life after having made a 'serious' suicide threat. Now hearers of such a threat can be held to account if they haven't done anything to prevent the threat leading to action. Second, if we are a member of the dead person's family, we also know that we may be blamed since people will surely say things like: 'Well what's the matter with the family?' (*LC1*: 14). Indeed, the suicide threat itself may be heard as a rebuke directed at us – for not caring, not listening, etc.

In these circumstances, we often seek a way out which will evade these moral dilemmas: a way we 'can go about refusing to give help without "refusing"' (*LC1*: 15). One common way out is to laugh at a suicide threat. This laughter need not be heard as a heartless refusal to give help. Rather, by laughing, we transform the meaning of 'I'm going to kill myself' from 'a cry for help' into a joke.

Our laughter means that we have honoured one kind of social duty: someone has told a joke and we have provided an appreciation of it. Moreover, our laughter (the appreciation) has the neat consequence of bringing the activity to an end (that is, the telling of a joke is completed by laughter) and we are now out of this topic. So a workable solution to this kind of moral dilemma is to turn a potentially challenging, non-routine 'cry for help' into one of the many ceremonial forms (like jokes or greetings) that are routine parts of the everyday world that we inhabit (*LC1*: 16).

If you are now prepared to concede that laughing at a suicide threat need not be irrational, you might still want to believe that threatening to take one's own life is the act of an irrational person. Surely there are rational alternatives to suicide?

Once again, Sacks suggests a way of discerning rationalities hidden behind apparently irrational acts. Sacks informs us that people who may potentially commit suicide and who call telephone helplines (like the Samaritans in Britain) often produce the following statement: 'I have no one to turn to' (1972a: 53–5).

The telephone counsellor then usually asks a series of questions such as 'do you have a spouse or partner?', 'do you have a mother or father?', 'do you have a best friend?' Sacks notes that these questions follow a regular sequence, beginning with parties who might be assumed to have the strongest obligation to help and ending with parties with far fewer obligations.

Many callers to suicide helplines respond negatively to these questions. Moreover, whether or not they are asked such questions, callers routinely imply that they too have posed themselves these questions and have posed them *in the self-same sequence.*

Sacks suggests that the uniformity in the way in which we seek to find people who might have an obligation to help us implies that contemplating suicide may be the outcome of a procedure every bit as rational as contemplating, say, purchasing a car. So, although suicide clearly offers an escape from the routine world, the decision to take one's life is fully embedded in that world. Indeed, in terms of routine decision-making, suicide can be a fully rational choice – the result of an *analysis* organized in a way that anybody might follow.

'Pick-ups'

Up to now, you may feel that Sacks concentrates on depressing situations in a rather heartless way. In fact, I chose the example of suicide only as a way of indicating Sacks's ability to illuminate a widespread social problem. It turns out that Sacks also has a great deal to say about the most mundane, apparently unimportant activities.

Take the example of socializing. The ability of some people to be able to enter into conversations with attractive strangers is something that puzzles a lot of us. Indeed, books with titles like 'How to Win Friends' usually sell very well. What is the knack involved?

Have you ever said 'hello' to a stranger and been rebuffed? The problem is that such a greeting implies that you already knew the person concerned and hence had 'an initial right to use "Hello"' (LC1: 103). Hence a stranger need not return your greeting.

As Sacks says, one solution to this problem is to begin with *questions* to a stranger such as: 'Don't I know you from somewhere?', 'Didn't I see you at such-and-such a place?', 'Aren't you so-and-so?' The advantage of the question form is that it is properly receipted by an answer. So not to answer a question, even if you suspect the motives of the questioner, is a difficult act to bring off. Moreover, having got that answer, the questioner properly may ask *another* question. In that way, conversations get started.

All this means that questions can be an effective 'pick-up' device. Indeed, in an exercise where Sacks asked his class to provide examples of utterances which might start conversations with members of the opposite sex, around 90 per cent were questions (*LC1*: 49).

Among such questions, routine requests are a particularly powerful device. In addition to the obligation to provide an answer to a question, there is the expectation that we should not be needlessly rude to a stranger making a request for something as mundane as, say, the time. Moreover, the requester knows that she or he will get a standard, quick response and thus will soon be in a position to ask a further question which may start a longer conversation, for example:

A: When does the plane arrive?
B: 7:15
A: Are you going to San Francisco also? (*LC1*: 103).

So questions can be good pick-up devices when you happen to find yourself in physical proximity to a stranger. However, things get more complicated when the person you are interested in is part of larger crowd involved with you in a multi-party conversation. In this situation, Sacks asks, how do people get involved in a two-party conversation?

One possibility is to ask if anyone wants a drink and then to return with the drink to sit next to the particular target of your attention (*LC2*: 130). In this way, the right 'territorial' situation can be created. Alternatively, one can try waiting until everybody other than the targeted party has left or, more reliably, if there is music, offer an invitation to dance (*LC2*: 131). Indeed, the institution of the dance can seen as a nice solution to the problem of transforming multi-party into two-party conversation (although the noise of modern discos may limit this possibility).

Telling News

These various devices underline Sacks's point that the achievement of a two-party conversation is a skilful, collaborative accomplishment (*LC2*: 130). But such collaboration is not limited to talk between strangers.

Take the case of friends telling and receiving news from each other. It is sometimes noted that we have less news to give to someone we haven't spoken to for, say, six months, than to someone to whom we speak nearly every day. As Sacks asks:

> Now how in the world would it be that you could have something to talk about every day with somebody, and not have something to talk about when you talk to them every six months? Why is it that you don't have six months of news? You could figure that the less you talk with somebody, say a friend who lives in another city, the more you'd have to talk about. (*LC2*: 16)

The answer to this puzzle is that, as every reporter knows, what counts as news depends on its immediacy. An item that may happily be reported to a friend the day after it happened, no longer appears to be newsworthy after six months. If something is not mentioned soon after it happened, then it can 'amount to nothing'. So the items of news that you can tell after six months are only things that are worthy of attention over such a long period. And, 'if you don't have them, you have nothing to talk about' (*LC2*: 172). To be able to manage a conversation after a long break as though it were a daily event is a special skill which is worthy of remark (*LC2*: 16).

Telling news is also responsive to a recurrent rule of conversation: don't tell others what they already know. How is this rule managed in multi-party conversations when one's partner is present – who may be assumed to know a lot that you know?

Sacks suggests two solutions. First, in such situations one could elect only to tell new things. But, as Sacks points out, this solution 'has massive troubles involved in it which are reflected in ... having their spouse complain "How come you never told me that"' (*LC2*: 439).

Given this 'trouble', a preferred solution often chosen is for spouses actively to adopt the role of a hearer of 'old' news. They can do this by monitoring a partner's talk for whether it is correctly presented and putting in corrections (often in overlapping positions). However, this solution can also be a subsequent cause for complaint (the teller may say 'why did you keep on correcting me?' and the listener may say: 'why did you tell the story so badly?') (*LC2*: 443).

Sacks's discussion of conversational news reporting shows that news is presented and heard as constructed for a particular audience. One implication of this is that, as recipients of news, we have to provide 'appropriate' responses. Along these lines, Sacks reports a telephone call where the called party has just reported a stay in hospital for an operation. This report is received by 'Oh:::' by the caller. After further details, the call concludes as follows:

Emma: but I'm <u>be</u>tter I wz, lying on the couch out'n front
Bernice: Oh::: I'm sorry Em<u>ma</u>? (*LC2*: 573)

Out of this apparently mundane conversation, Sacks generates a puzzle. Why don't we hear 'I'm sorry' as 'I'm sorry that you're better'?

It turns out that the first expectation on hearing such announcements is that the recipient will mark it as 'newsworthy' (as by the first drawn-out 'Oh'). For, if we don't at least do that (and do it first), the announcer can hear that we are not treating their announcement as particularly remarkable and hence challenging their credibility as proper newstellers. For instance, think of the impact of saying nothing after an announcement of good or bad news or even just saying 'mm', 'I see' or, still worse, 'so?'

Sacks argues that only after we have fulfilled our role as a news recipient can we properly engage in other activities such as the expression of sympathy. So this caller's 'I'm sorry' in this late position is not heard as meaning 'I'm sorry that you're better' but as a properly delayed expression of sympathy.

'Everyone Has to Lie'

If we look back at these examples, we can see how Sacks's analysis is powerfully counter-intuitive. Ordinarily, if we think about it at all, we assume that what we say reflects our state of mind. However, what Sacks is showing us is that, in practice, we construct our talk by reference to how it will be heard. By saying what we do, positioned in a particular place, we thus make available to our hearer(s) a particular *reading* of what we mean.

The implication is that speaking and hearing are *activities* rather than the passive transmission of thought processes. Moreover, these activities happen so quickly that it is implausible to think that they are usually done strategically or even with prior thought.

Take the example of someone answering the question 'How are you?' by 'Fine' even if they actually feel lousy (*LC1*: 562). Why do we dissemble? If you think about it, if we truthfully answer 'lousy', the appropriate next utterance from the hearer is the question 'why?' So, by being truthful, we demand that the questioner should begin what Sacks calls a 'diagnostic procedure' (*LC1*: 560). Now this is hardly appropriate or polite in the many cases where 'How are you?' is to be heard as part of a greeting ceremony rather than as a 'real' question. Indeed, this may be the point of more formal greetings such as 'How do you do?' which properly elicit the same utterance from the other person.

As Sacks points out, a good guide to this matter are books of etiquette (*LC1*: 566). From these it becomes clear that the person who answers 'truthfully' to a ceremonial question has all the makings of a bore. By contrast, by sometimes 'lying' when asked such a question, we show proper concern for what we and others should properly do (*LC1*: 562).

Herein lies a paradox related to two opposing demands of proper behaviour. On the one hand, we are never supposed to lie. On the other, we would place other people in an unwelcome position if we failed to show concern with 'the different consequences of [our] alternative answers' (*LC1*: 564). It thus turns out, in the title of one of Sacks's published papers (1975), that 'everyone has to lie.' Given the case of 'honest' bores, this is not something to be sad about but something for which to be grateful.

Now, of course, the maxim 'everyone has to lie' will be heard as only appropriate to *certain* occasions. For instance, it is unlikely to help you if you are found to lie when giving evidence in a court of law. Moreover, 'everyone' sometimes only refers to a relatively small group (that is, people we know, or everyone who is 'anyone') (p. 63).

By contrast, we sometimes restrict assertions to certain classes of people: lawyers, males, women. But do members of such classes whose qualities don't fit our assertion *disprove* what we have said? For instance, can you disprove the assertion that 'lawyers are all greedy' by citing a case of one lawyer who often works for nothing? No, says Sacks. The failure of this person to conform to the assertion may simply reflect on 'his status as a proper member of that class' so the counter-example is represented as not 'really' a lawyer (p. 60). In this way, formal and everyday logic part company.

Part of the reason for this is that, in everyday logic, generalizations don't altogether work as statistical claims. For instance, if you are challenged about your actions, one effective response may be to say 'everyone does don't they?' (*LC1*: 23). Here the appeal to 'everyone' works as a rhetorical device rather than a statistical claim. As such, it serves to limit your accountability for your act because such behaviour can be seen as 'general'.

Similarly, invoking a proverb (say, 'better late than never') is a powerful conversational move for reasons quite unconnected with whether the proverb is 'true' or even 'true in this instance'. Sacks notes that using a proverb as a conversational opener typically produces a token of agreement from the hearer. In this respect, it may be yet another effective pick-up device.

By contrast, people who fail to agree with an invoked proverb will find that the conversation is abruptly terminated by the proverb reciter. This may be because proverbs are usually treated as unchallengeable and therefore as something any conversationalist will know (*LC1*: 25). Hence challenging a proverb is an effective means of resisting an intended pickup by means of a proverb statement.

Conversational 'Space'

As with the return of greetings, responses to reciting proverbs show that when we speak we do far more complicated things than simply confirming assertions and/or emptying out the contents of our minds. Instead, it seems that what we say will be heard in terms of its position in this particular conversational 'space' – after a previous turn and in the light of a possible next turn.

Take the mundane activity of ordering from a restaurant menu. Sacks asks why we so often have conversations that go like this:

A: I'm going to have X
B: Well I just had that so I'll have Y

or:

A: I'm going to have X
B: I don't like that

In such cases 'you deal with their choice as if they were proposing it for you' (*LC*1: 791). Why? The answer lies in the fact that, although A is addressing a waiter, you hear A as saying something of possible relevance to you. After all, it is likely to be your turn next.

So choices by two or more people from a restaurant menu, like greeting exchanges or proverb assertions, are cooperatively accomplished. This is seen even more clearly when you are being treated to a meal and your host says:

H: Why don't you have the roast beef it's great here?

Of course, this does not mean that you have to choose the beef – after all, you may be a vegetarian or worried about 'mad cow' disease. How then do you show that you attend to your host's invitation? Simply, you can treat it as setting the price limit of any dish you do choose (*LC*1: 792).

Talk and Morality

Such close attention to a previous turn at talk implies that we tend to be very much aware of the moral implications of utterances. Indeed, attention to moral implications is seen even in the case of natural events. Take the example of an earthquake – a fairly regular occurrence in the part of California where Sacks lived. When the room shakes, why do you apologize to your house guests? Or, to return to the restaurant example, perhaps you have just had an excellent meal. Why do you not congratulate the chef but congratulate your host instead?

Sacks argues that these two examples involve events that have occurred while one person has an obligation to another (*LC*2: 296). Events, natural or otherwise, are not just the silent back-drop to what we say but are used to inform us about what it is appropriate for us to do next, such as apologizing to our guests or congratulating our host.

Even silence can be an event holding moral implications. In everyday talk, one party's silence can show that they have recognized that another speaker has yet to finish an utterance or, in a multi-party conversation, has not selected them as next speaker. Conversely, inappropriate silences (say after the punchline of a joke) can reveal that one was not properly listening.

An altogether different implication of certain silences is often drawn in a court of law where lawyers can employ the assumption that answerers *own* any pause after they have been asked a question. Here some delays in answering a question, particularly in cross-examination, will be heard to imply doubt, defensiveness or downright lying (*LC1*: 310–11).

The court example has yet another counter-intuitive implication. Ordinary people and the medical profession tend to agree that people who think that others are reading their minds are odd and may even have symptoms of schizophrenia. But the lawyer who wants a jury to treat a lengthy silence as indicating an upcoming untruth is precisely claiming that anyone can read such a person's mind. Equally, lawyers, police and other professionals will treat particular kinds of answers as implying more than they actually say.

Look at this example, used by Sacks, of a telephone conversation between a caller to a social welfare agency and an agency worker (A). The caller (B) has, up till this point, only revealed that he has 'marital troubles' with his wife (referred to as 'she' below):

```
1   A:   Yeah, then what happened?
2   B:   When she stepped between me and the child, I went to move
3        her out of the way. And then about that time her sister
4        had called the police.
5   A:   Didn't you smack her one?
6   B:   No.
7   A:   You're not telling me the story, Mr B.
8   B:   Well, you see when you say smack you mean hit.
9   A:   Yeah, you shoved her. Is that it?
10  B:   Yeah, I shoved her. (LC1: 113, simplified)
```

Sacks asks us to note how the agency worker is able to work out a possible omission from B's account ('Didn't you smack her one?', line 5), to persevere even after B's denial (lines 6–7) and, finally, to obtain an admission from B (line 10). In this respect, A has indeed been able to read B's mind.

Reading People's Minds

Reading other people's minds is certainly not a skill reserved for professionals. Indeed, as Sacks points out, we learn about the ability of others to read our minds as children. Sometimes these others are teachers or even God. Most regularly, however, they are our mothers. For instance, when children are asked what they have been doing, they can find their answer denied by their mother – who wasn't there – saying '"No you weren't" and the child then corrects itself' (*LC1*: 115). So schizophrenics who believe that others can read their minds may only be mimicking adult–child or para-legal talk.

But what about the surely paranoid delusion that other people can *control* your mind? Sacks give the example of somebody saying to you: 'Remember that car you had?' Now, even though the car was not on your mind at all, you can't help remembering it. In that sense, the first speaker has indeed controlled your mind. As Sacks puts it: 'people aren't crazy for thinking that other people control their minds. That could not be a source of their craziness. That could only be a matter of wisdom' (*LC2*: 401).

Sacks wants to show us how, as hearers, we depend upon our ability to read the speaker's mind in order to work out the next action required of us. In this respect, even apparently private matters can be viewed as social and structural.

Take the apparently extreme case of 'memory'. Surely 'memory' is something contained inside our heads and therefore 'private'? In this regard, Sacks invites us to think about those occasions when we had wanted to make a point but the present speaker had continued or someone else had grabbed the floor. In such circumstances, don't we often 'forget' the topic that we wanted to mention? As Sacks observes: 'if you don't get a chance to say it, when you then get a chance to say it, you've forgotten it.' In this respect, memory is not at all private or personal but 'in some perhaps quite dramatic way at the service of the conversation . . . It is in some ways an utterance by utterance phenomenon' (*LC2*: 96).

'Banal' Explanations

Conversation works in two ways. First, we are influenced by what others say (as with memory and others controlling our minds). But, second, their talk can provide us with a set of resources for interpreting and influencing what they will say and do (reading others' minds).

Take the case of observing that somebody is looking glum. How do you read their minds in order to find the source of their gloom?

Sacks suggests a common response to such an observation: 'If you're sitting with somebody and they look glum, then one of the things you routinely do is try to figure out what it is about here and now that they might be glum about' (*LC2*: 96).

Wherever possible, then, we will seek what Sacks calls 'a local explanation' for anything untoward that happens. Moreover, this search for the 'here and now' extends from such trivial events as a gloomy expression to large-scale happenings. For instance, the initial reports of bystanders in Dallas at the time of the assassination of President Kennedy were not of shots but of hearing a car backfiring (1984b: 419).

Why do people work at producing banal explanations as their first thoughts? When interpreting a gloomy expression we probably look for some local cause because in the presence of the gloomy person we have a lot of clues to hand. But what about events like assassinations or, say, UFO sightings?

It seems that, although mental patients may be correct about *some* of their interpretations, few of us want to appear as crazy or even stupid people. Thus in any explanation we give we have an incentive to show that we have first sought the obvious, mundane reason for an out of the way event.

It is also probably the case that such large-scale happenings take on a special meaning when we can relate them to something local or personal. For instance, many older people will still talk about the Kennedy assassination in relation to what they were doing on that day in 1963. In this regard, Sacks asks us why people respond more to tragedies when they involve local people? For instance, for the American people during the Vietnam War, the deaths of local soldiers 'brought home the war'. As Sacks suggests:

> It turns out that a major way that a war comes to hurt the government doing the war, is by it happening that people from small places die . . . It's about the only way that they can come to seriously feel about it. For one, if everybody knows the parents of the person who died, then everybody has occasion to be told about it, and in talking about it come to talk about the war. (*LC2*: 246)

Sacks is showing us that, when we tell a story (unless we are a bore), we try to find an audience to whom the story will be relevant. Indeed, without such an audience, we may not even remember the story.

'Experiences'

Storytellers also prefer to display some kind of 'first hand' involvement in the events they describe. Indeed, people are only entitled to have experiences in regard to events that they have observed and/or which affect them directly. For instance, in telephone calls, events like earthquakes are usually introduced in terms of how you survived it, and they become newsworthy less in terms of when they happened but more in relation to when we last talked – our 'conversational time' (*LC2*: 564).

In this way, Sacks notes, we seek to turn events into experiences or 'something for us' (*LC2*: 563). However, this shows that telling someone our experiences is not just emptying out the contents of our head but organizing a tale told to a proper recipient by an authorized teller. In this sense, experiences are 'carefully regulated sorts of things' (*LC1*: 248).

Introducing the notion of 'regulation' into something so apparently personal as 'experience' is just one surprise that Sacks has in store for us. Moreover, for Sacks, in everyday life, we cannot even count on an objective realm of 'facts' to balance apparently subjective 'experience'.

Scientists usually assume that first they observe facts and then seek to explain them. But, in everyday life, we determine what is a 'fact' by first seeing if there is some convincing explanation around. For instance, coroners may not deliver a verdict of suicide unless there is some evidence that the deceased person had a reason to take their own life (*LC1*: 123). In that sense, in everyday life, only those 'facts' occur for which there is an explanation (*LC1*: 121).

Names

In producing accounts of 'facts' and 'experiences', we have already seen that we try to avoid telling others what they already know (*LC2*: 438). Sacks argues that this bias in storytelling relates not only to narrated events but to the characters in them. For instance, when we mention someone whom everyone can be assumed to know, we will be expected to use the simplest description of them, for example a first name (*LC2*: 445).

First names are an example of what Sacks calls a type 1 identification. In type 1, a speaker uses an identification which the hearer will then use to find some person that they already know (say, 'John'). By contrast, in type 2 identifications (e.g. 'a guy', 'someone'), a speaker is telling a recipient not to try to find out from it a person he knows that is being referred to. Moreover, Sacks argues that the usual rule is: use type 1 if you can, but correct or repair into type 2 if type 1 is inappropriate (*LC2*: 445).

This makes the point that identifications, like stories as a whole, are recipient designed. Let me now give two examples which show why this matters. Have you ever noticed that when people refer to celebrities they sometimes mention just the first name, hesitate and then give the surname (Paul ... McCartney)? What is going on here?

Straight off we can see that the speaker's initial selection of a first name ('Paul') is a type 1 identification. Thus the speaker can be heard to be instructing recipients to use this name to search for someone they know. However, the obvious problem is that, while we are likely to have heard of Paul McCartney, when we hear the name 'Paul' we will search for someone with whom we are much more familiar (maybe someone in the room or a mutually known friend called Paul). This explains why the speaker might repair the description by, after a pause, adding the surname.

But why not avoid the need to repair by giving the full identification at the start? The answer seems to be that the initial description of first name only (a type 1 identification) implies that both speakers and hearers are so familiar with the person so identified that they will all know to whom the name Paul refers. However, the subsequent pause allows the speaker to show that they have reflected further and realized that such an identification, although perfect for them, will be inadequate for their audience. Thus, in a few words, the speaker has displayed a privileged first-name relationship with a celebrity.

The second example of why naming matters is taken from a meeting where American teenagers are having group therapy:

1	Ther:	Hi, Jim//c'mon in
2	Jim:	H'warya
3	Ther:	Jim, this is uh Al
4	Jim:	Hi
5	Ther:	Ken,
6	Jim:	Hi
7	Ken:	Hi (*LC1*: 281)

The issue that Sacks raises here is why does Jim say H'warya (line 2) to the therapist but not to the other clients, Al and Ken? Jim has already had an individual interview with the therapist and will know him as Dr so-and-so. However, there are problems in deciding what to call him in a group therapy session. Jim *could* call him Dr so-and-so but then, because this is his first group session, he still doesn't know how the other group members call him. This could create the following problem: 'If he comes on with "Hi, Dr so-and-so" and they (the other clients) call him something more rough and ready, then he may well already have been seen to be a kind of pansy' (*LC1*: 285).

An alternative would be for Jim just to say 'hi' but that would only postpone the problem of naming. 'H'warya' may now be seen as a nice solution to this problem. It does not lack a name but 'ya' does not commit Jim to the implications of naming the therapist by his title.

Sacks points out that naming is an issue for people doing introductions as well as for Jim here who is receiving an introduction (*LC1*: 298). As the Paul ... McCartney example above showed, there are always implications of using certain categories rather than others in naming somebody. For instance, the therapist might have named the group members by their full name, called them Mister or even referred to them by their clinic numbers. Or he might have called them by their full title and name but referred to the new boy just as 'Jim'. By avoiding this, the therapist is creating a situation in which the clients are encouraged to use 'first name' terms and to treat each other (but not necessarily the therapist) as equals.

In both examples, when speakers name someone they create a series of impressions not just about the persons being named, but also about themselves and their audience. In this sense, our attention to the implications of choosing names shows the extent to which we are aware of the importance of appearances. As Sacks points out, this awareness has a biblical precedent:

> In our Judeo-Christian mythology, the first event characterized as being human is a response to an awareness of an appearance. That is, the first event after the eating of the apple in Eden is just that event of being aware. The first thing they have happen is being aware that they're naked. Before that they're not human, and before that they're not oriented to what can be seen by looking at them. (*LC1*: 369)

As early as the Book of Genesis, then, we notice that Adam and Eve become human by understanding that they can be observed and, therefore, described. Moreover, even the Bible provides names which are designed for particular audiences. In this regard, Sacks mentions chapter 14 of Genesis where Abraham is referred to as 'Abraham the Hebrew'. Since Israelites would know about Abraham's ethnicity, biblical scholars have suggested that the description 'the Hebrew' implies that this section of Genesis was not written by a Jew and hence might provide independent evidence of the historicity of Abraham (*LC1*: 171).

Exactly the same issues of observability/reportability recur in even the most mundane contemporary conversation. Returning to our group therapy session, Sacks notes how these teenage clients use the term 'hotrodders' to describe themselves when they are discussing driving cars. Why use this apparently esoteric term and not a more readily understandable term like 'kids in cars'?

As with the example of Abraham, Sacks suggests that we see descriptions as addressed to possible audiences. Sacks notes that we attend to our choice of descriptive categories even in those many situations where we are talking to strangers and there is no apparent battle over which category to use. He mentions the case of people telling interviewers doing surveys that they watch less television than they actually do. Sacks comments: 'It's interesting in that they're controlling an impression of themselves for somebody who couldn't matter less' (*LC1*: 580).

Sacks argues that this happens because we can be held responsible not only for our descriptions but for the *inferences* that can be drawn from them, that is, as to the sort of person who would say such a thing about themselves or others.

Returning to our 'hotrodders' example, we can now see that many alternative descriptions like 'kids in cars' or 'teenage drivers' have a drawback: because they are intelligible to anyone, they can be used by adults. By contrast, 'hotrodders' is not owned by adults. If adults choose to use the term, they lack knowledge about how to use it properly – not every car is a hotrod, not every teenager in a car is a hotrodder (*LC1*: 173).

Choosing to use 'hotrodders' rather than say 'teenage drivers' to describe themselves means that the young people in group therapy have shifted their description around to a category that they administer and enforce (*LC1*: 399–400). Thus, having multiple terms for one 'object' represents not just more 'interest' in that object but an attempt to enforce authority (*LC1*: 402). In that sense, the categories we use in our descriptions are instruments of social control, and contested categories are one way that one does 'rebellion' (*LC1*: 174).

Ordering Social Relations

Sacks's demonstration of how categories are involved in systems of social control has far-reaching implications for how 'prejudice' or 'discrimination' is done in practice. In this respect, he shows how a detailed attention to the language we use relates to much wider political issues than how people present themselves.

This is seen most clearly in Sacks's analysis (1979) of the methods used by racists to link particular 'evils' to the work of people with certain identities (such as Catholics, Jews, blacks). We identify people by choosing one of many categories that could be used to describe them. It then follows that

> any person who is a case of a category is seen as a member of a category, and what's known about that category is known about them, and the fate of each is bound up in the fate of the other ... [so] if a member does something like rape a white woman, commit economic fraud, race on the street, etc., then that thing will be seen as what a member of some applicable category does, not what some named person did. And the rest of them will have to pay for it. (p. 13)

Not only do Sacks's observations give us a useful hold on how racism works but they also provide a way of describing one aspect of another 'big' issue – social change. For Sacks, one way we could identify social change would be by noticing shifts in the properties of categories used in everyday language and in how these categories were actually applied (p. 14).

So Sacks can give us a grip on apparently 'important' issues like racism or social change. However, we have to be careful here because Sacks rejected 'the notion that you could tell right off whether something was important'. He uses the case of biology to show how the study of an apparently minor object ('one bacterium') can revolutionize our knowledge. Why assume, for instance, that you need to look at states and revolutions, when, as we saw earlier, some apparently tiny object like a maxim or proverb 'may give an enormous understanding of the way humans do things and the kinds of objects they use to construct and order their affairs' (*LC1*: 28)?

Of course, part of this ordering and constructing our affairs does create activities like racism. In a less sinister fashion, it also allows us to treat each other as professionals and clients. For instance, think back to how the therapist was given a professional identity through Jim's choice of 'you' to name him. Sacks shows us that we can look at how categories like this are applied in organizations in order to resolve some puzzles about how such institutions function.

For instance, Sacks asks, why do psychoanalytic sessions look so different from ordinary conversation? One answer is that psycho-analysts famously refuse to comment on their patients' stories. Instead, they prefer to ask a question or just to say 'mm'. This means that we never find such a person responding to a patient's story with one of their own. As Sacks notes: 'it is absolutely not the business of a psychiatrist, having had some experience reported to him, to say "My mother was just like that, too"' (*LC2*: 259).

This may explain two troubles of such patients. First, the minimal responses they get from the professional may seem to indicate only a weak 'claimed understanding' and maybe that they are not really listening. Second, patients may worry that, since their doctor doesn't report the same experience, nobody else does either and so they really are crazy. It may also explain reports of psychiatrists falling asleep during the consultation – since they know they can't tell their own stories, they really don't listen (*LC2*: 260).

Examples like the above might suggest that professionals have a much greater degree of latitude than their clients and may even hold all the chips. But this is not necessarily so. In a suicide helpline studied by Sacks, records were kept of all phone calls. This meant that counsellors were aware that it would create a problem if the record showed that a client did not take their advice when it later transpired that this client committed suicide. If clients are aware of this, they can use this information to turn the call in a direction they prefer (*LC2*: 394).

Psychoanalysts too have their own troubles – even if these are a little different from those of their patients. In the 'hotrodders' example, we saw that teenagers have a problem with who 'owns' descriptions of their activities. But Sacks shows how the same problem extends to professional disciplines such as psycho-analysis. Freud faced the difficulty that everybody considers themselves an expert in psychology. Perhaps this is why Freud sought to invent new terms and attempted to enforce how they were used (*LC1*: 202).

Children and Power

Many people (including many sociologists) remain convinced that, at least in some relationships, only one side has the power. At first glance, the position of adults vis-à-vis small children would seem to be a case in point. After all, most small children have limited rights and therefore need an adult to warrant certain activities.

However, as many parents know, children can use this rule to their own benefit. For instance, they can go to several adults with a request, without telling them that they have asked anybody else, till they get a 'yes' answer. Then they go back to the first person (often Mum or Dad) and say: 'He said okay' (*LC1*: 77). Now this person is in something of a fix. If they persist in their refusal, they will be contradicting another adult.

A second recurrent device that Sacks notes is used by children as young as three is to begin a piece of talk with the following kinds of questions: 'You know what, Daddy?'; 'You know something, Mommy?' (*LC1*: 256). Now the thing to remember is that small children have limited conversational rights. Indeed, their utterances can often be ignored by adults. The issue, then, is how can such children use the apparatus of talk as a way of getting their attention without having to use other means (such as pulling an adult's item of clothing or even kicking them)?

In order to understand the power of these utterances, Sacks points out two facts. First, if somebody asks you a question, it is expected that you give an answer. Thus, as already noted in the pick-up example, questions are an effective way of opening a conversation. Second, both the kids' questions above have an unusual kind of answer, a further question: 'What?'

Now Sacks asks us to look at what such questions achieve. Following 'what?' the child is *obliged* to speak (remember that answers properly follow questions) and can therefore talk about the topic which she or he wanted to talk about all along because this is required by an adult. Moreover, following a completed question-answer sequence, the questioner may ask a further question. This means that the adult is now back in charge of the trajectory of the conversation in a way which would not have happened if the child had stayed in the questioning role.

By this device, children as young as three routinely thread their way into conversations by *trading off* adults' superior conversational rights. As Sacks comments: 'that's very nice. Three-year-old kids are kind of clever' (*LC1*: 257).

Children's use of adult-imposed conventions for their own purposes is also seen when adults formulate rules of 'correct behaviour' for children. For example, children are told 'don't stick your hand on the stove' and also 'don't tell lies.' Now, as Sacks notes, adults know that there is a distinction between two kinds of rules: class 1 rules, where, for adults, the consequences flow naturally from the act (such as putting your hand on the stove); class 2 rules, where, unless your behaviour is seen and somebody does something, no negative consequences follow (as with lying) (*LC1*: 78–9).

Sacks points out that children recurrently have to decide whether what they are dealing with is a type 1 or type 2 rule. So 'they begin to discover that there are some things which they can violate, that, if the adult doesn't know, isn't told, doesn't find out about, nothing happens' (*LC1*: 79).

Now parents may try to buttress the weaker type 2 rules by appeals to the 'long-term' consequences of evading them or to an all-seeing deity. In this way, type 2 rules, for a while at least, may still seem very powerful so that when children break them they experience guilt. Conversely, small children may try to figure out for themselves which kind of rule they are dealing with. Sometimes, this is merely amusing – for instance small children may tell lies to see if God notices and punishes them. Sometimes, it is positively dangerous: children stick their finger into an electrical point and see if they still get a shock even when nobody is watching them.

Concluding Remarks

Let me reassure readers who may be feeling rather confused about the import of these varied examples. The rest of the book offers a much more systematic treatment of Sacks's work which will demonstrate why these examples matter. The illustrations above, drawn from Sacks's lectures, were used simply to whet your appetite by demonstrating that, unlike a lot of social theory, Sacks's ideas are anything but boring. If my demonstration has not succeeded, either I have failed in my task or Sacks is just not for you. If, however, any part of this chapter has intrigued you (or even angered you), then I hope that you will be encouraged to read on.

2

An Intellectual Biography

At the time of his death in 1975, Harvey Sacks's brief curriculum vitae might have looked something like this:

Education

1955	A.B. Columbia University, New York
1959	LL.B. Yale
1959–66	Department of Sociology, University of California, Berkeley; Ph.D. 1966

Employment

1963	Acting Assistant Professor, Department of Sociology, University of California, Los Angeles (UCLA) (seconded as Fellow at the Center for the Scientific Study of Suicide)
1964	Assistant Professor at UCLA
1968	Associate Professor, Department of Sociology, University of California, Irvine (UCI).
1974	Professor, UCI

Publications

Ten journal articles or chapters in books (including two foreign language translations).

At first sight, this CV seems to mark out a scholar of around average productivity. In regard to our narrow contemporary criteria of academic prowess, a record of one publication a year since obtaining a Ph.D. might even look a little thin and the absence of a book-length publication could appear to be potentially damning.

An imaginary appointments committee in 1975 might have detected another problem about Sacks's record. In some quarters, Harvey Sacks's work seemed to attract incomprehension and rage. For the British social anthropologist, Ernest Gellner (1975), he was part of a Californian flower-power 're-enchantment industry'. To a student on his own course, perhaps echoing the views of the contemporary sociological establishment, Sacks's analysis of talk seemed wilfully to be avoiding the 'topics of conversation' (*LC2*: 549).

In retrospect, Sacks's reply to this student gives us an answer to a sceptic reading his CV and a reason for wanting to read his work today. His reply is characteristically blunt. From anyone else, it may seem self-important. But Sacks was just being accurate:

> weird as it may be, there's an area called the Analysis of Conversation. It's done in various parts of the world, and I invented it. So if I tell you that what we're doing is studying conversation, then there's no place to turn, as compared to experimental psychology where you can say 'I want to know what the mind is like' and then you can choose to study humanistic psychology or something like that. There is no other way that conversation is being studied systematically except my way. (*LC2*: 549)

Of course, Sacks was right. He did invent the study of conversation. And conversation continues to be studied across the world according to methods that Sacks established, most obviously in the trail-blazing paper in *Language* (Sacks, Schegloff and Jefferson 1974).

However, from 1963 until his premature death in 1975, most of Sacks's papers appeared in relatively obscure publications. After his death, twelve more papers appeared but, until the publication of his lectures in 1992, no book-length work had been published. A major book projected as 'Aspects of the Sequential Organization of Conversation' (listed as Prentice Hall (forthcoming) in Schegloff and Sacks 1974) never materialized.

But Sacks's publication record does not tell the whole story. As his lectures make abundantly clear, Sacks was less concerned with fame than with being correct. His metier was the highly polished document, addressed to a small audience, usually in a formal language of numbered points, which got things definitively and incontrovertibly right. This explains why Sacks was reticent about attempting early publication of his work in familiar social science journals. Although he projected the publication of several books, his painstaking series of revisions did not lead to anything that he was prepared to regard as a finished work. So, despite the massive impact of his work, Sacks's publication record was, as already noted, relatively meagre.

The Lectures

It was through transcriptions of his lectures, delivered first at UCLA (1964–8) and then at UC Irvine (1968–72), that Sacks's work became known. For over a quarter of a century, mimeoed copies of these lectures circulated, like samizdat publications, among small groups who knew to ask to see them. There was nothing elitist in this method, however. As Sacks says: 'The lectures get taped, they then get typed and then they get sent around to whoever it is that writes me letters saying they're interested in seeing what's happening right now' (LC2: 336).

Faced with the requirement to teach an undergraduate course, Sacks thus used the opportunity to sort out his ideas and to communicate with his colleagues around the world. As he put it, the lectures serve 'to organize my current work and get it down on paper and then let my friends see where I am' (LC2: 335–6).

Indeed, as Schegloff points out, 'With but a few exceptions, the students ... can hardly have known what they were hearing' (Schegloff in LC1: xii). Certainly, the class were told that the course was 'about conversation'. But they were also informed that they would *not* be taught 'how to analyze conversation' (LC2: 335). Sacks offers two curious justifications for this. First, conversation analysis, unlike calculus, is not a skill that important institutions say you need to have. Second, it is a skill with no obvious personal benefits: 'I don't figure it's all that useful – I mean useful for doing better conversation, or useful for figuring out "what's wrong with my conversation?" or figuring out what somebody was trying to do when they did something or other' (LC2: 336).

In fact, Sacks is not altogether fair to himself here. As we saw in chapter 1, Sacks's lectures do reveal how his approach can bring better understanding of many everyday situations. However, there is no question that Sacks had any intention of providing a 'user-friendly' course on which students could obtain marketable grades or skills, or indeed a course primarily addressed to any kind of student requirement. And, as we see from the transcripts of his lectures, at least one student was prepared to question what was going on: 'Q: If we are incidental observers to what is your primary interest of appealing to your primary audience, why bother spending time with the class? Why bother stifling yourself with 40 people? Why can't you do what you do?' (*LC2*: 338).

Sacks's initial reply to this question repeats that the lectures help organize his thoughts. He also says he gets paid to do the lectures. However, he also points out that his own self-centredness might be useful to those students present who actually want to think for themselves:

> in some ways it's much more uplifting for the class. That is to say, instead of being treated as the people you think you are, you might be being treated as the people you might let yourselves be. I suppose that people are more serious than they are and I therefore don't spend much time talking down to the class. (*LC2*: 338)

No doubt even this reply would be another black mark in our age of student-centred learning, where presentation skills sometimes seem to rate above the content of lectures. However, this did not mean that Sacks's students were offered grand theory that went above their heads or, to any great extent, programmatic statements about Sacks's position vis-à-vis the social sciences. On the contrary, Sacks offered his students demonstrations of how he worked with small pieces of data. As he put it:

> Basically what I have to sell is the sorts of work I can do. And I don't have to sell its theoretical underpinnings, its hopes for the future, its methodological elegance, its theoretical scope or anything else. I have to sell what I can do, and the interestingness of my findings. (*LC2*: 3)

None the less, perhaps there was a 'take it or leave it' attitude here, depending on whether or not the audience found Sacks's findings (or the data they stemmed from) 'interesting'. As Sacks pointedly once put it in an introductory lecture: 'I decided to spend the first time telling people something that I take it could hardly *not* be of interest to them ... And I guess I should say if *this* isn't absorbing, you could hardly imagine how unabsorbing the rest will be' (*LC2*: 215).

Another potential trouble to an undergraduate audience arose precisely in Sacks's unwillingness to position his work so that its relation to the standard fare of other social science courses could become more apparent. Unexpectedly and unprecedentedly, Sacks's students were expected to become active listeners. Sacks told them from the outset that they were not going to be fed pap.

Instead, with only minimal instruction, they were asked to engage in 'exercises' whose pedagogic purpose was barely apparent (for instance, to observe people exchanging glances – *LC1*: 81–94).

For Sacks, real learning was active – it occurred through doing something oneself rather than passively reading a book or listening to a lecture. As he put it:

> Unless you do ... some research, you don't know what research looks like. You don't know how to read the results, you don't know their sense, you don't know whether anything's been learned or what's been learned. By doing the exercises you can come to see what you, yourself can do. (*LC2*: 17)

After the exercise was done, Sacks would usually pull some threads together. And his students were reminded of their rights: 'to ask for clarification, ask for better statements, ask me why or how I did that, or is there more of that or is there a better way of doing it, and I will try to help you out' (*LC2*: 337).

But the first requirement was that students should begin to learn for themselves. Through the exercises, the students were told:

> You'll see that you can do things at one point that you couldn't do at another, so you get a sense of what sort of progress in your own minds you have acquired. You also find that you learn something from what you did ... quite independently of what I'll be doing here, and the virtues of the sorts of things I do. (*LC2*: 17)

Above all, Sacks's students were offered that rare commodity, a spectacle of a mind at work. Each year that his course was taught, rather than the dry repetition of last year's lecture notes, he offered new data and/or new analyses. So Sacks's lectures derived from his current research and his students were invited to think them through with him – the very opposite strategy to that of deductive social theorizing.

Thinking data through does not mean that analysis comes easily. Sacks showed his students the sheer amount of time that he spent on careful inspection of the data that went into his lectures. For instance, in discussing a one-page transcript of a telephone call involving a story about an accident on the freeway (*LC2*: 241), Sacks tells his class: 'I'd been working on this story for a year and a half before I happened to notice that in fact she [the storyteller] didn't see the wreck, and to see that she had found the wreck story in the wreck aftermath' (*LC2*: 234).

For original thinkers, thinking data through usually means making lateral connections. One of Sacks's findings here was that this telephone caller only introduced narrative resources that were going to come up later. And Sacks's students were asked to compare this finding to certain Russian literature (Nabokov's analysis of a Gogol play, *LC2*: 238–9) and, thereby, to think more deeply about what we might call the 'economy' of storytelling (see chapter 6 below).

Volume 1 of the *Lectures on Conversation* is centrally concerned with the importance of the descriptive apparatus available to us to make sense of events (making them, in Garfinkel's terms, 'observable/reportable'). Here Sacks draws on data from his Ph.D. dissertation on calls to a suicide prevention centre, as well as a newspaper story telling the tale of a Vietnam pilot, and a child's story.

When Sacks began, he was working in completely virgin sociological territory. By the late 1960s, there was some other work to draw on (in particular, Schegloff's (1968) research on telephone conversations). Increasingly too, Sacks was now working with data-sets rather than individual conversations in an effort to build a cumulative body of knowledge (see Schegloff in *LC2*: xxxix–xl). So the later lectures, collected in volume 2, focus on such data-sets, using a method that Sacks was now calling 'conversation analysis'.

However, the lectures in both volumes are largely data driven, based on data extracts, some of which are repeatedly analysed over the eight-year period (for instance, a long extract from a group therapy session). These data include calls to a suicide prevention centre, reports of student exercises on glances, phone calls to a 'social agency', an arbitration report, a coroner's report, multiple telephone calls arising out of an observed fire at a department store and a radio call-in programme.

In this book, I hope to demonstrate to you that, as Schegloff has put it, Sacks's lectures present 'a most remarkable, inventive and productive account of a strikingly new vision of how to study human sociality' (*LC1*: xii). However, nothing is ever entirely new in the realm of human thought. As Schegloff himself points out, we can learn a great deal about Sacks's ideas by placing them in the context of his intellectual history. Drawing heavily on Schegloff's introduction to Sacks's lectures, I will now try to offer some historical background to Sacks's work.

Some Historical Background

Schegloff shows that several unlikely influences were important in the germination of Sacks's thought. For instance, C. Wright Mills was a member of the sociology faculty while Sacks was an undergraduate student at Columbia in the 1950s. Now Mills, sometimes nicknamed the 'Texas Trot' to signify the odd combination of his southern origins with his radical politics, was known for his interest in historical and political change. More important to Sacks, however, was the intellectual 'audacity' that he reported that he learned from Mills – as well as the faculty library card he obtained with his help. Again, his period at Yale working on a law degree was principally important for learning from Harold Lasswell the importance of focusing on how the law (and, by implication, any social institution) *worked*.

Schegloff (*LC1*: xiii) tells us that Sacks first met Harold Garfinkel in 1959 at Harvard, where Garfinkel was spending his sabbatical. However, direct collaboration with Garfinkel was to be postponed for four more years. In 1959–60, when Sacks began graduate work at Berkeley, he encountered Erving Goffman. As Schegloff reports, 'Sacks took Goffman more seriously than he did virtually any other member of the faculty' (*LC1*: xxiii). By 1962–3, Sacks was a graduate student of Philip Selznick's Center for the Study of Law and Society, where he made the acquaintance of two other sociologists influenced by Garfinkel, Schegloff himself and David Sudnow.

In 1963, Sacks moved to UCLA to work with Garfinkel as fellows at the Center for the Scientific Study of Suicide. Data derived from the Suicide Prevention Center data were central to Sacks's first set of UCLA lectures in 1964–5. By 1966, Sacks had obtained his Ph.D. from Berkeley – but only after Goffman agreed to step aside and allow Aaron Cicourel to chair the committee. Schegloff reports that Goffman found Sacks's argument 'circular' (*LC1*: xxiv, n. 18).

In 1968, Sacks moved to the University of California's Irvine campus where he continued to record his lectures until spring 1972. Finally, in 1974–5, Schegloff reports that he and Sacks were approached to move to UC Santa Barbara to establish an interdisciplinary programme on language, discourse and interaction. This new development was aborted in 1975 when Sacks was tragically killed in a car crash.

It is obvious that Sacks's most important teachers were Erving Goffman and Harold Garfinkel. Because of this, I shall shortly set out some preliminary reflections on his debt to each. However, as Schegloff's extensive introductions to each volume of the *Lectures on Conversation* make clear, Sacks's early work can also be seen as a dialogue with three other programmes of the 1960s, offered by Bales, Homans and Chomsky. I shall therefore begin by examining aspects of Sacks's response to these and other figures who provided the background to his thought. Further discussion of his debate with contemporary social science is to be found in chapter 3.

Background Figures

In the decade between 1955 and 1965, two of the most influential social scientists were the social psychologists Robert Bales and George Homans. Because both were treated as offering crucial methods of studying human interaction, Sacks felt it necessary to situate his work in relation to each of them. As we shall see, his response was hardly favourable.

Like Sacks, Bales (1950) aimed at a precise observational science. Unlike Sacks, he used laboratory studies as a basis to generate intricate sets of categories through which he aspired to report behaviour precisely. In one of his lectures, Sacks describes Bales's method as 'exceedingly foolish' (*LC1*: 28). The problem is that Bales makes the issue of categorization by an analyst seem to be far too easy. Sacks compares Bales's tendency to produce immediate categories of 'interaction process' with the relatively long time taken by experienced physicians to read the output of electro-encephalographs (EEGs). For Sacks, you should not 'categorize ... as it comes out'. Indeed, as we shall see shortly, our ability to categorize quickly is properly treated as a research topic rather than a research resource.

Like Bales, Homans (1961) aimed to replace commonsense with a scientific study of human behaviour based on the analyst's categorization of their interaction. In Homans's case, this led to an explicit contrast between common sense and sociology. As Sacks puts it, Homans 'starts off with the supposition that persons think they know about the thing he wants to study, so he finds a way to show that they don't' (*LC1*: 105).

This is particularly revealed in Homans's treatment of proverbs as usually inconsistent *propositions* about social reality. I came face to face with the importance of Homans's position in the American sociology of the 1960s when, in 1964, I was a teaching assistant on a SOC101 course (Introductory Sociology) at UCLA. I recall vividly the instructor telling students that proverbs like 'too many cooks spoil the broth' and 'many hands make light work' were self-evidently 'contradictory'. Students were informed that the role of social science was to use rigorous laboratory methods of inquiry to establish which proverb was more 'correct'.

By contrast, Sacks shows that the point is not the 'defects' or 'inconsistencies' of proverbs but 'what's done with them' (*LC2*: 422). For instance, uttering a proverb usually produces agreements (*LC1*: 25) and may have other functions such as terminating topics (see Drew and Holt 1988; Silverman 1997a: 138–9). In this way, proverbs are 'invoked to govern various situations' and are therefore 'correct about something' (*LC1*: 105). Instead of 'testing' them, we would, therefore, do better to examine the 'actual occasions of their use' (*LC1*: 106; see also Schegloff in *LC2*: xxxv–xxxvi).

Unlike Bales and Homans, Sacks had no time for attempts to begin with 'operational definitions' of phenomena. Indeed, he pokes fun at the way such definitions are used in Introductory Sociology textbooks (*LC1*: 30). Instead, he says, we need to see how participants themselves employ definitions, without assuming that it is immediately obvious what is important or most basic. For instance, in an answer to a question which asks how to use conversational data to address a traditional sociological problem, Sacks says: 'The first rule is to learn to be interested in what it is you've got. I take it that what you want to do is pose those problems that the data bears' (*LC1*: 471).

A more relevant theorist for Sacks in the early 1960s was the linguist Noam Chomsky. In a broad sense, both Chomsky and Sacks were interested in understanding the basis on which language worked. Moreover, Chomsky's (1965) concern with generative rules of grammar to some extent paralleled Sacks's attempt to construct an apparatus or 'machinery' that would generate observed interactional outcomes (see chapter 4). However, unlike Chomsky (and the earlier Swiss linguist Saussure (1974)), who were principally concerned with deciphering the structural rules of language beneath imagined cases, Sacks seeks to understand the rules that participants demonstrably attend to in actual sequences of conversation. So, for instance, while Saussure was interested in the organization of a menu, Sacks is concerned with the sequential implications of a particular order from the menu (for instance, how

'I think I'll have roast beef' is treated as a 'proposal' for others, as with 'Oh I just had roast beef last night', see chapter 1 above).

However, Sacks's lectures reveal a far wider range of influences, shaped by his enormously extensive range of reading. Philosophical ideas influenced Sacks, from the Greeks through to Wittgenstein. It is evident that Sacks took very seriously the dialogue about mathematics in *The Meno* involving Socrates and a slave boy. Like Socrates, his aim in some sense, was to remind us about things we already know.

Although Sacks only mentions Wittgenstein twice in his lectures, the latter's analysis of what we know already is also clearly relevant. As Wittgenstein put it: 'The aspects of things that are most important for us are hidden because of their simplicity and familiarity' (Wittgenstein 1968: para. 129). In a similar vein, Sacks remarks:

> I take it that lots of the results I offer, people can see for themselves. And they needn't be afraid to. And they needn't figure that the results are wrong because they can see them ... As if we found a new plant. It may have been a plant in your garden, but now you see it's different than something else. And you can look at it to see how it's different, and whether it's different in the way that somebody has said. (*LC1*: 488)

In contemporary philosophy, Sacks was attracted to speech-act theory which treated talk as an activity, as he did. However, Austin (1962) and Searle (1969) do not study actual talk but work with invented examples and their own intuitions about what it makes sense to say. For Sacks, on the contrary:

> One cannot invent new sequences of conversation and feel happy with them. You may be able to take 'a question and an answer', but if we have to extend it very far, then the issue of whether somebody would really say that, after, say, the fifth utterance, is one which we could not confidently argue. One doesn't have a strong intuition for sequencing in conversation. (*LC2*: 5)

One is continuously struck by the rich variety of sources that Sacks offered his students. I have already mentioned his sympathetic reading of the Greeks. But one also finds two unlikely sources. There are recurrent (favourable) references to Freud. And Sacks frequently pulls out some fascinating material from the Old Testament. For example, Adam and Eve are seen as instances of becoming 'observable' where 'to be observable is to be embarrassable' (Sacks 1972b: 281); the Ten Commandments throw light on the organization of agreements; and Sacks draws attention to Job's need to 'rewrite history' when his world is destroyed.

Of course, Sacks also covers more familiar territory, while shifting our focus in a most original way. For instance, he looks at the first two sentences of a child's story: 'The baby cried. The mommy picked it up.' Why do we hear the 'mommy' as the mother of this 'baby'? Sacks asks: 'Is it some kind of magic? One of my tasks is going to be to construct an apparatus for that fact to occur. That is, how we come to hear it in that fashion' (LC1: 236). (For Sacks's full answer, see p. 78 below.)

Based on examples like these, Sacks treats 'socialization' as embedded in the sets of skills learned and deployed when children play games and address adults, using his interest in the work of the folklorists Iona Opie and Peter Opie (1959). In particular, Sacks reveals the role of 'You know what, Mummy?' as a way of getting into conversation, while preserving the adult's control of its direction (see chapter 1 above).

However, in my attempt to situate Sacks's thought, I have so far dealt with background influences on his work. I will conclude this chapter by examining his relation to two figures who were far more important to the direction of his work: the American sociologists Erving Goffman and Harold Garfinkel.

The Influence of Goffman

Judging by the number of references to his work by others, Erving Goffman was probably the most influential sociologist working on face-to-face behaviour. His early work, based on a study of the Shetland Islanders in the 1950s, set out the arts of what Goffman (1959) referred to as 'impression management'. This involved people managing their own appearances by controlling the impressions they gave by, for instance, organizing what guests might see in their home. Goffman further distinguished 'face work', which smoothed interaction by maintaining a ceremonial order, from 'character work', which served to maintain or challenge the moral standing of particular indivuals.

Goffman (1961) charted this 'character work' in the special context of an ethnographic study of what he called 'the moral career of the mental patient'. Goffman suggested that mental hospitals, like other 'total institutions' such as barracks, prisons, monasteries and boarding schools, broke down the usual boundaries between work, rest and play through using various strategies to strip people of their non-institutional identities, dressing inmates in uniforms, for instance, and calling them by a number or institutional nickname.

Faced with what he called a 'mortifying process', Goffman argued that inmates were by no means passive. In particular, they engaged in various 'secondary adjustments' which served to preserve a non-institutionally defined identity. These adjustments ranged from minor infringements of rules ('make-dos') to actively 'working the system' for their own benefit by making skilful use of 'free places' and establishing private and group 'territories'.

Goffman's later work builds on these two earlier studies to describe what he calls the 'interaction order'. For Goffman, social order is based on the collective maintenance of particular definitions of the situation which allow the systematic exclusion of 'troubles', as with the various functionaries who maintain 'proper' appearances at a wedding ceremony. Particularly important here are how events are 'framed' through defining what is and is not relevant and how speakers and hearers take on certain mutual alignments or 'footings' (Goffman 1974).

Unlike Bales, who mainly used laboratory data, Goffman was interested in the complexities of naturally occurring behaviour. Unlike Homans, he did not want to 'correct' everyday understandings but to show the complex way in which they functioned. In fact, Goffman cites as his intellectual ancestor the German sociologist Georg Simmel, commending his penetrating analyses of the 'forms' of social interaction.

One can now start to see why Goffman's work was important to Sacks. Like Goffman, Sacks took Simmel's work very seriously, referring to him as 'one of the greatest of all sociologists' (*LC2*: 132). Like Goffman, Sacks had no interest in building data-free grand theories or in research methods, like laboratory studies or even interviews, which abstracted people from everyday contexts. Above all, both men marvelled at the everyday skills through which particular appearances are maintained.

We can catch sight of Sacks's use of Goffman's ideas in his paper 'Notes on police assessment of moral character' (Sacks 1972b), which was originally written as a course paper for Goffman's course at Berkeley in the early 1960s (p. 280n). For Sacks, police officers face the same kind of problem as Goffman's Shetland Islanders: how are they to infer moral character from potentially misleading appearances?

To solve this problem, police 'learn to treat their beat as a
territory of normal appearances' (p. 284). Now they can treat slight
variations in normal appearances as 'incongruities' worthy
of investigation, working with the assumption of the appearances
of 'normal' crimes (cf. Sudnow 1965).

The link with Goffman is strengthened at various places in the
first volume of Sacks's lectures. For instance, his discussion of the
organization of appearances in someone's home is very close
to that of Goffman (1959): 'the magazines on somebody's coffee
table are routinely seen to be intended to suggest that they are
intellectuals, or whatever else' (*LC*1: 329).

Moreover, Sacks develops this example by trading off
Goffman's (1959) discussion of how a visitor can contrast such
appearances to the appearances they were unable to control but
'gave off'. As Sacks puts it: 'And you can walk out of a house and
say that somebody's a phoney by virtue of some lack of fit between
what you figured you could infer from various things in their
house, and what you've found out about them other than that'
(*LC*1: 329).

In the same volume, we see Sacks drawing on Goffman (1959)
by referring to how people 'control impressions' (*LC*1: 580), and
like Goffman's (1964) book on 'stigma', Sacks discusses the 'covers'
which people such as mental patients may use to conceal stigmat-
ized identities (*LC*1: 592). Finally, in a winter 1970 lecture, Sacks
offers a Goffmanesque discussion of how 'excuse me' rather than
'hello' works as an effective 'ticket' to talk to strangers (*LC*2: 195;
see Goffman 1981: ch. 1).

These kinds of intellectual affinities show why, as a graduate
student at Berkeley, Sacks may have sought out Goffman as his
Ph.D. supervisor. But, as already noted, Goffman turned out to be
very resistant to the ultimate shape of Sacks's dissertation and
eventually withdrew from his committee.

In his own later writings (notably Goffman 1981), Goffman was
to make clear the reasons for this break, referring to what he called
conversation analysis's 'systems engineering' perspective which
failed to do justice, as Goffman believed, to the often non-verbal
organization of 'ritual'. Can we catch any glimpses of the reasons
for this difference of view in Sacks's own work?

First, consider Sacks's interest in Goffman's (1959) work on
ceremonial orders. Although parts of Sacks's early lectures draw
directly from Goffman, it soon becomes clear that Sacks wants to
understand 'ceremony' not by reference to concepts like

'impression management' or 'frames' but to the sequential analysis of conversations.

For instance, we know that the proper return to 'how are you feeling?' is 'fine'. This means that if you want to treat it as a question about your feelings you have to request permission (maybe by saying 'it's a long story' where the next party may say 'that's alright, I have time'). This means that 'everyone has to lie' because people attend to 'the procedural location of their answers' and, in part, produce answers by reference to 'the various uses that the answer may have for next actions that may be done' (*LC1*: 565).

This focus on 'procedural organization' means that Goffman's (1981) attempt to separate the 'ritual' and 'system' requirements of interaction would have been a non-starter for Sacks. Contrary to Goffman's suggestion that Sacks has the focus of a 'systems engineer', Sacks shows that behaviour is *not* rule-governed but rule-guided. In this sense, you can do what you like but you will be held accountable for the implications of your actions. Moreover, unlike an engineering model, social order is merely a *by-product* of social interaction, an 'offshoot of a machine designed to do something else or nothing in particular' (*LC2*: 240).

There are also clear differences in the style of the two sociologists' work. Goffman writes in a very direct way, using hosts of examples, many of them invented or extracted from novels. By contrast, Sacks's publications are written in a very formal style which, unlike his lectures, are accessible only to specialists. Even Sacks's Goffmanian term paper is, in published form, written in a series of numbered points (Sacks 1972b). Perhaps this stylistic difference may be one of the reasons why Goffman came to think of Sacks's work as 'circular' and mechanistic.

But the difference between the two was undoubtedly more than stylistic. Sacks's stock in trade was not anecdotes or invented examples but detailed transcriptions of tape-recorded conversations (see chapter 4 below). By using this kind of data, Sacks claimed that he was able to look at interaction in a much more detailed way.

A good example of this is when a student at one of Sacks's lectures suggests that Sacks's example of a visitor reading appearances in a household is fully explained by Goffman's concept of the incongruous impressions that people 'give off'. Sacks replies that, in fact, he has a basic difference from Goffman's approach. As he puts it:

> Goffman talks about responses to incongruity but he does not tell us what incongruity is. That's what I think I'm beginning to see here in this stuff [data]. *How* it is that one sees it. He has not analyzed how it is that you do 'an incongruity', what makes it an incongruity. (*LC1*: 92)

Another way of putting this is that Sacks wanted to study the local production of social order in far greater detail than Goffman. To do that, as we shall now see, a crucial resource was Harold Garfinkel's ethnomethodology.

The Influence of Garfinkel

Sacks's first publication, 'Sociological description', acknowledges his indebtedness to Garfinkel not only for his funding (from a US Air Force grant) but for 'the stimulus for these thoughts'. Indeed, in this paper, Sacks acknowledges his use of Garfinkel's concepts of 'the commonsense perspective', 'practical theorizing', the 'etcetera principle' and the topic/resource distinction (1963: 10, 16).

Similarly, in his paper called 'An initial investigation of the usability of conversational data for doing sociology', Sacks acknowledges Garfinkel's 'pervasive impact on me' (1972a: 32n). Even in the published form of Sacks's Goffman-inspired early paper on policing, Sacks had noted that he was 'much indebted' to Garfinkel (Sacks 1972b: 280n).

To summarize Garfinkel's position in a page or two is a far more daunting task than was the case with Goffman. It is no coincidence, for instance, that Goffman's book called *Asylums* (1961) was that rare sociological commodity a popular bestseller, while Garfinkel's *Studies in Ethnomethodology* (1967) is, at least initially, a daunting treatise even for experienced scholars (but see Heritage 1984 and Sharrock and Anderson 1986 for guidance). So it may be more helpful in an introductory volume like this to proceed step by step, linking some of Sacks's arguments to Garfinkel as we go.

Sacks's critique of Bales's categories of 'interaction process analysis' is a useful place to begin. Say we are an ethnographer interested in the 'measuring system' of a particular tribe. How are we to study that system? As Sacks says:

> The overwhelming tendency is to use some 'real' – that is, defined as scientifically correct – system, in terms of which one can formulate how it is that the natives go about measuring whatever it is that they're

measuring. So, for example, color terms may be mapped onto the 'real' spectrum known by Western science. (*LC1*: 436)

Ethnographers who measure natives' measuring systems by some 'scientifically correct system' have adopted a Balesian solution. However, the solution generates a further problem: aren't we assuming some stable 'phenomenon' (like 'measurement') to which natives respond? By contrast, Sacks suggests that people should not be seen as 'coming to terms with some phenomenon' (*LC1*: 437) but as actively *constituting* it.

Take the phenomenon of 'speeding' – how does one know one is speeding? One solution is to look at your car's speedometer. However, another well-used method is to compare your movement relative to other traffic. And 'traffic' is a phenomenon that is actively organized by road users. As Sacks suggests:

> persons can be seen to clump their cars into something that is 'a traffic', pretty much wherever, whenever, whoever it is that's driving. That exists as a social fact, a thing which drivers do ... [so] by 'a traffic' I don't mean that there are some cars, but there is a set of cars that can be used as 'the traffic', however it's going; those cars that are clumped. And it is in terms of 'the traffic' that you see you're driving fast or slow. (*LC1*: 437)

Sacks here is suggesting that, rather than being a natural fact, 'the traffic' is a self-organizing system, in which people adjust their speed by reference to 'the traffic'. The traffic thus serves as a metaphor for how social order is constructed by reference to what can be inferred. It also shows how the ability 'to read other people's minds' (in this case, the minds of other drivers) is not a psychotic delusion but a condition for social order.

For Sacks, then, 'traffic' and 'speed' are not natural facts but locally assembled phenomena (see also Pollner 1987). As he notes, the self-same features can be seen in medical interviews, where what is 'normal' is attended to by doctors on the basis of their elicitation of what is normal for you (*LC1*: 57–8). Moreover, while illnesses may be 'erasable', this doesn't usually apply to speeding fines or suicide attempts – hence, for instance, people's reluctance to identify themselves when calling an emergency psychiatric service (*LC1*: 61).

In each of these examples, Sacks's discussion of how phenomena are locally assembled is intimately related to Garfinkel's (1967) account of the procedure through which societal 'members' transform context-bound (or 'indexical') activities into 'objective expressions' of some 'obvious' phenomenon. Garfinkel illustrates this procedure by a number of demonstrations of the way members hear answers to questions as relevant, routine and so on. Below, I set out three examples from Sacks's lectures in fall 1967 to see how he does the same.

Q: When did you have the cast taken off?
A: Tuesday   (*LC*1: 740)

Sacks asks: why isn't the answer November eleventh 1967?

Teacher: How many people don't have paper?
Pupils: ((raise their hands))   (*LC*1: 742)

Sacks asks: why doesn't a pupil look round and answer 'five'?

I'll be there at 9.30   (*LC*1: 742)

Sacks asks why doesn't this speaker say: 'I'll be there at 9.32'?

The alternative answers are logically correct – indeed they are more precise than the answers actually given in all three cases. Yet 'under certain circumstances . . . November eleventh is an answer that would get you committed' (*LC*1: 741). The pupil who answers 'five' is likely to get a rebuke from the teacher and comments like 'smart-ass' from fellow pupils, while, if you say 9.32, people will wonder why you're giving such a precise number.

These three examples show that we select answers not in terms of logic but in relation to 'relevancy constraints' (*LC*1: 743). For instance, in the first example speakers may meet every Saturday, in the second the teacher's question is hearable as asking which pupils need paper, and in the third example you know that people's announced times of arrival are imprecise.

Such 'relevancy constraints' are employed by members in order to discover some 'reality' beneath the 'appearances' of everyday phenomena (like questions). As Garfinkel (1967) argues, this search for 'reality' employs a method whereby appearances are interpreted as 'documenting' some underlying reality – the 'documentary method of interpretation'.

Moreover, not any 'reality' will do. Closely following Garfinkel's use of Alfred Schutz's (1962) argument that everyday life is our 'paramount' reality, Sacks shows that 'ventures out of being ordinary have unknown virtues and unknown costs' (*LC2*: 219). In this sense, we all have to work at being ordinary. As Sacks puts it: 'It's not just that somebody *is* ordinary, it's perhaps that that's what their business is. And it takes work, as any other business does' (*LC2*: 216).

So, for instance, we scan the appearances of scenes in order to see the ways in which they are usual. If we observe something we can tell others (a 'story'), we first look for its 'ordinary' aspects and search for 'ordinary' explanations. So, if we can, we will report that we first heard what turned out to be gunshots as a car backfiring or tell about a plane hijack as a joke (*LC2*: 220).

Following Garfinkel, through such activities, everyday reality is 'accomplished' and made 'observable/reportable' or 'storyable' as Sacks (*LC2*: 218) puts it. Through this accomplishment, we permit ourselves routine ways of dealing with scenes which allows you to read strangers' minds (*LC2*: 221). And these 'routine ways' are embedded or, as Garfinkel (1967) put it, 'incarnate' or 'reflexive' in whatever we do.

Contrary to many social scientists who use 'reflexivity' to refer to self-consciousness (about values and the like), for Garfinkel the term points to the way understanding is constituted locally, *in situ*. As Sacks suggested in a joint lecture, it is a question of 'what forms of social organization get participants to occasions of talk to do the work of understanding the talk of others in the very ways and at the same times as they do that work?' (Moerman and Sacks 1971: MS 3).

However, as Garfinkel suggests, this kind of reflexivity is unavailable for conventional social science, including sociology. Garfinkel (1967) argues that this is because such social science confuses the distinction between what he calls 'topic' and 'resource'. Because it treats its members' knowledge of the everyday world as a tacit 'resource', it cannot, even if it would want to, make the accomplishment of that world a research 'topic'.

This is precisely how Sacks characterizes what he terms 'conventional social science'. Taking the example of social surveys of religious belief, he comments: 'at the end of a survey, when you try to decide that you've got decent findings, you will say "Well, we know that religion counts for politics, and if we've got that kind of correlation, then we can say, 'See? We understand it.' Because we know that it counts." ("We" being "any Member")' (*LC1*: 487).

By contrast, like Garfinkel, Sacks wants to 'turn that around' by treating such 'findings' as a 'topic'. So what Sacks wants to do is 'to use what "we" know, what any Member knows, to pose us some problems. What activity is being done, for example. And then see whether we can build an apparatus which will give us those results' (*LC*1: 487).

Sharing Garfinkel's disdain for ironic comparisons, Sacks preferred to treat conventional social science's ability to produce its findings as an 'accomplishment' rather than as a cause for direct criticism (see *LC*2: 339). Of course, this only served to infuriate such social scientists who, in their terms, knew a criticism when they saw one.

Not only did Sacks want to abstain from criticism, he also refused to respond to suggestions that social science must justify itself by its contribution to 'society'. We see this very clearly in a question and answer session with a student. This passage about Sacks's analysis of Members' categories occurs at the end of one of his spring 1966 lectures:

> Q: Will it ever have any possible relevance to the people who were involved in producing it?
> A: It needn't have any relevance ... I take it that there's an enormous amount of studies that are not intended to be relevant. For example, studies of how cancer does cancer is not intended to build better cancer ... (*LC*1: 470)

In this answer, Sacks closely follows what Garfinkel terms 'ethnomethodological indifference' to questions of how things (whether cancer, social problems or, indeed, social science itself) *should be*. Of course, his answer depends on a degree of sophistry – presumably the student did not intend that research should help cancer!

Sacks's answer also looks a little dangerous today when funding bodies seem to demand 'relevance' for any piece of research. However, we might defend Sacks's argument in two ways. First, if ethnomethodology has some claim to be 'basic' research, then it may demand support whether or not any short-term social benefit can be shown. Second, recent applied work using methods that ultimately derive from Sacks can, in my view, undoubtedly claim to contribute to the solution of several practical issues, most notably in the field of organizational interaction (see Drew and Heritage 1992; Peräkylä 1995; Silverman 1997a).

Today, there is some debate about the relative positions of Garfinkel and Sacks as the 'founding fathers' of ethnomethodology and conversation analysis (see chapter 9). As we have seen, Sacks acknowledged a great debt to Garfinkel. It is interesting, then, that Schegloff, when listing writers concerned with 'other processes' (than Sacks was concerned with), includes not only Bales but Schutz (concerned with 'interpretive strategies') *and* Garfinkel (commonsense methods) (*LC1*: xviii). So, for Schegloff, Sacks's project needs to be separated from ethnomethodology's philosophical ancestor and its founding father.

To some extent, there is evidence that Sacks himself went some way towards agreeing with Schegloff's assessment. For instance, in his earliest publication, after acknowledging his indebtedness to Garfinkel, he added that 'he is far from agreeing with all that I have to say' (1963: 1n).

Clearly, Sacks's work was driven by a concern (to do a systematic science) absent from Garfinkel's project (cf. Schegloff in *LC1*: xxxii). We can get some sense of this by examining the response of the two writers to the work of the French sociologist of the late nineteenth century Émile Durkheim (see also chapter 3 below). Garfinkel (1967) acknowledges a debt to Durkheim's conception of the 'moral order'. But Garfinkel also makes clear that, unlike Durkheim, his aim was to discover the reflexive moral order 'within' whatever members were doing.

Durkheim is much more relevant to Sacks than to Garfinkel. Not only does Sacks share Durkheim's anti-psychologistic thrust, but, unlike Garfinkel, Sacks makes no bones about doing a 'science' aimed at understanding 'culture', albeit in a very different sense. For Sacks, you no longer need to use such a gloss as 'culture' when you can closely observe the 'machinery' that members use to produce particular outcomes. When studying a conversation, as Sacks clearly shows:

> our aim is ... to transform ... our view of what happened here as some interaction that could be treated as the thing we're studying, to interactions being spewed out by machinery, the machinery being what we're trying to find; where, in order to find it, we've got to get a whole bunch of its products. (*LC2*: 169)

Unlike Garfinkel, then, Sacks aims for a cumulative science of conversation, through offering what Schegloff terms a way of obtaining 'stable accounts of human behavior [through] producing accounts of the methods and procedures for producing it' (in *LC1*: xxxi). As Schegloff puts it, the task then is based on the observation of actual talk with actual outcomes. The question one poses is simply: how was this outcome accomplished? The method is straightforward: 'begin with some observations, then find the problem for which these observations could serve as ... the solution' (*LC1*: xlviii).

Conclusion

As Schegloff implies, in working out an intellectual heritage it is difficult to separate the facts from the politics of the situation. In particular, he draws our attention to how his own editing of the transcripts of Sacks's lectures may have imposed a particular reading with possible political consequences (*LC1*: x-xi). Indeed, Schegloff's own observations imply a positioning of Sacks's work which others have contested. In particular, this is seen in Schegloff's view that Sacks abandoned parts of his analysis of members' descriptions because 'of an incipient promiscuous use of them' (*LC1*: xlii) (see chapter 5 below).

Ultimately, however, attempts to draw final boundaries between different approaches to social science serve to work against the very kind of lateral thinking that original minds like Sacks encourage. So this chapter is intended to give a context to Sacks's work rather than to position it for all time.

Perhaps the most telling part of Schegloff's comments relates not to such a positioning but to the sense of difficulty that Sacks and he felt as they tried, in the mid–1960s, to establish conversation analysis. Garfinkel's injunction to make the familiar 'strange' involved the difficult task of needing to see 'around the corner'. Moreover, at the time, it was not at all clear how to build a discipline from the observations that Sacks and he were making (Schegloff in *LC1*: lix). Indeed, they felt an ever-present danger of 'lapsing back into a mundane, vernacular, commonsense hearing/understanding' (*LC2*: xvii).

Schegloff's observations carry an important message to those of us who write and read the kind of intellectual histories offered in this chapter. As Thomas Kuhn (1970) showed, the history of thought is not a seamless web. Although, as we shall see in chapter 4, Sacks recommended his method as a method anyone could use, it was a method that was hard-earned.

3
Social Science

Readers of this book will, I hope, be drawn from a range of backgrounds. In this chapter, I will try to help to position Sacks's work within a range of approaches and disciplines, including anthropology, linguistics and ethnography. However, bearing in mind Sacks's presence in a sociology department, I also return to Sacks's relationship to Émile Durkheim as a key classical figure of sociological thought.

First, however, I want to give a context to Sacks's position in relation to a view of social science conceived of as a 'machine'. For reasons that will become clear, the 'machine' metaphor was very important for Sacks.

The Social Science 'Machine'

All social scientists have, wittingly or unwittingly, a sense of what social science is as a project. Some follow directly from others' orientations, sometimes even conceiving their research topics in terms of popularly recognized social problems. This is the conservative view of social science. Other, more radical spirits, shift gears dramatically and form entirely new projects from a discipline. This often transforms received wisdom and existing terminology and moves them into new directions with new sets of meanings.

We can see the conservative view of social science by examining which kind of research topics appear to get funding by public agencies. As a gross generalization, I suggest that funded research often claims to focus on the *causes* of some apparently important social problem or issue (crime, unemployment, entrepreneurial activity, etc.). Although the media have a highly selective concern with social research, this focus is seen as I write in newspaper reports of a psychological study of the causes of 'compulsive shopping syndrome'. So such research begins with a 'fact' like this (usually as measured by statistical indices) and then hunts down whatever may have caused that fact.

As Sacks puts it, in such research 'one has to find some indices, and build an apparatus that would maintain the indices in whatever way they seem to stand – or fall' (*LC1*: 484). This apparatus or 'machinery' consists of sets of 'causes' which are used to explain the stability or variability of indices of given social problems. If there are no such indices (or no readily measurable causes), then, says Sacks, we assume that there is no 'nice stuff' to be found. Hence it is assumed we must be dealing with something 'random' and therefore non-researchable (or 'garbage'). So, for Sacks, the social science 'machine' looks like 'a machine with a couple of holes in the front. It spews out some nice stuff from these holes, and out of the back it spews out garbage' (*LC1*: 484).

Above all else, the social science machine attacks social problems, which are seen to constitute what Sacks says we call 'big issues'. By contrast, activities which are 'terribly mundane, occasional, local, and the like' (*LC1*: 484) are not viewed as big issues.

Now, as Sacks notes, it is not as if social science usually fails in its stated project. It routinely succeeds in what it attempts to do, that is, its 'machine' does describe and explain what we take to be 'social order'. For instance, social surveys, despite their statistical limits, get orderly results. And, at the other extreme, sociolinguistics appears to be able to build grammars of a particular language simply by a researcher talking to one native speaker, as in Whorf's work on the Navajo (*LC1*: 485).

Is all this an example of the genius of social scientists? Or rather may it not depend on a sleight of hand? For instance, we can respond to Whorf's account of Navajo grammar by saying: '"Isn't that fantastic? What a genius he must have been." But then we could say, well, how many people does any given Navajo encounter when he learns to do Navajo? Are they such geniuses?' (*LC1*: 485).

In this sense, the accomplishments of sociolinguists and social surveyors are cast in a new light. For their apparent 'answers' to 'big' questions may turn out to depend on the deeply mundane skills that we all use in everyday life. And these skills remain unexplicated by research both because they are not seen as 'big' problems and because such research demands that they be used as a resource rather than as a topic (see Garfinkel 1967).

Sociology and Durkheim

In many respects, the work of the French sociologist Émile Durkheim at the end of the nineteenth century provides a provoking example of these issues. To attempt a crude simplification, for Durkheim behaviour is seen to arise from social conventions or norms. Given any aspect of social action, Durkheim then wants to examine how it is shaped by norms, and how, in turn, norms are reinforced by social action. So, for instance, to Durkheim, communal responses to crime or public disasters appear to have an integrative function for society.

As Sacks notes, Durkheim's argument appears to be plausible in the light of our personal experience. For instance, when strangers put their arms around each other after witnessing some disaster, we don't have any trouble in working out what they are up to (LC2: 194). But, as with the Navajo, the question for Sacks is what everyday skills all of us (including Durkheim) are using to *see* a norm together and know that we saw the same thing (LC1: 93). Once again, the trick is not to look for 'big' issues such as societal processes but rather at how we see and do whatever we see or do. For instance, in the case of response to disasters, Sacks notes how such publicly observable situations provide a 'ticket' for strangers to talk (LC2: 196–7).

The reader may now be in a position to see why, in his earliest publication (1963), Sacks would have aimed 'to make current sociology strange' because 'the stance it adopts towards its subject matter seems so peculiar to me' (p. 1). For Sacks, sociology's stance is 'peculiar' not because it is counter-intuitive but precisely because it *is* intuitive and commonsensical.

Take the case of how sociologists use informants to support their findings, for instance in interview studies or by means of 'respondent validation'. By doing so, Sacks suggests that they treat people's ability to give and receive 'sensible' descriptions in different contexts as entirely non-remarkable. As he puts it: 'The essential "message" of this paper is: even if it can be said that persons produce descriptions of the social world, the task of sociology is not to clarify these, or to "get them on the record" or to criticize them, but to describe them' (p. 7).

Sacks's paper is rightly famous for the example of a machine with its own built-in commentator. He tells us that this hypothetical machine might be described by the layman in the following terms: 'It has two parts; one part is engaged in doing some job, and the other part synchronically narrates what the first part does ... For the commonsense perspective the machine might be called a "commentator machine", its parts "the doing" and "the saying" parts' (p. 5).

For a native speaking sociologist, the 'saying' part of the machine is to be analysed as a good, poor or ironical description of the actual working of the machine (pp. 5–6). However, Sacks points out that this sociological explanation trades off two kinds of unexplained knowledge: '(a) knowing in common with the machine the language it emits; and (b) knowing in some language what the machine is doing' (p. 6).

But to know 'what the machine is doing' ultimately depends on a set of pre-scientific, commonsense assumptions based on everyday language and employed to sort 'facts' from 'fancy'. It follows that our ability to 'describe social life', whether as laypeople or sociologists, 'is a happening' which it should properly be the 'job of sociology' (p. 7) to describe rather than tacitly to use.

We now see why Sacks should have referred to sociology's 'peculiar stance'. Quite properly, he suggests, sociology seeks to be a science. In doing so, it needs to seek a 'literal' description of its subject matter. However, this search is undercut, in Sacks's view, by sociology's use of concepts ('a descriptive apparatus') based on unexplained assumptions (p. 2).

This problem is readily seen in Durkheim's famous attempt to relate suicide to levels of social integration, using statistics (Durkheim 1952). For Sacks, the problem is not that the statistics may be distorted but that Durkheim treats the issue of identifying a suicide as resoluble by referring to a working or 'operational' definition. Sacks is worth quoting at length on this point:

> The crucial problem with Durkheim's *Suicide* is not that he employs official statistics, but that he adopts the problem of practical theory. 'Suicide' is a category of the natural language. It leads to a variety of practical problems, such as, for example, explaining particular suicides or explaining the variety of suicide rates. To say that Durkheim's error was to use official records rather than for example studying the variation in the reporting of suicides is to suppose that it is obvious that

events occur which sociologists should consider 'really suicide' ... An investigation of how it is that a decision that a suicide occurred is assembled, and an investigation of how an object must be conceived in order to talk of it as 'committing suicide', these are the preliminary problems for sociology ...

Till we have described the category, suicide, i.e. produced a description of the procedure employed for assembling cases of the class, the category is not even potentially part of the sociological apparatus. (Sacks 1963: 8, n. 8).

Sacks's insistence on the priority of describing the everyday 'procedure employed for assembling cases of the class' radically separates his position both from Durkheim *and* from interactionist or subjectivist sociologies (see the discussion of Goffman in chapter 2 above). Despite their apparent differences, both Durkheim and Goffman take for granted some social 'reality' to which people respond (such as 'suicide') or describe a process (such as 'labelling') identified on the basis of tacit commonsense reasoning. Their common failing is, as Sacks puts it, that they work with 'undescribed categories': 'To employ an undescribed category is to write descriptions such as appear in children's books. Interspersed with series of words there are pictures of objects' (1963: 8, n. 8).

For Sacks, most sociologists get by through simply 'pointing' at familiar objects (what philosophers call 'ostensive' definition). So they are able to give an account of what Sacks's 'commentator machine' is 'doing' by invoking 'what everybody knows' about how things are in society – using what Garfinkel (1967) refers to as the 'etcetera principle'. They thus pretend to offer a 'literal' description of phenomena which conceals their 'neglect [of] some undetermined set of their features' (Sacks 1963: 13).

Moreover, such neglect cannot be remedied, as some researchers claim, by assembling panels of judges to see if they see the same thing (for instance, inter-coder agreement as a basis for claiming that one's descriptions of data are reliable). Such agreement offers no solution because it simply raises further questions about the *ability* of members of society to see things in common – presumably by using the 'etcetera' principle as a tacit resource (see Clavarino, Najman and Silverman 1995).

Sacks's problem is to find a way to build a sociology that does better than this. In some way, sociology must free itself from the 'commonsense perspective' (1963: 10–11) employed in its use of 'undescribed categories'. For Sacks, the solution is to view such categories 'as features of social life which sociology must treat as subject matter' rather than 'as sociological resources' (p. 16).

What looks like a complicated theoretical solution turns out, however, to involve a quite straightforward direction for research. We must give up defining social phenomena at the outset (like Durkheim) or through the accounts that subjects give of their behaviour (Sacks's 'commentator machine'). Instead, we must simply focus on what people *do*. As Sacks puts it: 'whatever humans do can be examined to discover some way they do it, and that way would be describable' (*LC1*: 484).

Sacks concedes that this kind of research can seem to be 'enormously laborious' (*LC1*: 65). However, he denies critics' claims that it is trivial. You only need to look at the ability of both laypersons and conventional researchers consistently to find recognizable meaning in situations to realize that social order is to be found in even the tiniest activity. The accomplishment of this 'order at all points' (*LC1*: 484) thus constitutes the exciting new topic for social research.

As Sacks recognizes, however, no topic is ever entirely new in human knowledge. As we shall shortly see, there were varieties of sociology which Sacks saw as partially relevant to his task. But the most immediately relevant work was to be found in the disciplines of anthropology and linguistics. Let us consider each in turn.

Anthropology

In his 'commentator machine' paper, Sacks (1963) had made a great point of how native speakers could take for granted their own ability to make ready sense of what others 'meant'. In this respect, anthropology's 'problem' – understanding other cultures – can thus be seen to have great merit. Face to face with both languages and behaviours that do not permit ready understanding, the anthropologist is forced to ask basic questions about how 'order at all points' is achieved by native speakers.

This seems to be why Sacks's lectures have many approving references to anthropological studies. For instance, Sacks finds Max Gluckman's *Order and Rebellion in Tribal Africa* to be instructive because of its focus on 'the reasonable wrongdoer in Barotse law'. Gluckman's concern with how the Barotse construct their 'picture' of possibly unlawful behaviours allows Sacks to pose a question about the 'machinery' that is being used. For Sacks, the Barotse version of the 'wrongdoer' raises the issue of 'how a human gets built who will produce his activities such that they're graspable in this way' (*LC1*: 119).

For similar reasons, Sacks cites Evans-Pritchard's (1937) book on witchcraft among the Azande as 'one of the greatest books in the social sciences' (*LC1*: 34). According to Evans-Pritchard, the Azande don't have a notion of chance. They believe that everything that happens to them is ultimately caused by some other person or agency. Thus, when faced with an untoward event, the Azande consult the oracle to find out who is responsible.

Like Gluckman, Evans-Pritchard has described the procedures used by a community to describe the social world. Moreover, his focus on 'chance' illuminates a procedure taken for granted in most Western societies where 'chance' can be readily used to explain untoward events. Indeed, in our society, 'persons who do not have a notion of chance are persons who have the symptoms of paranoid schizophrenia' (*LC1*: 35).

However, the conclusion that studying other cultures can open our minds to our own is commonplace. Indeed, it can lead in a Durkheimian direction where behaviour is simply 'explained' as a product of 'culture' without problematizing the 'machinery' involved. Sometimes anthropology appears to appeal to 'culture' in this mechanistic sense. For instance, Sacks cites Ethel Albert's (1964) work on the Burundi for its fascinating focus on how the Burundi organize their conversations (in an apparently very hierarchical way). However, for Sacks, we still need to describe *how* this is done rather than to treat the rules of conversational sequencing as *given* by culture (*LC1*: 624–32).

Once we shift our focus away from the content of different cultures towards the machinery through which particular activities get recognizably 'done', we open up the possibility of cross-cultural *similarities*. For instance, sequences of returned greetings and of questions followed by answers do not seem to be at all culture-specific (*LC1*: 98). It follows that the regularities for which Sacks is looking may be basic to all social life. To that extent, following Chomsky, Sacks speculates whether biology or neurology may not be just as relevant for his task as anthropology. As he puts it: 'if you get that kind of stability, across fantastically different languages, then the social sciences and the biological sciences come to some close relationship' (*LC1*: 98–9).

Such an opposition to a deterministic model of 'culture' explains why Schegloff and Sacks (1974) reject a suggestion by the sociolinguist Dell Hymes that they might characterize their findings on the sequential organization of conversation as relating to 'conversation rules in American English' (p. 35). A focus on the local machinery of conversation means that we must forgo any quick recourse to explanations in terms of national and language identification.

On this basis, the anthropologists' concept of 'culture' is best approached as what Sacks calls an 'inference-making machine' (*LC*1: 119). So culture becomes a descriptive apparatus which is to be revealed in how descriptions are 'administered' and used in specific contexts.

Once again, this focus on behaviour rather than 'meaning' or 'thought' suggests that we should not have recourse to 'comment-ators' who interpret the 'meaning' of their culture. This implies a methodological problem for much anthropological research pre-cisely because so many anthropological ethnographies rely on native informants. As Sacks puts it: 'the trouble with their work is that they're using informants; that is, they're asking questions of their subjects. That means that they're studying the categories that Members use ... they are not investigating their categories by attempting to find them in the activities in which they're employed' (*LC*1: 27).

I shall return to this issue of 'investigating categories' in chapter 5. For the moment, it is sufficient to note Sacks's emphasis here on looking at 'activities' rather than 'asking questions'. In this respect, we see Sacks's sympathy for any form of human or biological science (from anthropology to linguistics and even psychology and biology) seriously concerned with understanding behaviour. As Sacks puts it: 'if you figure, or guess, or decide that whatever the human does, it's just another *animal* after all, maybe more complic-ated than others but perhaps not noticeably so, then whatever humans do can be examined to discover some way they do it, and that way would be describable' (*LC*1: 484, emphasis added).

Linguistics

Sacks cites linguistics as 'the most advanced social science' (*LC*1: 647). His praise for it seems to derive from its determination to build a model of social life from an empirical understanding of what Sacks calls 'actual linguistic events'. Linguists who treat the utterance as the basic unit for linguistic research allowed postwar linguistics to become an empirical field which, in a real sense, focused on the machinery through which we communicate with one another. As we shall see in chapter 6, the turn by turn organ-ization of utterances became the major direction for Sacks's research. In this way, linguistics was an important inspiration for the study of such empirical matters as utterance completion (*LC1*: 649), the organization of next turns by 'tying' mechanisms (*LC1*: 650) and, indeed, the whole topic of sequencing in conversation (*LC1*: 622).

However, Sacks also notes a problem with work then current in linguistics. Linguists tended not to look at conversations; indeed many did not go beyond the analysis of a sentence. In particular, when linguistics appeals to the linguistic organization that allows speakers to understand novel sentences, it may overlook the *social* organization of understanding in conversation.

To investigate this social organization, one must gather recordings of actual conversation rather than simply produce instances from the armchair like certain linguists and 'ordinary language' philosophers (such as J. L. Austin and John Searle). As Sacks argues: 'What we need to do ... is to watch conversations ... I don't say that we should rely on our recollection for conversation, because it's very bad ... One can invent new sentences and feel comfortable with them. One cannot invent new sequences of conversation and feel comfortable about them' (*LC2*: 5).

These issues were stated in a most pointed way by Moerman and Sacks in a lecture called 'On understanding in conversation', given to a symposium on the relation between anthropology and linguistics held at the seventieth annual meeting of the American Anthropological Association in New York in November 1971. Following Sacks's concern with the machinery of interaction, in this lecture Moerman and Sacks pose as the basic question: 'Why do people understand one another?' Both anthropology and linguistics do offer stimulating but incomplete answers to this question: 'Anthropology appeals to "culture", linguistics to the linguistic organization that allows speakers to understand novel sentences. But what about *social* organization?' (Moerman and Sacks 1971: MS 1).

Consonant with my earlier discussion, this social organization can be observed within the structures of conversation. So Moerman and Sacks rephrase their previous question: 'What forms of social organization secure the recurrence of understanding among parties to conversation, the central institution of language use?' (MS 3).

Using Moerman's work on conversation among the Lue, a Thai hill tribe, Moerman and Sacks show that 'culture' is an inadequate concept to explain this social organization. For instance, Moerman found many counter-intuitive similarities between Thai and American English speakers. In particular, the common conversational rule was: one speaker talks at a time with no gaps or overlaps. This was accomplished in both 'cultures' by a number of mechanisms:

- speakers noticing and correcting violations;
- collaboratively locating transition points;
- collaboratively locating next speaker;
- co-participants listening for completions, turn transitions, insults, etc. (MS 8)

Through these and other mechanisms, not only do Thai and English speakers communicate with one another but they do so in an apparently effortless way: 'continually, there and then – without recourse to follow-up tests, mutual examination of memoirs, surprise quizzes and other ways of checking on understanding – [participants] demonstrate to one another that they understood or failed to understand the talk they are party to' (MS 10).

By analysing this 'continual, there and then' demonstration, we can bring into focus the apparatus which is occluded by Sacks's hypothetical commentator machine. Moreover, by learning from linguistics and neurology about the sheer depth of human communication skills, sociologists can overcome their tendency to treat human action in terms of over-rationalistic or deterministic models. As Moerman and Sacks suggest: 'The instant availability of elaborate rules of grammar shows that our naive notion of how little the human brain can do quickly is wrong' (MS 11).

Ethnography

So far we have been looking at what Sacks took from other disciplines, given his critique of much of his own discipline of sociology. However, Sacks was too sophisticated a thinker to believe that any approach, including his own, could learn nothing from its predecessors. In particular, his lectures make many favourable references to the tradition of ethnographic work that originated in the 1930s in the sociology department of the University of Chicago. This work represented the first flowering of an empirical school of sociology concerned with observing what it termed the 'sub-cultures' to be found in the buildings and the streets of the modern city (see Hammersley 1989).

Despite taking a different theoretical tack, Sacks found much to admire in the Chicago School's attention to detail:

> Instead of pushing aside the older ethnographic work in sociology, I would treat it as the only work worth criticizing in sociology; where criticizing is giving some dignity to something. So, for example, the relevance of the works of the Chicago sociologists is that they do contain a lot of information about this and that. And this-and-that is what the world is made up of. (*LC1*: 27)

Like the older ethnographers, Sacks rejected the crass empiricism of certain kinds of quantitative sociology. In particular, as we have seen, its assumptions that research is based on finding some indices and explaining why they rise and fall by *ex post facto* interpretations of significant correlations.

Sacks was convinced that serious work paid attention to detail and that, if something mattered, it should be observable. For instance, in a fascinating passage, Sacks noted the baleful influence on sociology of G. H. Mead's proposal that we need to study things which are not available to observation, such as 'society' and 'attitudes' (see Mead 1934). As Sacks comments: 'But social activities are observable, you can see them all around you, and you can write them down. The tape recorder is important, but a lot of this can be done without a tape recorder. If you think you can see it, that means we can build an observational study' (*LC1*: 28).

However, the ethnographers' praiseworthy attention to detail rarely satisfied Sacks's rigorous methodological demands, informed by his critique of the naive sociology of the 'commentator machine'. In the box overleaf, I offer a summary list of Sacks's specific points of departure from the ethnographic tradition (including sociolinguistics and cognitive anthropology as well as the Chicago School). Much of this argument is drawn from Sacks's early lecture called 'An impromptu survey of the literature' (*LC1*: 26–31). In addition, his lecture 'On doing "being ordinary" ' (*LC2*: 215–21) should be read by every ethnographer.

Sociology

As already noted, for Sacks the ethnography of the 1960s had the merit of searching for detail. It also was beginning to pose what for him was a crucial issue: the problematic character of how we

Methodological imperatives for an observational social science

1 Avoid summary representations of the data in favour of providing detailed transcripts. In this way 'the reader has as much information as the author and can reproduce the analysis' (*LC1*: 27).

2 Pursue data-sets which allow study of the fine details of behaviour. This will usually mean taping conversations: 'My research is about conversation in only this incidental way, that conversation is something that we can get the actual happenings of on tape ... If you can't deal with the actual details of actual events then you can't have a science of social life' (*LC2*: 26).

3 Question the reliance of so much ethnography on interview data: 'the trouble with their work is that they're using informants; that is, they're asking questions of their subjects. That means that they're studying the categories that Members use ... they are not investigating their categories by attempting to find them in the activities in which they're employed' (*LC1*: 27). This means that Sacks is concerned with what he calls 'understanding as displayed' in actual behaviour rather than 'understanding as tested' (for instance, by sociological interviews) (*LC2*: 30–1).

4 Analyse the most basic details of interaction rather than relying on glosses of what-everyone-knows ('If you're going to have a science of social life, then, like all other sciences of something or other, it should be able to handle the details of something that actually happens') (*LC2*: 26).

5 Reject the anti-scientific position of some interactionists (such as Blumer 1969). Sacks wanted to do a *better* science. For instance, he criticized laboratory studies only for their lack of success, not for their aim of producing a 'science of society'. So lab studies of, say, 'short-term memory' fail because they ask the wrong question, namely 'do people understand what somebody else says?' Instead, researchers should be asking: 'is there some *procedure* people use which has, as its product, a showing that they heard and understood?' (*LC2*: 30, emphasis adapted).

6 Make common sense, as Garfinkel (1967) put it, a 'topic' not just a tacit 'resource'. Thus the problem with *both* survey research and much ethnography is that they fail to topicalize their understandings. As Sacks says: 'Now [w]hat I want to do is turn that around: to use what "we" know, what any Member knows, to pose us some problems. What activity is being done, for example. And then we can see whether we can build an apparatus which will give us those results' (*LC1*: 487).

describe our observations. Put at its simplest, this relates to what categories we use. As Sacks says:

> Suppose you're an anthropologist or sociologist standing somewhere. You see somebody do some action, and you see it to be some activity. How can you go about formulating who is it that did it, for the purposes of your report? Can you use at least what you might take to be the most conservative formulation – his name? (*LC1*: 467)

As Sacks suggests, this apparently trivial problem is actually not resoluble by better technique, like detailed note-taking. Rather it raises basic analytic issues: 'The problem of strategy . . . may not be readily handleable by taking the best notes possible at the time and making your decisions afterwards. For one, there is an issue of when it is for the Members that it turns out who did the thing' (*LC1*: 468).

In fact, many contemporary ethnographers, now aided by advanced software packages, ignore this problem. In the way Sacks suggests, they simply put in some set of categories derived from lay usage (*LC1*: 629). By doing so, of course, we are no wiser as to how, *in situ*, categories are actually deployed and enforced or as to how violations in category use are actually recognized (*LC1*: 635–6).

The limits of ethnography reveal the limits of much contemporary sociology. For Sacks, the discipline of sociology has failed to grasp the analytic nettle. As he puts it: 'All the sociology we read is unanalytic, in the sense that they simply put some category in. They may make sense to us in doing that, but they're doing it simply as *another Member*' (*LC1*: 41–2, emphasis added).

The availability of alternative category collections (for example, first names, surnames, occupational or family titles) means that any sociology that aspires to do more than reiterate commonsense understandings must specify how members categorize (*LC1*: 803). Only in this way, can sociology can be 'a natural observational science' (*LC1*: 802).

By contrast, much sociology has sheltered behind commonsense understandings dressed up as scientific explanations, using 'concepts' which ultimately derive from what we already know in common without understanding that everyday 'classes and categories permit you to see' things in the first place (*LC1*: 83, 87). For instance, as we saw in the case of public responses to disasters, sociologists will appeal to norms as explanations of behaviour while trading off their own native ability to see such a norm in action

(*LC1*: 253). Even when such sociology uses transcripts of talk rather than statistical arrays as its data, it will focus on the *content* of what is said, deciding what is remarkable and unremarkable by using lay standards dressed up as a sociological method (*LC1*: 312).

Sacks's lectures are, in part, a plea for the social sciences to reconsider their subject matter and, thereby, its analytic purpose. Beginning with the observability of 'order at all points', our first task should be to inspect the 'collections of social objects – like "How are you feeling?" – which persons assemble to do their activities. And how they assemble those activities is describable with respect to any one of them they happen to do' (*LC1*: 27).

As Sacks's example 'How are you feeling?' shows, this means that sociology will have to reject its prevalent assumption that only 'macro' structures are important. A quarter of a century later, very little has changed in this regard. In 1995, I can recall an eminent British sociologist asking me how I could defend our work on videos of AIDS counselling (Peräkylä 1995; Silverman 1997a) as properly sociological! Yet, as we saw in chapter 1, thirty years earlier Sacks had rejected 'the notion that you could tell right off whether something was important' (*LC1*: 28).

Conclusion

In developing this characterization of Sacks's view of the social sciences, I have drawn highly selectively on his writings and lectures. Using this approach, I am very wary of having given a highly partial view of his concerns. To the extent that Sacks is polemical, he is trying to excite the interest of an audience. This is why his broad-brush, critical comments on other social scientists are largely found in the opening lecture of each of his courses.

In fact, consonant with his rigorous methods, Sacks is usually much more cautious in how he approaches what others have written. His response below to a question from a student shows how he was very careful about appearing to take a global 'position':

> If you really want me to talk about what sociology ought to be about, or what relation any of these things has to what I do, I wouldn't want to do it in class, because that's like taking a position. These can't be handled *seriously* unless one takes them as the kind of issues they are; like take a line out of a book and *try to see how that fellow came to write that*. (*LC1*: 31, emphasis added)

In part, Sacks's appeal to 'serious' handling of such issues reflects scholarly caution. In part also, he was following his teacher, Harold Garfinkel, who always denied that he was trying to make ironic comparisons between his work and other varieties of sociology. So it would do a fundamental disservice to Sacks's achievement to pretend that it derives from entering the continuing war between competing social science paradigms. Instead, Sacks is altogether more positive.

As we shall see in the next chapter, this positive focus in part derives from the methodological 'toolkit' that Sacks offers the novice researcher. At the same time, he would never reduce research to sets of tools and techniques. Social science is nothing unless it begins with some vision of its purpose. While sociology has often derived this vision from apparently *political* purposes, by contrast Sacks offered an *aesthetic* vision. As he said to his students: 'One of the basic things I want to be able to give you is an *aesthetic* for social life. By that I mean in part we should have some sense of where it is deep, and to be able to see, and to pose, problems' (*LC1*: 113, emphasis added).

We now need to describe how this aesthetic vision allows us to identify, in Sacks's terms, what is 'deep' about social life. Through this identification, we can pose, and try to answer, analytically interesting research problems.

4

Method

All social research ultimately derives its vision from some theory and set of related concepts about how social reality works. Although Sacks was conscious about what we could learn from earlier research, as we saw in the last chapter, he came to reject many much-used social science concepts. Anthropology looks for explanations in terms of 'culture' and sociology often appeals to 'social structure'. Yet, for Sacks, neither concept helps in explaining the fine detail of how people interact. The attention of linguistics to the linguistic organization that allows speakers to understand novel sentences certainly appears to offer a more 'ground level' approach to human interaction. But it necessarily deflects the analyst's attention from the *social* organization through which people communicate.

For Sacks, we start to see what is 'deep' about social life by focusing relentlessly on what people do and analysing how they do it. As he puts it: 'whatever humans do can be examined to discover some way they do it' (Sacks 1984a: 22). This means that we must forgo appeals to concepts like 'culture' and 'social structure' which rush us towards explanations of phenomena which have barely been identified, except in commonsense terms. Instead, we must examine *how* people achieve whatever they do achieve by focusing on the social organization of members' mundane practices (see Silverman and Gubrium 1994).

A concern, in this sense, with 'how' questions means that we must avoid the temptation to start off any analysis by bringing problems to the data, using categories derived from conventional social science and/or common sense, such as 'culture', 'power' or 'gender'. Instead, we ought to proceed inductively. For Sacks, in practice, this meant carefully transcribing a tape of some naturally occurring data and trying to identify how it is socially organized (Sacks 1984a). As he put it, we 'make a bunch of observations and see where they will go' (p. 27).

Although Sacks referred to this method as an 'unmotivated examination' of data (p. 27), we should not think that he was an apostle of the impossible dream of a purely inductive science. For, of course, we can only make 'observations' if we know the kinds of 'things' we are looking for. In fact, his guiding assumption was that wherever we approached social reality, we would find 'order at all points' (p. 22). The pervasiveness of social order is shown by Sacks's example of how children learn what things mean and what is appropriate behaviour. They do all this despite initially having very little contact with the outside world apart from their immediate family and its social circle. Despite this limitation, most children 'come out in many ways much like everybody else' (p. 22).

Somehow, then, children learn about 'society' from apparently very little contact with it. In other words, at every point, however minimal or seemingly trivial, children encounter social order. Following the example of how children learn, the nice message for novice researchers is that, in a sense, they will find evidence of social order wherever they look. As Sacks puts it: 'given the possibility that there is overwhelming order, it would be extremely hard *not* to find it, no matter how or where we looked' (p. 23). This is why Sacks suggests that social research might employ the 'same resources' used by children. Whatever our data, social order should be apparent. As he argues: 'tap into whomsoever, wheresoever and we get much the same things' (p. 22).

Novice researchers who worry about the 'significance' of their data may be heartened by Sacks's indifference to the assumption that some (naturally occurring) data are better than others. But they may still wonder about what, in practice, it means to look for social order in data. Sacks's answer is that we can start to raise 'deep' questions about the social order in our data by shelving both conventional social science and commonsense concerns. In regard to the latter, we are tempted to ask ourselves questions about individuals' motivation and personality. Instead, we need to locate what Sacks calls the 'machinery' through which they are able to *do* whatever they do and to *see* whatever it is that they see. So, if our data is a transcript of a conversation, we need to transform our view of 'what happened': 'from a matter of a particular interaction done by particular people, to a matter of interactions as products of a machinery' (p. 26).

In order to see exactly what Sacks meant by the concept of 'machinery', let me present you with a version of Sacks's position in terms of a set of seven methodological rules. I offer these rules as a didactic device. As you study them, you must always bear in mind that these rules are theoretically grounded rather than free-floating techniques. In other words, to appreciate fully what these rules imply and to use them properly, you need to context them in Sacks's particular version of how social order works (see chapters 2 and 3 above).

Seven Methodological Rules

1 Gather observational data

Sacks's work is always driven by data. Rather than sit in his arm-chair and construct grand theories about society, he preferred, like the early ethnographers, to 'get his hands dirty' with some data. As we have seen, this was not because he was necessarily fascinated by such data in themselves. Instead, it was because any data raised for him basic questions about the machinery of interaction. As he commented: 'We are trying to find the machinery. In order to do so we have to get access to its products' (Sacks 1984a: 26–7).

Wanting 'access' to the 'products' of this machinery meant that Sacks rejected the use of hypothetical examples as a helpful method of social science. This was not because such examples might not be compelling. Rather the problem is that, precisely because such examples make sense, they conceal the sense-making abilities of both scientists and their audiences (*LC2*: 419).

Equally, interview data gathered by the researcher is not necessarily helpful. This is because the interview method *generates* categories instead of looking at how categories are ordinarily deployed. As Sacks argues, in a piece already quoted in chapter 3: 'the trouble with [interview studies] is that they're using informants; that is, they're asking questions of their subjects. That means that they're studying the categories that Members use ... they are not investigating their categories by attempting to find them in the activities in which they're employed' (*LC1*: 27).

By contrast to both interview-based and hypothetical data,

Sacks stressed, like the ethnographers of his time, the potential of observation. As he put it: 'I want to encourage the sense that interesting aspects of the world, that are as yet unknown, are accessible to observation' (*LC2*: 420). These 'interesting aspects of the world' may be very far away from what an everyday perspective finds interesting. So, from Sacks's point of view, we turn to observational data 'as a basis for theorizing' about things we could never imagine: 'Thus we can start with things that are not currently imaginable, by showing that they happened' (1984a: 25; see also *LC2*: 420).

2 *Making recordings*

'The kind of phenomena I deal with are always transcriptions of actual occurrences in their actual sequence' (Sacks 1984a: 25): while the earlier ethnographers had generally relied on recording their observations through fieldnotes, why did Sacks prefer to use an audio-recorder? Sacks's answer is that we cannot rely on our recollections of conversations. Certainly, depending on our memory, we can usually summarize what different people said. But it is simply impossible to remember (or even to note at the time) such matters as pauses, overlaps, inbreaths and the like.

Now whether you think these kinds of things are important will depend on what you can show with or without them (see chapter 6). Indeed, you may not even be convinced that conversation itself is a particularly interesting topic. But at least by studying tapes of conversations, you are able to focus on the 'actual details' of one aspect of social life. As Sacks put it:

> My research is about conversation only in this incidental way, that conversation is something that we can get the actual happenings of on tape and transcribe them more or less, and therefore have something to begin with. If you can't deal with the actual detail of actual events then you can't have a science of social life. (*LC2*: 26)

Tapes and transcripts also offer more than just 'something to begin with'. In the first place, they are a public record, available to the scientific community, in a way that fieldnotes are not. Second, they can be replayed and transcriptions can be improved and analyses take off on a different tack unlimited by the original transcript. As Sacks told his students:

> I started to play around with tape recorded conversations, for the single
> virtue that I could replay them; that I could type them out somewhat,
> and study them extendedly, who knew how long it might take ... It
> wasn't from any large interest in language, or from some theoretical
> formulation of what should be studied, but simply by virtue of that; I
> could get my hands on it, and I could study it again and again. And
> also, consequentially, others could look at what I had studied, and make
> of it what they could, if they wanted to disagree with me. (*LC1*: 622)

A third advantage of detailed transcripts is that, if you want to,
you can inspect sequences of utterances without being limited to
the extracts chosen by the first researcher. For it is in these
sequences, rather than in single turns of talk, that we make sense
of conversation. As Sacks points out: 'having available for any
given utterance other utterances around it, is extremely important
for determining what was said. If you have available only the
snatch of talk that you're now transcribing, you're in tough shape
for determining what it is' (*LC1*: 729).

3 *Being behaviourist*

As I have already noted, a popular activity in everyday life is to
wonder about people's motives. Indeed, in the case of talk-shows,
the motives of the rich, famous or just plain unlucky or deviant
become a central topic. Yet, in many respects, social science has
picked up this habit, taking as its task the revelation of other
people's 'motives' and 'experiences'. Elsewhere, I have noted this
'Romantic' tendency in social science (Silverman 1993a; Atkinson
and Silverman 1997).

Even in the 1960s, Sacks seemed fully aware of these issues. His
kind of social science always turned away from the insides of
people's heads and towards their observable activities. In this
sense, Sacks was a self-proclaimed behaviourist who announced
that his task was to elucidate how members did whatever they did.
As he put it:

> For Members, activities are observables. They see activities. They see
> persons doing intimacy, they see persons lying, etc. ... And that poses
> for us the task of being *behaviourists* in this sense: finding how it is that
> people can produce sets of actions that provide that others can see such
> things. (*LC1*: 119)

As examples of such 'sets of actions', Sacks offers 'describing' and 'questioning'. These are interesting examples because each may be seen as a *resource* for social scientists as when ethnographers 'describe' cultures and 'question' informants. However, Sacks wants to make both activities a *topic* by examining them as forms of behaviour which, through some methods awaiting inspection, are produced and recognized.

4 Members' methods

It follows that how societal members (including social researchers) 'see' particular activities is, for Sacks, the central research question. In this respect, together with Garfinkel (1967), he offers a unique perspective in social science which 'seeks to describe methods persons use in doing social life' (Sacks 1984a: 21).

When researchers 'describe' and 'question', the problem is that they are tacitly using members' methods. If we are to study such methods, it is, therefore, crucial that we don't take for granted what it is we appear to be 'seeing'. As Sacks says: 'In setting up what it is that seems to have happened, preparatory to solving the [research] problem, do not let your notion of what could conceivably happen decide for you what must have happened' (*LC1*: 115). Here Sacks is telling us that our 'notion of what could conceivably happen' is likely to be drawn from our unexamined knowledge as members. Instead, we need to proceed more cautiously by examining the methods members use to produce activities as observable and reportable.

Put at its simplest, researchers must be very careful how they use categories. For instance, Sacks quotes from two linguists who appear to have no problem characterizing particular (invented) utterances as 'simple', 'complex', 'casual' or 'ceremonial'. For Sacks, such rapid characterizations of data assume 'that we can know that without an analysis of what it is [they] are doing' (*LC1*: 429). Such an analysis needs to locate particular utterances in sequence of talk (*LC1*: 430, 622). So an ethnographer who reports that she or he heard someone tell a 'story' only raises a further question: how the ethnographer (and presumably the members of the group studied) heard an activity as a 'story'.

As we shall see in chapter 6, for Sacks an account only becomes a 'story' when displayed and monitored as such by teller and recipient: 'We want to see: Is the fact that someone is telling a story something that matters to the teller and the hearer? How can it matter, and why does it matter, and of course when does it matter?' (*LC2*: 223). So the category 'story' must be treated as what Sacks calls 'a candidate name' and we are only interested in what has happened as a 'story' if we can show how an activity is produced as a 'story'.

5 Concepts in social science

At this point, the experienced researcher might respond that Sacks has characterized conventional research as over-naive. In particular, most researchers are aware of the danger of assuming any one-to-one correspondence between their categories and the aspects of 'reality' which they purport to describe. Instead, following Weber (1949), many researchers claim that they are simply using hypothetical constructs (or 'ideal types') which are only to be judged in relation to whether they are *useful*, not whether they are *'accurate'* or *'true'*.

However, Sacks was aware of this argument. As he notes:

> It is a very conventional way to proceed in the social sciences to propose that the machinery you use to analyze some data you have is acceptable if it is not intendedly the analysis of real phenomena. That is, you can have machinery which is a 'valid hypothetical construct', and it can analyze something for you. (*LC1*: 315)

By contrast, the 'machinery' in which Sacks is interested is not a set of 'hypothetical constructs'. Instead, Sacks's ambitious claim is throughout 'to be dealing with the real world' (*LC1*: 316). The 'machinery' he sets out, then, is not to be seen as a set of more or less useful categories but the *actual* categories and mechanisms that members use. In this sense, he points out: 'I intend that the machinery I use to explain some phenomenon, to characterize how it gets done, is just as *real* as the thing I started out to explain' (*LC1*: 315, emphasis added).

6 Locating the machinery

Let me try to clarify the nature of the machinery in which Sacks is interested. As Sacks argues in the quotation above, the machinery is what allows some 'phenomenon' to 'get done'. In this sense, social research must seek to construct the *machinery* that would produce any naturally occurring event. As Sacks puts it:

> The kind of phenomena we are dealing with are always transcriptions of actual occurrences, in their actual sequence. And I take it our business is to try to construct the machinery that would produce these occurrences. That is, we find and name some objects, and find and name some rules for using those objects. (*LC1*: 113)

The implication is that Sacks is interested in 'occurrences' only in so far as they can be studied as outcomes of particular members' methods. Take the case of a telephone call. The interest is not specifically in the mundane contents of the call. So it is unlikely that Sacks's analytic purposes could be satisfied by, say, listing the topics people are talking about. Instead, Sacks is interested in such calls 'as really one machine product. That is to say, it's not this conversation that we're really interested in, but we can begin to see machinery that produces this as a series of moves' (*LC2*: 169).

Sacks's language of 'machinery' and 'production' fits his rejection of over-rationalistic models of human action (see chapter 3). So, for instance, people don't intend to grab the floor in order to tell a story, yet somehow they do it (see chapter 6 below). This also means that, for Sacks, it is an error to assume that the machinery is somehow rationally designed to achieve certain ends or products. Instead, Sacks argues:

> Most of the things that we [other social scientists, laypeople] treat as products, i.e. the achieved orderliness of the world of some sort, are *by-products*. That is, there is machinery that produces orderly events, but most of the events that we come across that are orderly are not specifically the product of a machine designed to produce them, but are off-shoots of a machine designed to do something else or nothing in particular. (*LC2*: 240)

So it is a gross error to assume that Sacks uses the term 'machinery' to identify some all-determining apparatus like, say, 'culture'. Admittedly, his references to 'machinery' and sometimes to 'the technology of conversation' (*LC2*: 339) do seem to imply that he is working with a deterministic model. This may be why Goffman (1981: 17) criticized what he took to be Sacks's perspective of a 'systems engineer'. And there does seem evidence for this in certain parts of his lectures where Sacks seems to imply a very mechanical model. For instance, he describes interactions 'as being spewed out by machinery, the machinery being what we're trying to find; where, in order to find it we've got to get a whole bunch of its products' (*LC2*: 169).

However, a fuller reading of the lectures shows, by contrast, that Sacks is consistently interested in how members *use* the machinery. As he puts it: 'the idea is to take singular sequences of conversation and tear them apart in such a way as to find rules, techniques, procedures, methods, maxims [which] can be used to generate the orderly features we find in the conversations we examine' (*LC2*: 339).

Bearing in mind Sacks's insistence that his machinery 'is just as real as the thing I started out to explain' (*LC1*: 315), the rules, procedures and so on that Sacks identifies here are members' rules and procedures used by members to 'generate . . . orderly features'. For instance, Sacks argues that members, just like analysts, treat 'the positioning of an utterance' as 'a resource for finding what it's talking to' (*LC2*: 427) and, thereby, use that positioning to display an understanding of something (as an invitation, a question, and so on).

7 *Building a data analysis*

How do we actually go about inspecting some data in order to identify the locally employed machinery used to produce them? Sacks offers an important warning that apparently simple phenomena may need complex explanations. As he puts it: 'There is no necessary fit between the complexity or simplicity of the apparatus you need to construct some object, and the face-value complexity or simplicity of the object. Just because something seems 'pretty routine', we cannot assume that it is not difficult to explain. As Sacks points out: 'the activities that molecules are able to engage in quickly, routinely, have not been described [even] by enormously brilliant scientists' (*LC1*: 115).

Now replace molecules with a social activity like issuing invitations. The aim then is 'to build a method which will provide for some utterance as a "recognizable invitation"' (*LC1*: 300). Moreover, 'since invitations stand in alternation to rejection', we need to be able 'to discriminate between the two'. What our analysis is looking for is a method that will

provide for the recognizability of 'invitation' for some cases and for the recognizability of 'rejection' for others. And if we get a method, then we ought to be able to use it to generate other cases than this one; where, then, the ones that we generate ought to be equally recognizable as invitations or rejections. (*LC1*: 301)

In chapter 6 , we will see precisely how Sacks builds an analysis of exactly how invitations are 'recognized' in this sense. However, it should not be assumed that Sacks is merely seeking understandings of discrete or isolated activities like invitations. On the contrary, his investigation of a particular piece of data is always intended as part of a cumulative enterprise where one finding leads to another, as we will see below: 'recurrently it happens that some piece of data is analyzed, and when you're analyzing something else you find that the machinery built and tested to analyze one thing is now important for this other thing. That permits you to tie things together' (*LC1*: 316).

So the overall aim is to 'tie things together'. But, contrary to Goffman, this does not mean that we can ever lose sight of the fact that we are trying to identify a machinery built *in situ* to produce a particular data-set: 'the core point is that when you introduce a piece of machinery, that piece of machinery in the first instance [is] introduced where it, itself, analyzes the things of which it's built' (*LC1*: 316).

Moreover, even when you set out this way and, as sometimes happens, discover that you cannot explain your original problem, this does not mean that you should be discouraged or assume that 'you've got nothing'. In fact: 'You may have learned an enormous amount, as you've fitted various pieces of machinery together, [learned] about what they're doing, about other data' (*LC1*: 316).

So, somewhat reassuringly, Sacks reminds us that our original research problem may be forced to change. And, providing the analytic thrust remains, this need not be a problem because we can then go on to discover new, perhaps even 'deeper' things.

But how 'deep' are Sacks's discoveries? Clearly, I would not be writing this book (and you would not be reading it) without some belief in the 'deepness' and importance of Sacks's approach. However, precisely because that approach is so different from the rest of social science, it has not been without its critics. In chapter 9, I will offer an overall assessment of the contemporary significance of Sacks's work in the context of more conventional social science. In the final part of this chapter, I set out on the more limited enterprise of examining how Sacks defended himself against criticisms of his method.

Answering the Critics

In his lectures Sacks posed (and answered) five criticisms that might be made of his method. Were his research topics trivial? Were his data trivial? Did it matter that his selection of data was not random? Were his data incomplete? Where was 'social structure' in his analysis? To conclude this chapter, I will review below Sacks's response to each of these criticisms.

1 Trivial topics?

As will already be apparent, Sacks was largely preoccupied with conversation. This might provide one possible line of attack for potential critics. After all, could it not be argued that there are more *important* social events than 'mere' talk – revolutions, murders, new laws and so on?

However, social scientists have been relatively reluctant to follow up this line of attack. First, it is difficult to resist the argument that conversation is a major medium of social interaction and, as such, merits study. Second, as the social sciences have expanded, researchers have accepted a division of labour in which it is recognized that it is quite legitimate for each to focus on different 'slices' of social reality.

None the less, it might be asked why, having taken conversation as his topic, Sacks appeared to make so little of the topics about which people were actually talking? For instance, as he himself notes, conventional approaches like 'content analysis' would set out to list and count the topics present in conversations (*LC*1: 752). Today, we might add that qualitative software programmes are often used in this way, particularly in relation to interview responses (Richards and Richards 1994).

Sacks's answer to this criticism is that, by focusing on 'topics', researchers may simply replicate everyday concerns. For instance, not only ordinary conversationalists but professionals like doctors, lawyers and psychiatrists may listen to others in this way. If social science is to be any more than a 'lay' analysis, Sacks argues that it must approach talk in a different way. In particular, rather than simply describe the topics that people talk about, it might 'try to extract relatively formal procedures which persons seem to use in doing whatever they are doing' (*LC*1: 752).

One way of looking at this is to say that Sacks is more concerned with 'form' than with 'content'. A more accurate characterization is to state that his approach is focused on the interpersonal machinery that we use in the *production* of particular recognizable features of social reality. Of course, these features include 'topics in conversation'. So, as we shall see in chapter 6, Sacks was very much concerned with how topics are assembled in talk (by choosing categories, by 'tying' turns, and so on).

2 Trivial data?

Even if we set aside the problems critics might have with Sacks's focus on particular aspects of talk, they might still worry about what appears to be a very limited data-set from which Sacks builds his lectures. In a moment, we will look at this issue in terms of social science's conventional concern with 'random' samples of data. For now, I want to examine how Sacks deals with the complaint that he makes too much of apparently trivial data. For instance, why does he devote so many lectures to a therapy session for American adolescents and to the first line or two of a child's story? As he says: 'People often ask: "Why do you choose the particular data you choose? Is it some problem that you have in mind that caused you to pick out this group therapy session?"' (*LC*1: 292).

Sacks answer is uncompromising: he happily works with any data that he happens to find: 'I'm very insistent that I just happened to have it [the group therapy data], somebody had found this segment, it became fascinating, and I spent some time at it' (*LC*1: 292).

As we have already seen, once a piece of data turned up, Sacks worked at it inductively to see if he could generate from it issues that were relevant to his theoretical position. He notes:

> it's not that I attack it by virtue of some problem I bring to it ... but [there is] the possibility that some first-level analysis of a piece of data can set up another consideration which will turn out to address, say, some theoretical or methodological problems that we know exist in the field ... [but] how interesting what you come up with will be, is something you cannot in the first instance say. (*LC*1: 292–3)

Because what is 'interesting' about data cannot be said prior to its 'attack', Sacks responds to his critics ('trivial' data) by adopting what he calls 'a counter-strategy' of choosing specifically *uninter-esting* data (*LC1*: 293). The advantage of such data is that, by using them, it is relatively easy to resist the temptation to pursue issues that fascinate us in everyday life (and concern many social scient-ists). As Sacks argues: 'Things like an exchange of greetings are kind of ideal, rather than, say, the discourse of kings or salon con-versation, where we know ... that it's important and interesting, and it's very hard in the first instance to ignore "what they say", which you have to do' (*LC1*: 293).

Using this counter-strategy, Sacks aims to develop 'criteria of interestingness' out of his theoretically informed analysis. In this way, he aims to build a social science which generates its own topics while handling the details of something that actually happens, that is, mundane conversation (*LC1*: 293; *LC2*: 26).

3 Non-random data?

It will already be apparent that Sacks had a strategy of working with any data that crossed his path. This clearly conflicts both with the standard approach of quantitative social scientists, who usually work with random samples from particular populations, and with the common defensiveness of their qualitative brethren about the representativeness of the cases that they study.

Sacks's lack of defensiveness on this issue stems from his argu-ment about the obvious pervasiveness of the social forms (or 'machinery') with which he is concerned. Thus, as we have seen, Sacks notes the ability of a child to learn a culture from very limited contacts and of the sociolinguist Whorf to build a Navajo grammar from talking to just one person (*LC1*: 485).

The pervasiveness of structures which these examples suggest implies to Sacks that it does not matter what data you select. As he argues:

> Now if one figures that that's the way things are ... then it really wouldn't matter very much what it is you look at – if you look at it care-fully enough. And you may well find that you got an enormous general-izability because things are so arranged that you *could* get them; given that for a Member encountering a very limited environment, he has to be able to do that, and things are so arranged as to permit him to. (*LC1*: 485)

So we see that, in common with many contemporary qualitative researchers (such as Mitchell 1983; Silverman 1993a), Sacks argued that the validity of a piece of research did not depend on how a data-set was selected but on the, theoretically derived, quality of the analysis. However, this did not mean that Sacks totally dismissed quantitative researchers' concerns with how phenomena were distributed. Sacks notes, for instance, that he was 'really heavily interested in trying to distributionalize things' (*LC2*: 570).

Sacks pursued this interest on his conversational data by a three-step sequence. First, by seeking to identify any utterance as 'a sort of thing', for example a question; second, by trying to work out the place in which it went; and third, by trying to find an explanation of why it went in that place. This meant that his interest in distributions was not statistical. As he put it: 'So, instead of just counting the range of places something goes ... locate a version of the place and then see if you can come up with an account of why it goes there; some explanation or proof' (*LC2*: 570).

As his studies show, Sacks's opposition to counting coexisted with a careful inspection of many instances in order to confirm the existence of some phenomenon. However, because of his belief in the pervasiveness or omnipresence of the features with which he was concerned, Sacks insisted that we should not be surprised if such an inspection failed to yield deviant cases. As he wrote:

> Omnipresence need not ... only set off a search for exceptions or variation. Rather, we need to see that with some such mundane occurrences we are picking up things which are so overwhelmingly true that if we are to understand that sector of the world, they are something we will have to come to terms with. (1987: 56)

Such omnipresence must, for Sacks, be treated as significant. Returning to the previous charge ('trivial questions'), Sacks offered this rebuttal: 'omnipresence and ready observability need not imply *banality*, and, therefore, silence' (1987: 56, emphasis added).

4 Incomplete data?

As Sacks himself recognized, there was a stronger charge against his data than their apparent non-randomness. This was the charge that his data, based mainly on audio-recordings, were incomplete. In his fall 1968 lectures, we see Sacks's response to this issue when a student asks a question about 'leaving out things like facial expressions' from his analysis (*LC2*: 26). Sacks at once concedes that 'it would be great to study them. It's an absence.' None the less, he constructs a two-part defence of his data.

First, he suggests that he has not set out 'to develop anything like a comprehensive analysis of what actually happened, but to begin to set minimal constraints on what an explanation or a description of talking or doing things together would look like' (*LC2*: 26). At this early stage of his work, Sacks is here prepared to describe it in terms of developing a methodology rather than a set of clear findings. Since elsewhere he does indeed confidently display such findings, Sacks seems to be somewhat on the defensive in this first part of his argument.

His second point raises some of the undoubted technical problems involved in camera positioning and the like if you were to use videos (*LC2*: 26–7). These are the very issues that have been addressed, if not resolved, by more recent work based on video-recorded data (see Heath 1986; Heath and Luff 1992; Heath 1997).

With the advantage of hindsight, we may make two observations about Sacks's response to this problem. First, in the 1960s Sacks was working in an entirely new terrain. Therefore, to argue that his data were 'incomplete' seems rather petty. Second, more important, the idea of 'completeness' may itself be an illusion. Surely, there cannot be totally 'complete' data any more than there can be a 'perfect' transcript? Rather, as always in science, everything will depend on what you are trying to do and where it seems that you may be able to make progress. As Sacks put it: 'one gets started where you can maybe get somewhere' (*LC2*: 26).

5 *Social structure?*

The charge that such work on conversation leaves out reference to 'social structure' is the most common rebuke offered not only to Sacks but to ethnomethodology in general (see Sharrock and Anderson 1986: 100–5). Because the issue is so important, I will return to it in the context of Sacks's aesthetics of research in chapter 9.

At the moment, we can note that Sacks himself deals with this rebuke at its most polite where he refers to other sociologists who term his work 'microscopic' (*LC1*: 65). To some extent, we have also seen how Sacks constructs an answer by his attempt to distance himself from global notions like 'culture' (see chapter 3 above). As he argues, we simply do not need to appeal to a concept like 'culture' when we find a regularity: 'we needn't at all suppose, to begin with, that these are other than two or more people doing some interaction' (*LC2*: 169). To the extent that we need to look any further, 'we should seek only the local *apparatus* that has them being able to do that' (Sacks 1987: 65).

Sacks insists that this apparatus is context-free. So, for instance, 'caller–called' are identities 'that the conversation itself makes relevant' (*LC2*: 361). Although you can imagine a world where some social status held by the speakers determined how they could talk to one another (see his references to Albert's work on the Burundi in *LC1*: 624–32), almost universally: 'Conversation is independently organized – from such other things as social class etc. ... it has a sequential organization which employs identities that it determines' (*LC2*: 361–2).

Sacks's analysis of this sequential organization will be enlarged on in chapter 6.

5
Membership Categorization Analysis

In the previous chapter, we saw that Sacks's claim to offer an original perspective in social science was based upon his attempt 'to describe [the] methods persons use in doing social life' (Sacks 1984a: 21). This stands in contrast to the work of many social scientists, whose 'notion of what could conceivably happen' (*LC1*: 115) is likely to be drawn from their unexamined members' knowledge. Instead, for Sacks, we need to proceed more cautiously by examining the methods members actually use to produce activities as observable and reportable. As it turns out, among those methods are ways of generating categories in order to make sense of particular events.

At its simplest, we can see categories being generated in early parts of conversations between strangers. Here, as Sacks notes, we commonly find questions like 'What do you do?' and 'Where are you from?' (see chapter 1 above on 'pick-up' questions). Such questions invoke categories, like occupation and residence, which are what Sacks calls 'inference-rich' (*LC1*: 41). These categories allow us to find out a great deal about people.

For instance, the assassination of President Kennedy was still fresh in the minds of Sacks's students when he gave his lectures of autumn 1964 to spring 1965. As Sacks points out, people tried to discover the meaning of this event by invoking such categories: 'If you have access to a variety of materials from that time, you can see persons reporting themselves going through "Was it one of us right-wing Republicans?", "Was it one of us Negroes?", "Was it a Jew?", etc.' (*LC1*: 42).

By posing such questions, people relied on their commonsense knowledge of how particular categories like 'Jew', 'Negro' or 'right-wing Republican' were tied to certain presumed characteristics or activities. These characteristics give you immediate explanations by making 'some large class of activities immediately understandable' (*LC1*: 337). Moreover, the process works the other way as well. When you spot some activity, you often know immediately the kind of person who might have done it (*LC1*: 338).

As Sacks suggests, such explanations are so powerful that they cannot be disproved simply by introducing one contrary case. For instance, knowing one 'generous' Scotsman will not demolish the common English assumption that 'all Scotsmen are mean'. In this sense, category-based explanations are what Sacks calls 'protected against induction' (*LC1*: 336).

Of course, it is always possible that when we invoke category-based explanations, other people may accuse us of 'prejudice'. One way to protect yourself against such a charge is simply to use a category and let others construct the explanation. In this way, if necessary, you can deny that you intended that explanation to be derived while knowing that that was *precisely* the explanation that people would derive.

For instance, Sacks shows how the Soviet Union used to publish the names of 'profiteers'. Given the state ideology, this would be a legitimate activity. However, people could see that these were Jewish names. Given this, people could produce an explanation: profiteering is the work of Jews because Jews seek to make money at the expense of the rest of us. Because the Soviet state did not actually say this, it could continue to deny that it was anti-semitic, while deflecting grievances at its own economic inadequacies (*LC1*: 338).

In chapter 1, we saw that such categorization is also present in much more innocent activities. People who feel suicidal and call telephone helplines (such as the Samaritans) often produce the following statement: 'I have no one to turn to' (1972a: 53–5) or 'I am nothing' (*LC1*: 67). The telephone counsellor then usually asks a series of questions such as 'do you have a spouse or partner?', 'do you have a mother or father?', 'do you have a best friend?' Sacks notes that these questions follow a regular sequence, beginning with persons who might be assumed to have the strongest obligation to help and ending with parties with far less obligation. Moreover, callers routinely imply that they too have posed themselves these questions and have posed them *in the self-same sequence.*

Using data from his Ph.D. dissertation on calls to a suicide prevention centre, Sacks points out that people may only become suicidal *after* they have reviewed various categories of people and found 'no one to turn to'. So a caller's statement 'I'm nothing' is not to be heard as having a purely psychological reference or as indicating some mental disturbance but as the outcome of a procedure 'arrived at properly and reproducibly' (*LC1*: 67) by suicidal persons. This suggests that both parties, despite their different stake in the issue of suicide, work with a common set of categories in order to offer explanations of why someone might consider taking their own life.

Recall also Sacks's example of a telephone conversation between a caller to a social welfare agency and an agency worker (chapter 1 above). In this case, the agency worker was able to work out a possible omission from the caller's account and, eventually, to obtain an admission from him about his violent behaviour towards his wife. Like the suicide counsellor, this agency worker did not need any special skills to work out what 'really' might be going on or even to read the caller's mind. In both cases, we glimpse a highly powerful apparatus which somehow allows us to come up with workable explanations of all kinds of social events.

Indeed one way of determining whether something happened is to see if we can come up with a convincing explanation for it. For instance, coroners may not deliver a verdict of suicide unless there is some evidence that the deceased person had a reason to take their own life (*LC1*: 123). In that sense, in everyday life, only those 'facts' occur for which there is an explanation (*LC1*: 121).

Now one might say that none of this is very original. It simply derives from what social scientists have long known and termed 'culture' or 'common knowledge'. The issue for Sacks, however, is whether such 'common knowledge' is 'just lists of items that persons know in common' (*LC1*: 23).

This certainly seems to be the version of 'common knowledge' that most ethnographers use. We can see this in the way in which many ethnographies tend to use lay categories as a tacit resource. Sacks notes, for instance, how the anthropologist Ethel Albert, whose account of Burundi society he so admires, none the less relies upon 'categories of actors formulated in terms that the society has of them or translations of that into categories of actors formulated in the names our society has, and categories of actions formulated in the same way' (*LC1*: 629).

The problem with this approach, as Sacks points out, is that it fails to give you any deeper understanding of how it is, in actual interactions, that people actually choose between (and invoke) particular categories. This meant that he was deeply suspicious about social science's claims to be an analytic approach, different from common sense. Sacks puts the issue succinctly:

> Suppose you're an anthropologist or sociologist standing somewhere. You see somebody do some action, and you see it to be some activity. How can you go about formulating who is it that did it, for the purposes of your report? Can you use at least what you might take to be the most conservative formulation – his name? Knowing, of course, that any category you choose would have the[se] kinds of systematic problems: how would you go about selecting a given category from the set that would equally well characterize or identify that person at hand? (*LC*1: 467–8)

Sacks shows how you cannot resolve such problems simply 'by taking the best possible notes at the time and making your decisions afterwards' (*LC*1: 468). As he put it, in an extract I used in chapter 3: 'All the sociology we read is unanalytic, in the sense that they simply put some category in. They may make sense to us in doing that, but they're doing it simply as *another Member*' (*LC*1: 41–2, emphasis added).

The alternative that Sacks proposed means analysing what he calls 'the structural properties' of commonsense knowledge (*LC*1: 23). This involves using 'what any Member knows, to pose us some problems. What activity is being done, for example. And then we can see whether we can build an apparatus which will give us those results' (*LC*1: 487).

Following Sacks, then, our aim should be to try to understand when and how members do descriptions, seeking thereby to describe the apparatus through which members' descriptions are properly produced. The rest of this chapter is devoted to setting out the descriptive apparatus that Sacks sought to build. This is a *membership categorization* apparatus because it generates the categories that members of society use in their descriptions.

Membership Categorization

Much of this section will be concerned with definitions of the many concepts that Sacks introduces in order to understand the apparatus of membership categorization. However, because I am aware that lists of definitions may be indigestible, I will begin with an example from which Sacks derived many of his concepts.

Consider this description in which the identities of the parties are concealed: 'The X cried. The Y picked it up.' Why is it that we are likely to hear the X as, say, a baby but not a teacher? Furthermore, given that we hear X as a baby, why are we tempted to hear Y as an adult (possibly as the baby's mother) (*LC1*: 248–9)?

In fact, Sacks looks at the first two sentences of a story by a child: 'The baby cried. The mommy picked it up.' Why do we hear the 'mommy' as the mother of this 'baby' (*LC1*: 236)? Why do we hear the baby's cries as the 'reason' why the mommy picks it up?

Not only are we likely to hear the story this way, but we hear it as 'a possible description' without having observed the circumstances which it characterizes. Sacks asks: 'Is it some kind of magic? One of my tasks is going to be to construct an apparatus for that fact to occur. That is, how we come to hear it in that fashion.' No magic lies behind such observations. Instead: 'What we want to do then . . . is to provide for how it is that something that's done is recognized for what it is' (*LC1*: 236).

Returning to the way we read the child's story, Sacks observes that our reading is informed by the way we infer that the categories 'baby' and 'mommy' come from a collection of such categories which we call 'family' (*LC1*: 238). While the 'family' collection can include many categories (not just 'baby' and mommy' but also 'daddy', 'daughter', 'grandmother', etc.), some categories are or can be built as two-set collections, as with gender (male and female) or race (black and white) (*LC1*: 47–8).

Of course, not any set of categories will be heard as a collection. As Sacks says: 'We only talk about a collection when the categories that compose it are categories that members do in fact use together or collect together, as "male" and "female" go together' (*LC1*: 238).

Sacks notes that, as here, younger children's stories may have just one collection of categories – the 'family'. Young children apply this collection to virtually everyone, parents' friends coming to be called 'aunt' and 'uncle' (*LC1*: 368). However, for children, like any population, there are always at least two collections of categories available (1972a: 32). This means that young children can at least choose between, say, 'auntie' and 'woman' as a way of categorizing a female.

Of course, one only has to read accounts of the 'same' event in two different newspapers to realize the large number of categories that can be used to describe it. For instance, as feminists have pointed out, women, but not men, tend to be identified by their marital status, number of children, hair colour and even chest measurement. Such identifications, while intelligible, carry massive implications for the sense we attach to people and their behaviour. Compare, for example, 'Shapely, blonde, mother of five' with 'Thirty-two-year-old teacher'. Both descriptions may 'accurately' describe different aspects of the same person. But each constitutes very definitely how we are to view that person (for instance, in the first, largely in terms of certain ways of constructing gender).

Each identity is heard as a category from some collection of categories. For instance, in the two versions above, we hear 'mother' as a category from the collection 'family'. By contrast, 'teacher' is heard as located in a collection of 'occupation'.

Sacks calls such a collection a *membership categorization device* (or MCD). This device consists of a collection of categories (such as baby, mommy, father = family; male, female = gender) and some rules about how to apply these categories. A definition of an MCD is as follows.

- *Membership categorization device* 'any collection of membership categories, containing at least a category, which may be applied to some population containing at least a member, so as to provide, by the use of some rules of application, for the pairing of at least a population member and a categorization device member. A device is then a collection plus rules of application' (1972c: 332).

What are these 'rules of application' to which Sacks refers? First, returning to the child's story, we can note that the characters are described by *single* categories ('baby', 'mommy'). So we are not told, as we might be, about, say, the baby's age or gender or the mommy's occupation or even hair colour. And this did not cause us a problem when we first saw 'The baby cried. The mommy picked it up.'

The intelligibility of single category descriptions gives us what Sacks calls *the economy rule*.

- *The economy rule* 'a single category from any membership categorization device can be referentially adequate' (LC1: 246).

Of course, single category descriptions are not confined to children's stories – sometimes categories like 'man', 'nurse' or 'pop star' are entirely referentially adequate. Nonetheless, the economy rule gives us a very interesting way of addressing how children's socialization may occur. First, children seem to learn single names ('mommy', 'daddy'). Then they learn how such single categories fit into collections ('family') and come to understand various combinatorial tasks (for instance, man = daddy or uncle). So, even at this early stage of their lives, say before they are two years old, children have already learned 'what in principle adequate reference consists of' (1972a: 35) and, in that sense, entered into society/been 'socialized'.

A second rule of application of MCDs suggests that once one category from a given collection has been used to categorize one population member, then other categories from the same collection *may* be used on other members of the population. Sacks refers to this as *the consistency rule*. It is formally defined as follows.

- *The consistency rule*   'If some population of persons is being categorized, and if some category from a device's collection has been used to categorize a first Member of the population, then that category or other categories of the same collection may be used to categorize further members of the population' (1972a: 33, emphasis added; see also *LC1*: 225, 238–9, 246).

The import of the consistency rule may be seen in a simple example. If we use an abusive term about someone else, we know that a term from the same collection can be used on us. Hence one of the reasons we may avoid name-calling is to avoid the development of this kind of slanging match.

However, any category can belong in more than one collection. For instance, as Sacks points out, 'baby' can belong to the collection 'stage of life' ('baby', 'child', 'teenager', 'adult') as well as the 'family' collection (*LC1*: 239). 'Baby' also used to be a term of endearment heard in Hollywood movies; here it belonged to a different collection ('romance'?).

Sacks suggests a 'hearing rule' (*LC1*: 239) or *consistency rule corollary* (*LC1*: 248) which provides a way for members to resolve such ambiguities. When a speaker uses two or more categories to describe at least two members of a population and it is possible to hear the categories as belonging to the same collection, we hear them that way. That is why, in the story with which Sacks begins, we hear 'baby' and 'mommy' in relation to the collection 'family'.

- *Consistency rule corollary*   'If two or more categories are used to categorize two or more Members to some population, and those categories can be heard as categories from the same collection, hear them that way' (LC1: 247).

The consistency rule and its corollary have explained why we hear 'mommy' and 'baby' as part of the same 'family' collection but it remains to be seen 'how "the mommy" is heard as "the mommy of the baby"' (*LC1*: 247). The answer stems from the way in which 'the family' is one of a series of collections that be heard as constituting a 'team', that is, as part of the same 'side'. In this respect, 'mommy' and 'baby' belong together in the same way as, say, 'defender' and striker' in a football team. Sacks suggests that one of the central properties of teams is what he calls *duplicative organization*.

- *Duplicative organization*   We treat any 'set of categories as defining a unit, and place members of the population into cases of the unit. If a population is so treated and is then counted, one counts not numbers of daddies, numbers of mommies, and numbers of babies but numbers of families – numbers of "whole families", numbers of "families without fathers", etc.' (1972c: 334; see also *LC1*: 225, 240, 247–8).

Duplicative organization helps us in seeing that 'mommy' and 'baby' are likely to be heard as part of the same 'unit'. But a further rule suggests that this is not just likely but required (in the sense that if you saw things differently then your seeing would appear to other members to be 'odd'). This rule is *the hearer's maxim for duplicative organization*.

- *The hearer's maxim for duplicative organization*   'If some population has been categorized by use of categories from some device whose collection has the "duplicative organization" property, and a Member is presented with a categorized population which *can be heard* as co-incumbents of a case of that device's unit, then hear it that way' (*LC1*: 248).

Given that the MCD 'family' is duplicatively organized, the hearer's maxim shows us how we come to hear 'the mommy' as not anyone's 'mommy' but as 'the mommy of this baby' in the child's story (*LC1*: 248).

However, 'mommy' and 'baby' are more than co-incumbents of a team; they are also a pair of positions with mutual rights and obligations (such as the baby's right to be fed but, perhaps, obligation not to cry all the time). In this respect, mothers and babies are like husband–wife, boyfriend–girlfriend and even neighbour–neighbour. Each party has certain standardized rights and obligations; each party can properly expect help from the other.

Sacks refers to such groupings as *standardized relational pairs* (SRPs). SRPs in turn are found in *collection R*.

- *Collection R* A collection of paired relational categories 'that constitutes a locus for a set of rights and obligations concerning the activity of giving help' (1972a: 37).

One aspect of the relevance of such paired relational categories is that they make observable the *absence* of the second part of any such pair. In this way, we come to observe that a player in a sporting team is 'missing' or, more seriously, treat non-incumbency of, say, a spouse as being a criterion of suicidalness (see the discussion of suicide earlier in this chapter, pp. 75–6, and Sacks 1972a: 38–40). Such absences reveal what Sacks calls the *programmatic relevance* of collection R.

- *Programmatic relevance* 'if R is relevant, then the non-incumbency of any of its pair positions is an observable, i.e. can be proposedly a fact' (1972a: 38).

Just as collection R consists of pairs of categories who are supposed to offer each other help, there are also categories of 'experts' who offer specialized help with particular 'troubles'. When paired with some 'troubled' person (such as a client), they constitute what Sacks refers to as *collection K*.

- *Collection K* 'a collection constructed by reference to special distributions of knowledge existing about how to deal with some trouble' (1972a: 37).

Collection R and its programmatic relevance allow someone to analyse their situation as, say, properly 'suicidal'. Collection K then allows such a person to know who can offer dispassionate 'advice'.

Collection K implies something about the proper activities of particular categories of people like professionals and clients. This helps to resolve one further issue in our reading of the child's story.

Why do we have no trouble with the description: 'The baby cried. The mommy picked it up'? To put it more pointedly: why might it look odd if the story read: 'The mommy cried. The baby picked it up'?

The answer, of course, lies in the way in which many kinds of activities are commonsensically associated with certain membership categories. So if we know what someone's identity is, we can work out the kinds of activities in which they might engage. Similarly, by identifying a person's activity (say, 'crying'), we provide for what their social identity is likely to be (in this case, a 'baby').

Sacks refers to activities which imply identities as *category-bound activities* (CBAs). His definition is set out as follows.

- *Category-bound activities* 'many activities are taken by Members to be done by some particular or several particular categories of Members where the categories are categories from membership categorization devices' (*LC1*: 249).

CBAs explain why, if the story had read 'The X cried. The Y picked it up', we might have guessed that X was a baby and Y was a mommy. Crying, after all, is something that babies do and picking up (at least in the possibly sexist 1960s) is something that mothers did. Of course, as Sacks points out, no description is ever completely unambiguous. For instance, 'crying' is not confined to 'babies' and an adult can sometimes be called a 'baby' (*LC1*: 584).

Members employ their understandings of category-bound activities to recognize and to resolve such ambiguities. Above all, everyday understanding is based on the assumption that, as Sacks puts it, 'they' (that is, some category of people) do such things (*LC1*: 179). As we already noted, such an understanding was skilfully used in Soviet news items about 'profiteers'.

Sacks shows how what we know about CBAs allows us to construct what he calls 'a search procedure' when some problematic occurrence appears to have occurred. For instance, he shows how, at the end of 1963, the claim that the possible assassin of President Kennedy was a 'communist' clinched the case for many people – after all, assassination of capitalist leaders appears to be category-bound to the category 'communist infiltrator'. In this way, CBAs allow us to 'tie' certain activities to particular categories. As Sacks puts it: 'if somebody knows an activity has been done, and there is a category to which it is bound, they can damn well propose that it's been done by such a one who is a member of that category' (*LC1*: 180).

So even though we know that people other than babies do cry, we are unlikely to say 'the baby cried' if we mean 'the baby of the family'. In this way, the selection of a category makes many potential ambiguities 'non-arisable' (*LC*1: 585).

However, on the face of it, when we observe an activity, there could be ambiguity as to the category to which the activity might be bound. Take the case of a 'confession'. As Sacks points out, we know that *both* Catholics and criminals often 'confess'. Have we observed a Catholic or a criminal?

We see at once that, in everyday life, there is rarely such an ambiguity. For, of course, we all know that a Catholic confessional 'looks' very different from a criminal confessing (*LC*1: 584–5). So if we read about a 'confession', the surrounding features of the story (for example, as part of a 'criminal' story) will tell us immediately how we are to understand it. And all this happens without any sense of problem or ambiguity.

For instance, we do not have any problem with seeing a struggle between two adults (a man and a woman) and a younger person as a 'family fight' (*LC*1: 90–1). Ambiguity about this interpretation is much more likely to appear when parties subsequently review an incident. It may be that in a legal context, what unambiguously appeared to be merely a 'family fight' can be transformed into a 'kidnap'. At the time of the incident, however, witnesses properly treat things as 'normal' partly because they assume it's not their job but the police's to note crimes (*LC*1: 92). Thus we invoke our knowledge of category-bound activities and standardized relational pairs as ways of resolving incongruity.

Returning to our child's story, 'baby' is also a member of a class which Sacks calls *'positioned' categories* (such as baby ... adolescent ... adult) in which the next category is heard as 'higher' than the preceding one. This creates the possibility of praise or complaint by using a higher or lower position to refer to some activity. So an adolescent can be described as acting in a very 'adult' way or as acting just like a 'baby'.

- *Positioned categories* A collection has positioned categories where one member can be said to be higher or lower than another (as with baby ... adolescent ... adult) (*LC*1: 585).

The fact that activities are category-bound also allows us to praise or complain about 'absent' activities. For instance, a baby that does not cry where it might (say at a christening) can be properly praised, while an older child that does not say 'thank you' when passed some food or given a present is properly blamed (*LC1*: 585). In both these cases, certain activities become remarkable because of the way their presence or absence is tied to a stage of life. Stage of life is important not only, say, around the dinner table but also in the compilation of official statistics. As Sacks points out, statisticians, like the rest of us, know that, for instance, being unmarried or unemployed are not usually descriptors appropriate to school-age children (*LC1*: 68).

As we have seen, because of the category-bound character of many activities, we can establish negative moral assessments of people by describing their behaviour in terms of performing or avoiding activities inappropriate to their social identity. For instance, it may be acceptable for a parent to 'punish' a child, but it will usually be unacceptable for a child to 'punish' a parent.

Notice that, in both cases, 'punish' serves as a powerful picture of an activity which could be described in innumerable ways. Social life, unlike foreign films, does not come with subtitles attached. Consequently, how we define an activity is morally constitutive of it. So if, like other sociologists, Sacks is talking here about norms, unlike them (and members) he is not treating norms as descriptions of the *causes* of action. Instead, he is concerned with how 'viewers use norms to provide some of the orderliness, and proper orderliness, of the activities they observe' (1972a: 39).

How viewers use norms takes us back to the way we read 'the baby cried'. For instance, babies can be boys or girls. Why then, might not a 'cry' be reported as, say, 'the boy cried'? The answer, says Sacks, lies in a *viewer's maxim* for category-bound activities.

- *Viewer's maxim* 'If a Member sees a category-bound activity being done, then, if one sees it being done by a member of a category to which the activity is *bound*, see it that way' (*LC1*: 259, emphasis added).

Through the viewer's maxim, we can understand why we would see a 'baby' rather than 'a boy' crying, since a 'baby' is a category that we treat as having 'a special relevance for formulating an identification of its doer' (*LC1*: 259).

Finally, why do we treat it as unremarkable that the story reports as the next activity: 'The mommy picked it up'? As we have already seen, part of the answer lies in the way in which we hear 'mommy' and 'baby' as part of a 'team'. In this respect, duplicative organization is relevant here. In addition, however, picking a baby up is likely to be heard as a norm such that where a baby cries, a mother properly picks it up. In this regard, we have, therefore, a *second viewer's maxim* as defined below:

- *Second viewer's maxim* 'If one sees a pair of actions which can be related by the operation of a norm that provides for the second given the first, where the doers can be seen as members of the categories the norm provides as proper for that pair of actions, then (a) see that the doers are such Members, and (b) see the second as done in conformity with the norm' (*LC*1: 260).

Through this second viewer's maxim, viewers provide the 'proper orderliness of the activities they observe' in at least two ways: (1) explaining the occurrence of one activity given the occurrence of the other; and (2) explaining the sequential order of the two activities (first one, then the other) (*LC*1: 260).

Most readers, I suspect, will by now be pretty sated with concepts. I therefore want to slow up the pace somewhat and offer some illustrations and applications of these concepts that Sacks himself uses. Later, I will conclude this chapter by reflecting on the *status* of the MCD apparatus that Sacks describes. In particular, I will explain why, despite any apparent similarities, MCD work has little resemblance to anything that anthropologists or sociologists might refer to as 'culture'.

Applications

To readers used to dealing with conventional social science concepts (such as 'power', 'cognitive dissonance', 'norms'), MCD analysis can present a tricky problem. The problem arises because we are tempted to use MCDs, like these other concepts, in order to understand things *better* than members. However, for Sacks, the MCD apparatus is entirely a members' apparatus. This means that it exists not as another social science concept but only in and through the way in which it is demonstrably used by lay members.

Members do not have to consult a textbook before analysing the world. They just do it. One way of getting a clearer understanding of this is to look at how Sacks discusses the *functions* of membership categorization for resolving members' problems. Take the case of being a host at a party where we have to introduce a number of guests (*n*). How do we introduce an *n*th person where that person is not the first?

Here Sacks tells us we have a simple solution: use the consistency rule (*LC1*: 326). So if we have introduced earlier guests by their first names or by their titles and/or occupations, we can do the same for the *n*th person. Indeed, if we do anything else, we may need to invoke a special warrant if we do not want to puzzle (or insult) our other guests!

But what if you are dealing with a single person and hence the consistency rule does not apply? If that person is engaged in some activity, one obvious solution is to retrieve the category bound to that activity. For instance, one sees a cricketer take a catch and might then ask: 'Who is that fielder?'

But how do we properly invoke a category where the only activity being done is identifying itself? One solution is to be found in a piece of data:

A: ((a little girl)) Who's that?
B: ((her mother)) That's Rita. Remember when you went to the party last
      week and met Una? Well that's Una's mother (*LC1*: 326)

B's solution is to treat Rita 'as the second person of a pair for which the first [Una] is known' (*LC1*: 327). Of course, as Sacks points out, such standardized relational pairs are not always available when you are searching for a single person category. But note also how, in this data extract, B seeks to offer more than just a name (Rita). As Sacks suggests: 'a name is not treated as an adequate identifier, but when *any* category, perhaps, is offered, the identification *is* treated as adequate. If the world works that way, that's extraordinarily lovely' (*LC1*: 327).

Sacks eventually seems to have recognized that this 'loveliness' (appealing to a standardized relational pair in order to identify someone) could not be a *universal* solution to the problem of single person identification: as Schegloff points out, not any SRPs would do (for instance, stranger/stranger would not work) and the categories chosen have to be recognizable to the person asking for an identification (Schegloff in *LC2*: xxxvii–xxxviii).

None the less, even posing the question raised a number of fascinating issues about how membership categories are resourcefully used by members in the most mundane situations. To get his students to analyse how 'the world works' in these kinds of ways, Sacks instructed them to observe how strangers exchanged glances. After this exercise, he pointed out how strangers might shrug their shoulders and smile at a woman smoking a pipe or at a 'couple' composed of a worn old man and a young pretty girl.

In both cases, the exchange of glances between strangers seemed to mark 'incongruity'. And this incongruity was observable through the viewers' use of the MCD apparatus. So, in the first example, in the USA at least, pipe-smoking is category-bound to 'male'. In the second example: 'What one is doing is employing the procedure by which persons properly come together and finding that this does not produce these two persons as a *pair*' (*LC1*: 90, emphasis added).

Given this perceived incongruity, one can then search for appropriate category-bound activities such as being 'a dirty old man', 'gold-digger', etc. MCDs can thus work as ways of identifying and resolving incongruity.

Until now, you may have got the impression that because membership categorization allows people to make sense of people and events, Sacks is implying that everything always proceeds smoothly in the best of all possible worlds. Far from it. First, we have already seen, in the example of Soviet identification of profiteers, how categorization can just as easily serve to maintain racism as to preserve harmony. Second, the use of quite innocent knowledge of category-bound activities can unintentionally allow horrible crimes to be committed.

For instance, in the case of the young British boys who murdered the child Jamie Bulger, witnesses who had seen Jamie holding the hands of his two assassins reported that they had assumed they were watching a child with his two older brothers. Similarly, as Sacks notes, people working in organizations, faced with possibly life-threatening events, do not take remedial action themselves but report what they have seen to the next person up the hierarchy (*LC1*: 64). This is because in organizations categories are organized into hierarchies. So people assume that they need to refer to another category to confirm some act or to take some action.

The kind of ordered sequence we find here is replicated, in a less dramatic way, in two examples discussed earlier in this chapter. First, in calls to a suicide prevention centre, Sacks revealed how professionals and clients appealed to collections R and K in a remarkably ordered sequence. In the second example, a worker at a social agency could work out that if, in a family dispute, the police had been called, then the husband is likely to have hit his wife ('did you smack her one?', he asks) (*LC1*: 114). In both cases, the parties use the MCD apparatus to produce what Sacks calls 'presumptively correct descriptions' (*LC1*: 118).

Moreover, such descriptions are not just invoked for the user but are produced in such a way as to be appropriate to the hearer or reader. In this respect, categories are 'recipient designed' (*LC1*: 790–1). For instance, as we saw in chapter 1, there is a place in the Book of Genesis where Abraham is referred to as 'Abraham the Hebrew' (*LC1*: 171). Since Israelites would know about Abraham's ethnicity, biblical scholars have suggested that this implies that this section of Genesis was not written by a Jew.

A similar example of recipient design, also discussed in chapter 1, is a group therapy session in which participants use the term 'hotrodders' to describe themselves. For hotrodders, the aim is to produce and ride in fast cars. Hence when challenged about your car, to say it's 'the hottest thing in town' serves as a *password*, that is, it affirms a prototype 'good motive', serving to maintain group solidarity (*LC1*: 116). So, as with Abraham, this description is addressed to others.

Sacks shows how alternative descriptions like 'kids in cars' can be used by adults. Conversely, 'hotrodders' is not owned by adults. So, if adults use this term, they are constrained by members' knowledge about what it takes to be a member, that is, not every car is a hotrod, not every teenager in a car is a hotrodder (*LC1*: 173).

In much the same way, as we saw in chapter 1, these kids' problem with who 'owns' descriptions extends to scientific disciplines. One of Freud's problems was that so many people consider themselves experts in psychology. So, like 'kids in cars', Freud invented new terms and tried to enforce how they were used (*LC1*: 202).

Moreover, any category (including such new terms as 'psychoanalysis' or 'hotrodder') is not just haphazardly invoked, anyhow and anywhere. Instead, recipient design means that members pay detailed attention to the implication of using a particular category in a particular place. For instance, in a therapy group transcript containing the hotrodders data, a participant called Ken remarks 'we were in an automobile discussion.' The transcript shows how this utterance occurs after the introduction of a new member to the group. As Sacks shows (*LC1*: 300–1), Ken's categorization of the preceding activity can be heard as an *invitation* by:

1 describing a category-bound activity;
2 implying a category that it is bound to ('teenage boys'); and
3 through the consistency rule, implying that the new member of

the group can appropriately be characterized by a category from the same collection.

As Sacks observes, Ken might equally have produced a *rejection* by proposing a category relevant to the pre-present persons but not to the entrant (*LC1*: 301–2). In another context, we can hear a rejection in the following example:

> a man comes home [and] his wife is there talking to a friend of hers. She says, 'We're discussing the sewing circle.' It's a rejection. He says 'Oh excuse me.' That is to say, that thing is bound to 'adult females' and he's a male. It provides for them as members, and not for him. (*LC1*: 302)

The force of both Ken's and the wife's remarks arises in their positioning immediately after a new person is available as a co-conversationalist. This underlines the point that categories are not somehow plucked out of space according to certain timeless 'rules'. Instead, categorizers and categorized closely attend to the positioning of categories.

This has two important implications. First, it suggests the inescapable link between MCD analysis and conversation analysis (CA). For instance, Sacks's MCD work on invitations and rejections is, as we shall see, inseparable from his CA work on 'pre-invitations' (*LC1*: 304–5). Second, as I argue below, it emphasizes that membership categorization analysis, in Sacks's hands, is very different from how most sociologists and anthropologists use concepts like 'norms' and 'culture'. Instead, MCDs are local, sequentially organized devices designed and administered by members.

MCDs as Local Devices

In chapter 3, we saw that Sacks approached 'culture' as an 'inference-making machine': a descriptive apparatus, administered and used in specific contexts. The issue for Sacks was not to second-guess members but to try to work out 'how it is that people can produce sets of actions that provide that others can see such things ... [as] persons doing intimacy ... persons lying, etc.' (*LC1*: 119).

Given that many categories can be used to describe the same person or act, Sacks's task, as we have seen, was 'to find out how they [members] go about choosing among the available sets of categories for grasping some event' (*LC1*: 41). Of course, Sacks does not mean to imply that 'society' determines which category one chooses. Instead, he wants to show the active interpretive work involved in rendering any description and the local implications of choosing any particular category.

A particularly telling example of this is to be found in Sacks's analysis of a *New York Times* story about an interview with a navy pilot about his missions in the Vietnam War (*LC1*: 205–22, 306–11). Sacks is specially interested in the navy pilot's answer to a question in the extract from the newspaper's report:

> 'How did he feel about knowing that even with all the care he took in aiming only at military targets someone was probably being killed by his bombs?
>
> "I certainly don't like the idea that I might be killing anybody," he replied. "But I don't lose any sleep over it. You have to be impersonal in this business. Over North Vietnam I condition myself to think that I'm a military man being shot at by another military man like myself."' (*LC1*: 205)

Sacks invites us to see how the pilot's immediate reply ('I certainly don't like the idea...') shows his commitment to the evaluational scheme offered by the journalist's question. For instance, if the pilot had instead said 'Why do you ask?', he would have shown that he did not necessarily subscribe to the same moral universe as the reporter (and, by implication, the readers of the article) (*LC1*: 211).

Having accepted this moral schema, Sacks shows how the pilot now builds an answer which helps us to see him in a favourable light. The category 'military man' works to defend his bombing as a category-bound activity which reminds us that this is, after all, what military pilots do. The effect of this is magnified by the pilot's identification of his co-participant as 'another military man like myself'. In this way, the pilot creates a standardized relational pair (military man/military man) with recognizable mutual obligations (bombing/shooting at the other). In terms of this pair, the other party cannot properly complain or, as Sacks puts it: 'there are no complaints to be offered on their part about the error of his ways, except if he happens to violate the norms that, given the device used, are operative' (*LC1*: 206).

Notice also that the pilot suggests 'you have to be impersonal in this business.' Note how the category 'this business' sets up the terrain on which the specific SRP of military men will shortly be used. So this account could be offered by either pair part.

However, as Sacks argues, the implication is that 'this business' is one of many where impersonality is required. For 'if it were the case that, that you had to be impersonal in this business held only for this business, then it might be that doing this business would be wrong in the first instance' (*LC1*: 208). Moreover, the impersonality involved is of a special sort. Sacks points out that we hear the pilot as saying not that it is unfortunate that he cannot kill 'personally' but rather that being involved in this 'business' means that one must not consider that one is killing persons (*LC1*: 209).

But the pilot is only proposing an SRP of military man–military man. In that sense, he is inviting the North Vietnamese to 'play the game' in the same way as a child might say to another 'I'll be third base.' However, as Sacks notes, in children's baseball, such proposals can be rejected: 'if you say "I'll be third base", unless someone else says "and I'll be ..." another position, and the others say they'll be the other positions, then you're not that thing. You can't play' (*LC1*: 307).

Of course, the North Vietnamese had indeed rejected the pilot's proposal. Instead, in shooting at him they proposed the identification of the pilot as a 'criminal' and defined themselves as 'doing police action'. As Sacks observes, these competing definitions had implications which went beyond mere propaganda. For instance, if the navy pilot were to be shot down then the Geneva Conventions about his subsequent treatment would only properly be applied if he indeed were a 'military man' rather than a 'criminal' (*LC1*: 307).

Even if there is consensus about how a person or an act is properly described, some latitude remains and people may try to avoid the normally category-bound implications of certain activity descriptions. For instance, Sacks discusses the American South where, according to some whites, even when blacks engage in activities appropriate to anybody, they are not to be seen as 'anybody, but as 'blacks-*imitating*-whites'.

Moreover, this attention to descriptive categories occurs even in far less politically charged situations where we are talking to strangers and there is no apparent battle over which category to use. Sacks mentions the case of people telling interviewers doing surveys that they watch less television than they actually do. He comments: 'It's interesting in that they're controlling an impression of themselves for somebody who couldn't matter less' (*LC1*: 580).

Sacks argues that this happens because we can be held responsible not only for our descriptions but for the *inferences* that can be drawn from them. Given the way in which activities are category-bound, we all have an interest in the inferences others will draw about the sort of person who would say such a thing about themselves or others.

Moreover, as I have already stressed, descriptions are not just assembled for ourselves but are recipient designed for others. In chapter 1, I gave a relevant example of this in relation to Sacks's discussion of 'naming'. Using descriptions like 'Joe', 'Tom' or 'Harry' allows hearers to search for someone already known. In this way, we help others infer certain things from our descriptions by indicating whether the hearer should seek to use them to find some person already known to them. These type 1 descriptions (first names) are different from type 2 descriptions (like 'a guy' or 'someone') where we signal that the description should *not* be used by the recipient to find out who is being referred to (*LC2*: 445).

As we also saw in chapter 1, naming is an issue for people doing introductions. When speakers name someone, they create a series of impressions not just about the persons being named, but also about themselves and their audience. In this sense, our attention to the implications of choosing names shows the extent to which we are aware of the importance of appearances.

A further interesting example of the effect of how we name people arises in Sacks's discussion of a young woman talking to a male audience in a therapy session. The woman tells a story in which she implies that she had sex with a 'guy'. But her story begins:

One night– (1.0) I was with this guy that I liked a real lot. (*LC2*: 453)

Sacks notes how 'guy that I liked a real lot' alerts hearers that such a story does not mean that she is available to anyone. In this sense, the woman's story is 'defensively designed', that is, oriented to the possibility that a hearer might say: 'That's not what happened really, is it?' (*LC2*: 505). Such stories can thus be heard as 'fragile' because they can be seen as 'ordering materials out of alternative versions of what happened, such that a recipient could, from the materials nonetheless left in there, pick away at it as to whether what happened is other than your *version* of it' (*LC2*: 505, emphasis added).

Hearably 'fragile' stories are an excellent example of how members use the MCD apparatus to build and to challenge particular versions of reality. Central to such stories is the way they construct (or reconstruct) particular identities that can be associated with the activities they describe.

As a further example of this process which he calls 'identification reformulation' (*LC2*: 126), Sacks offers the story of a student called Nancy. In this extract, Nancy is talking to Agnes about a meal she had with students in her class at college:

N: ... so a bunch of us went over, and there were three of us gals and five or six fellas. And then one of the girls had to leave, about half an hour later 'cause she had to go home and let her roommate in. And uh, one of the other girls had to leave for something. And there I sit with these young fellas. I felt like a den mother.
A: Are you the oldest one in the class?
N: Oh by far. (*LC2*: 126)

Sacks invites us to notice how, in the first sentence, gender is relevant to Nancy's account and how Nancy also gives the approximate number of 'gals' and 'fellas'. As Sacks points out, in social activities relative numbers of each gender can be hearably relevant. For example, equal numbers can turn into pairs (*LC2*: 127).

However, as it turns out, the gender-relevant issue that Nancy wants to raise is what it means when she is left alone with the men? Now how will it look to an observer? A solution is to provide an identification reformulation which will legitimate the co-presence at a social event of one woman and several men. Her comment 'I felt like a den mother' provides just that legitimation as it reformulates the identities of those present away from any sexual undertones and firmly places all parties in a family SRP (mother:sons).

Although Sacks does not point this out, we might also note that Nancy's identification reformulation in terms of 'den mother' is presaged by her earlier reference when she is left alone with the men to 'all these *young* fellas'. Here we might infer that Nancy is making a point about her being much older than the 'fellas' since, if she were the same age, they might not be recognizably 'young'. Indeed, this is precisely how Agnes monitors Nancy's account, asking: 'Are you the oldest one in the class?'

The 'defensive' design of both Nancy's story and the earlier account of a young woman about 'a guy that I liked a real lot' helped to pre-empt a potential challenge to their moral status. In these cases, then, such a challenge was not actually made. However, as Sacks points out, such challenges can arise in at least two different ways. First, a hearer of a story can offer a direct challenge, for instance asking 'Why did you do this?' and the storyteller will then know that there is something they have to defend (*LC2*: 22). Second, a hearer can offer a candidate 'reason' for what you say which Sacks refers to as a 'correction-invitation device' (*LC2*: 21–5).

In the following police interview, A is a police officer and B is a woman who has called the police about her fourteen-year-old daughter who has not been coming home at night. I have marked challenges as [C] and correction-invitation devices as [CI].

A:	Do you have a gun at home?	
B:	A forty-five	
A:	You do have a forty-five.	
B:	Uh huh, loaded.	
A:	What's it doing there. Whose is it.	[C]
B:	It's sitting there.	
A:	Is it yours?	[CI]
B:	It's Dave's.	
A:	It's your husband's huh	
B:	I know how to shoot it.	
A:	He isn't a police officer.	[CI]
B:	No.	
A:	He just has one	
B:	Everyone does, don't they? (*LC1*: 21)	

The difference between the two forms ([C] and [CI]) is noted by Sacks:

> If you say to somebody 'Why did you do this?' then what they are being asked to present is something they may well know they have to defend. And you set up a different situation when ... you're not asking for an account they have to defend, but you're 'inviting a correction'. (*LC1*: 22)

From a police point of view, Sacks suggests, the use of the correction-invitation device is usually to be preferred. First, because its aggressive character is not so obvious, it can lull a suspect into providing fresh material because its offer of one member of a class (as, in the interview above, a 'police officer') might elicit another more incriminating alternative. Although this does not happen here (B does not say 'No he's a such-and-such'), I shall return shortly to B's final line in this extract.

The second reason why the police prefer correction-invitation devices is that, by offering hypothetical answers, they can trap suspects into a vicious circle where it is difficult for them to avoid incriminating themselves. As Sacks notes, in murder investigations, police interviewers may avoid directly asking a suspect whether they are the murderer. Instead 'they say "Did you hit him with a tire iron?" And the guy says "No", and then they say "Well what did you hit him with?" where the guy hasn't admitted yet that he did it' (*LC*1: 22).

However, as we have seen, correction-invitation devices do not guarantee that a police suspect will offer an incriminating version of their activities or identity. Moreover, as Sacks notes, a very powerful device that storytellers can use in the face of potential or actual challenge is to be found in the extract above. Indeed, Sacks refers to B's 'everyone does, don't they?' as 'one of the most fabulous things I've ever seen' (*LC*1: 23).

B's question serves to cut off her accountability (for the presence of a gun in the household) by claiming generality. If, indeed, such situations are general, no further account can be called for. In the same way, but even more strongly, invoking a proverb can terminate a topic (Drew and Holt 1988: 411; Silverman 1997a: 138–9) since resisting a proverb is a sure way to make interaction break down (*LC*1: 25) (see chapter 1 above).

Both correction-invitation devices and direct challenges make use of members' knowledge of certain things that are known about any category, for instance, people of a certain age or gender. Such categories are used routinely (particularly within families) as a means of social control. For instance, mothers may say, as Sacks suggests: '"Remember you're a such-and-such" (a lady, an American, a Negro, a Catholic, etc.). That is, any action you take is exemplary' (*LC*1: 42).

But, once again, the organization of descriptions is subject to continuous, mutual interpretive work. So, if you want to escape such category-bound implications (for instance about your age), you can counter by accounting for why the category should not be read in this way here ('I'm forty-eight but . . .') (*LC*1: 44). However, people use sayings like 'boys will be boys' to serve as 'anti-modifier modifiers', asserting that, in the last instance, the category is omnirelevant (*LC*1: 45, 587).

The precise relevance of a category is also established by categorizing the categorizer, that is, if B categorizes C as 'old', you might categorize B in order to decide how *you* would categorize C.

Concluding Comments

The examples that we have just been considering demonstrate that membership categories are far from being the inert classificatory instruments to be found, say, in the more rigid forms of content analysis or in Bales's categorizations of 'interaction process' (see chapter 2 above). By contrast, membership categorization devices are local members' devices, actively employed by speakers and hearers to formulate and reformulate the meanings of activities and identities.

However, Sacks had little interest in *positioning* his ideas within a social science lexicon. As we saw in chapter 4, he recommended his approach as offering a method anyone could use. In this sense, his lectures offer a toolbox rather than a museum exhibition. Consonant with this position, chapter 7 will be mainly concerned with how subsequent social scientists have *used* categorization analysis. There, I shall follow Watson (n.d.) in arguing that Sacks's work on membership categorization is wholly consonant with his analysis of the sequential organization of conversation. (The reader unfamiliar with conversation analysis (CA) will by then have read chapter 6 to help with an understanding of the import of this observation.)

At this stage, however, it is worth remarking that many of the examples we have just been looking at are susceptible to a combination of CA and MCD analysis. For instance, correction-invitation devices fit fully with Sacks's discussion of conversational 'repair' (see pp. 122–3 below). And the organization of storytelling points to the importance of how tellers and recipients of stories obtain the floor by 'tying' their talk to a previous turn (pp. 117–18). In both examples, CA and categorization analysis help us to home in on the precise accomplishment of what Sacks refers to as 'order at all points'.

However, to appreciate this argument, we must examine in some detail Sacks's account of conversation analysis. As already noted, this is the task of chapter 6.

6

Conversation Analysis

In his very first transcribed lecture, given in fall 1964, Sacks begins with data from his Ph.D. dissertation on telephone conversations collected at an emergency psychiatric hospital. In the following two extracts, A is a member of staff at the hospital and B can either be somebody calling about themselves or calling about somebody else.

6.1 [*LC*1: 3]
A: Hello
B: Hello

6.2 [*LC*1: 3]
A: This is Mr Smith may I help you
B: Yes, this is Mr Brown

Sacks makes two initial observations about these extracts. First, B seems to tailor his utterance to the format provided by A's first turn. So, in 6.1, we get an exchange of 'hellos' and, in 6.2, an exchange of names. Or, as Sacks puts it, we might say that there is a 'procedural rule' where 'a person who speaks first in a telephone conversation can choose their form of address, and ... thereby choose the form of address the other uses' (*LC*1: 4).

Sacks's second observation is that each part or turn of the exchange occurs as part of a pair (Hello–Hello). Each pair of turns may be called a 'unit' in which the first turn constitutes a 'slot' for the second and sets up an expectation about what this slot may properly contain. Given this expectation, A is usually able to extract B's name (as in 6.2) without ever having to ask for it directly. The beauty of this, as Sacks points out, is that it avoids a problem that a direct question might create. For instance, if you ask someone their name, they may properly ask 'Why?', and in this way require that you offer a proper warrant for asking (*LC*1: 4–5). By contrast, providing a slot for a name cannot be made accountable. So to answer a phone with your name has a function in institutions where obtaining callers' names is important (*LC*1: 5–6)

Of course, the fact that something may properly happen once a slot has been created, does not mean that it *will* happen. Take this further example cited by Sacks:

6.3 [*LC*1: 3]
A: This is Mr Smith may I help you
B: I can't hear you.
A: This is Mr <u>Smith</u>.
B: Sm<u>i</u>th.

Sacks's two procedural rules do not mean that speakers are automatons. What seems to happen in 6.3 is that B's reply 'I can't hear you' means that the slot for the other party to give their name is missed. This does not mean that their name is 'absent' but rather that the place where it might go is closed. As Sacks puts it: 'It is not simply that the caller ignores what they properly ought to do, but something rather more exquisite. That is, they have ways of providing that the place where the return name fits is never opened' (*LC*1: 7).

Sacks returns to the issue of 'place' or conversational 'slot' in his spring 1966 lectures. Slots are places where certain second activities may properly occur after a particular first activity. But how do you demonstrate this? Is 'slot' simply an analyst's category invoked only to explain what the analyst sees? Sacks answers these questions by showing that members themselves routinely attend to the issue of whether a slot is properly used. One good example of this is the way in which all of us are able to recognize the 'absence' of proper uses of slots. For instance, where someone does not return our 'hello' (and they clearly heard it), we have no problem in seeing that something is absent (*LC*1: 308). Indeed, we may properly recount this incident to someone else as an example of a 'snub'.

This example of an 'absent' greeting can be readily seen because returned greetings are part of a category of 'paired objects' which include not only 'greetings' but, for instance, questions-and-answers (*LC1*: 308–9). When the first part of such a paired object has been completed, any pause by the second party is seen as *their* pause, that is, their responsibility. This is because such a first part is hearable as an 'utterance completer' where, once provided, it is the other party's turn to speak and to speak in a way that properly attends to the first part (*LC1*: 311).

Such proper attention means that it will be hearably 'odd' if we reply 'hello' to a recognizable question. However, this does not mean we are bound to act in the expected way, or even that a non-expected reply will always be heard as 'odd' (see my discussion of 'insertion sequences' below).

So far, we have been assuming that there are only two speakers. As Sacks points out, this simplifies matters considerably since two-party conversations usually have the structure A-B-A-B as above. However, it is not the case that multi-party conversations necessarily or even usually take the form A-B-C-A-B-C (*LC1*: 309–10).

This raises the issue of how the next speaker gets to speak at a possible turn-transition point in a situation where there are others who might speak. One option is for the present speaker to choose the next speaker (*LC1*: 527) by, for instance, asking a question with her gaze turned towards a particular person. A second possibility is that using someone's name will be heard by them as involving their possible nomination as next speaker as in the following extract:

6.4 [*LC1*: 665]
Dan: Well, Roger uh
Roger: Hm?
Dan: – introduced a kind of topic when he uh . . .

Even though, as it turns out, Roger is not specifically being selected as next speaker (as we see in Dan's use of 'he' to refer to Roger), 'the very use of the name "Roger" seems to involve him in seeing that he has been selected' (*LC1*: 665).

A third possibility is that the next speaker self-selects. However, as Sacks notes, it is a bit more complicated than this. First, the next speaker may only properly speak after an 'utterance completer' (like a question) or at some other recognizable possible turn-transition point (for example, a silence after a topic is possibly completed). Second, where more than one speaker then talks and, therefore, you get overlapping talk, the apparent rule here is: 'first starter goes' (*LC1*: 527).

However, as Sacks points out, this does *not* mean that the second starter, having allowed the first starter to speak, then gets the next turn as of right. Given that the present speaker can choose the next speaker, there is no reason why the late starter will necessarily get to speak at the next available turn-transition point (*LC1*: 527).

All this means that people in a multi-party conversation who want to speak next have to listen out for when a turn is completed in order to try to get the next turn for themselves. Moreover, the possibility that you may be named by the present speaker means that even those with nothing to say have to listen at all times in case they don't respond properly (or at all).

In this way, Sacks invites us to see that utterances which are apparently meaningless, like Roger's 'Hm?' (6.4), or obvious (like the exchange of 'hellos' in 6.1), can be seen as 'social objects' (*LC1*: 10). Such objects get used to construct a range of activities which include, as here, recognizing that it is your turn to speak and/or to do a greeting. In this respect, as Sacks puts it in his earliest transcribed lecture: 'we can go about beginning to collect the alternative methods that persons use in going about doing whatever they have to do' (*LC1*: 11).

However, as I pointed out in chapter 4, we should not take Sacks's use of terms like 'methods' (or, elsewhere, 'apparatus') to imply that he is assuming that conversation follows some 'rational' plan. First, like Garfinkel, Sacks is not referring to conscious strategies but to members' everyday methods – their 'ethnomethods'. This means, second, that we don't need to worry about how quickly people are able to do things. As Sacks said:

> Don't worry about how fast they're thinking. First of all, don't worry whether they are 'thinking'. Just try to come to terms with how it is that the thing comes off. Because you'll find that they can do these things. Just take any other area of natural science and see, for example, how fast molecules do things. And they don't have very good brains. (*LC1*: 11)

Conversational Sequencing: Some Basics

To look at how people 'do these things' requires empirical investigation of how people actually talk together. Such investigation shows that one person's talk does not necessarily correspond to a sentence. It may be much shorter ('Hm?' in 6.4) or contain several sentences. This means that members do not limit themselves to grammatical notions like 'sentences' when they talk.

However, as Sacks recognized, no empirical study can or should ever be theory-free. So, for instance, Sacks replaces the concept of the 'sentence' with the concept of an 'utterance' (*LC1*: 647) which, as we have seen, is hearably terminated by some 'utterance completer'. As it turns out, the idea of 'hearability' is very important. For Sacks searched for a theory which members demonstrably employed without ever necessarily thinking about it. As he put it: 'I have a bunch of stuff and I want to try to see whether an order for it exists. *Not that I want to try to order it,* but I want to see whether there's *some order* to it' (*LC1*: 622).

In this search for (a member's) order, Sacks looked for (a member's) 'unit'. As he told his students: 'We want to construct some unit which will permit us to study actual activities. Can we construct "the conversation" as such a unit? Can we in the first place make of it a "unit" – a *natural* unit and an *analytic* unit at the same time?'(*LC1*: 95, emphasis added).

Such a 'unit' has to be an analyst's construction of a member's unit (that is, a 'natural' unit). Given that, Sacks asks himself what we (and members) need to construct such a unit. The answer that Sacks provides is deceptively simple. We need just two things. First, we need rules of sequencing in conversation through which single utterances 'turn out to be handleable' (*LC1*: 622). Second, we need to understand the objects handled by these rules (*LC1*: 95).

Sacks offered this general definition of what he meant by 'the sequential analysis of conversation'. It means 'that the parts which are occurring one after the other, or are in some before and after relationship, have some organization as between them' (1987: 54).

We saw some aspects of these before and after relationships in Sacks's analysis of the extracts above. Some 'grossly apparent' general features of the sequential organization of conversation (*LC2*: 32) are set out by Sacks in a number of lectures (such as *LC1*: 95–9; *LC1*: 621–3; *LC2*: 32–43; *LC2*: 223–6). For ease of reference, I have listed these features in a box.

Two initial points need to be made about the list. First, in Sacks's early writing, turn-taking issues were not fully separated

---

Some features of the sequential organization of conversation

1 People talk one at a time.
2 Speaker change recurs.
3 Sequences that are two utterances long and are adjacently placed may be 'paired' activities.
4 Activities can be required to occur at 'appropriate' places.
5 Certain activities are 'chained'.

---

from issues relating to the sequencing of actions. Drawing upon this work, the list addresses both turn-taking *and* sequencing. Later in this chapter, I focus more specifically on turn-taking.

The second point is that the list refers to features of conversation which are not always necessarily present in any empirical instance. However, their absence will be attended to and made accountable. Moreover, their power is shown by the way they are invariant whatever the number of co-conversationalists, their age, gender, occupation or political preference. For instance, as Sacks puts it:

> it's not particularly a feature of, e.g., male conversation or female conversation or female–male conversation that one party talks at a time and speaker change recurs. They hold across types of conversations – arguments, business talks, whatever else. They hold across the parts of a conversation – beginnings, middles, ends. They hold across topics.
> (*LC2*: 34)

Sacks's comment suggests the force (and boldness) of his claim about these 'formal features of conversation'. Quite explicitly, social scientists are being asked to put on one side their theories about how what people do is shaped by social structures (such as class or politics) or by non-conversational interpersonal processes (from 'role distance' to 'cognitive dissonance' and 'distorted communication').

Given the boldness of this claim, you will be in a better position to judge what Sacks is saying if I now fill in a little of the detail that he provides for each of the five elements listed in the box.

1 People talk one at a time

We have already come across the argument that people monitor a present speaker's utterance to find a point at which it may have terminated. As we saw, if it turns out that there is overlap between the talk of two or more speakers, either because the initial speaker continues or because other speakers' talk overlaps, then the rule is that the first speaker is allowed to continue. So, despite speaker change, one-party-at-a-time is preserved (*LC*2: 32).

Moreover, the fact that overlaps don't occur all the time suggests that speakers display (and listeners hear) features which indicate that a current turn is about to end so that the other party can hear that it is their turn to speak (*LC*2: 33). Where there is no obvious marker such as a greeting (such as 'hello'), listeners may, for instance, inspect a pause to see whether it is:

– a pause within a turn (the current speaker's pause);
– a pause between turns (a possible turn-transition point);
– 'their' pause (because they have been nominated as next speaker).

2 Speaker change recurs

Given that people attend to the rule that, as far as possible, they should only speak one at a time, how does speaker change occur? Clearly, what Sacks calls 'coordinative work' is required to locate appropriate 'completion-transition points' (*LC*2: 33). Such work is most transparent in the turn-taking organization found in many traditional classrooms. Here, when a teacher has asked a question, students simply raise their hands and the teacher selects one of them to be next speaker (see Mehan 1979).

In less structured conversations, there are three possible ways of coordinating speaker change:

1 Current speaker can select next speaker. For instance, in a multi-party conversation, the current speaker can name someone else (*LC*2: 40). As we have seen, this carries the implication that 'the obligation to listen is built into conversation' (*LC*2: 41).
2 Current speaker can select a next action. For instance, by asking

a question, current speaker selects an answer as the next action (*LC2*: 42).
3 Second speakers can self-select themselves and the action they will do (*LC2*: 42). However, as Sacks adds, what a second speaker says will be related in some way to the previous talk (see the discussion below, pp. 117-18, of 'tying').

Moreover, these three ways of organizing speaker change are 'ordered' in a sequence (*LC2*: 40). So (2) only applies if (1) does not occur. And (3) can happen only if (1) and (2) are absent.

3 Adjacency pairs

As returned greetings show, consecutive activities may be grouped in pairs. This constrains what the next speaker may do but it also constrains the initiator of the first part of the pair. So, for instance, if you want to receive a greeting, you may have to offer one yourself first (*LC1*: 673).

Not only greetings but also such adjacent activities as questions-and-answers and summons-and-responses are also paired. This has two consequences. First, the two parts are 'relatively ordered' (*LC2*: 521). This means that 'given a first, a second should be done' and what should be done is 'specified by the pair organization' (*LC2*: 191). Second, if the indicated second is not done it will be 'seen to be absent' (*LC2*: 191) and a repeat of the first will be offered. For instance, Sacks suggests that quite young children who say 'hi' to someone and then get no reply will usually only go about their business after they have repeated their first 'hi' and obtained a 'hi' in return (*LC1*: 98).

The organization of these kinds of two consecutive utterances provides the concept of 'adjacency pairs' – sequences that are two utterances long and are adjacently placed (greeting–greeting, question–answer, summons–answer). As we have seen, adjacency pairs are 'relatively ordered' because one always goes before the other. They are also 'discriminatively related' in that the first part defines (or discriminates between) appropriate second parts (*LC2*: 521).

Adjacency pairs can now be seen as a powerful way of organiz-ing a relationship between a current utterance and a prior and a next utterance. Indeed, by constituting a next position which admits only one utterance type (*LC2*: 555), Sacks suggests that 'the adjacency relationship between utterances is the most powerful device for relating utterances' (*LC2*: 554)

The power of this device is suggested by two examples relating to the 'summons–answer' adjacency pair. As Cuff and Payne point out, 'the recipient of summons feels impelled to answer.' As they note, one unfortunate consequence of this is that in Northern Ireland, when their front doorbell rings and, thereby, constitutes a 'summons', 'persons still open the door and get shot – despite their knowledge that such things happen' (1979: 151).

The second example arises in Sacks's discussion of a child's question: 'You know what, Mommy?' (*LC1*: 256–7, 263–4). As he points out, the child's use of 'Mommy' establishes another summons–answer sequence, where a proper answer to the summons is for Mommy to say 'What?' This allows the child to say what it wanted to at the start, but as an obligation (because questions must produce answers). Consequently, this utterance is a powerful way in which children enter into conversations despite their usually restricted rights to speak.

However, Sacks warns us to avoid the assumption that adjacency pairs, like summons–answer, necessarily work in a mechanical way. For instance, he notes that questions can sometimes be properly followed by further questions, as in 6.5:

6.5 [*LC2*: 529]

1 A: Can I borrow your car?
2 B: When?
3 A: This afternoon
4 B: For how long?
5 A: A couple of hours
6 B: Okay.

Here B provides the second part of the question–answer pair in line 6 not in line 2. Citing Schegloff (1972), Sacks calls lines 2–5 an 'insertion sequence' (*LC2*: 528). Such sequences are permissible in question–answer pairs on the understanding that B will provide the answer when A has finished (*LC2*: 529). However, Sacks suggests that in greetings, unlike other adjacency pairs, insertion sequences are unusual (*LC2*: 189).

To summarize: 'An adjacency pair first pair part can go *anywhere* in conversation, *except* directly after a first pair part, *unless* the first pair part is the first pair part for an insertion sequence' (*LC2*: 534). Moreover, since adjacency pair first pair parts can go anywhere, we see, once more, that people have to listen at all times – this time in case they are called upon to do a second pair part (*LC2*: 536). Indeed, we should not assume that adjacency pairs only consist of two utterances. Not only may there be insertion sequences but sometimes chains of adjacency pairs may be constructed.

As an instance of such a chain, Sacks notes how we often say things like 'What are you doing tonight?' where our companion knows that an answer like 'Nothing in particular' is pretty certain to lead to a further adjacency pair of 'invitation–response'. In this way, the first question–answer pair serves to 'pre-signal "invitation to come"' (*LC2*: 529).

4 Activities occur at 'appropriate' places

If Sacks emphasizes that objects like adjacency pairs are not used mechanically, it is because all the 'objects' and 'rules' that he describes owe their status to how they are recognized and used by members. Take the example of the utterance 'hello'. Sacks points out that 'hello' need not always be heard as a 'greeting'. For instance, saying 'hello' in the middle of a phone conversation will probably be heard not as a greeting but as checking out that the other person is still on the line. It follows that members distinguish 'greeting places' from 'greeting items' (*LC1*: 97).

The placement of particular activities at a particular place in a sequence, as we have seen, allows members to identify what is absent from a particular 'place'. So, for instance, where a 'joke' is recognizably completed, the non-appearance of laughter or some appropriate substitute (such as 'I've heard that one before') will be heard to be 'absent'.

Moreover, one joke can lead to another since doing any activity may allow another party to do the same (*LC1*: 99–100). So one way in which activities occur at 'appropriate' places is as a repeat of a first activity by another speaker. Of course, this applies not just to jokes but also to activities like inquiries about someone's health and also to announcements and invitations.

5 Certain activities are 'chained'

As we have seen, questions and answers are an example of an adjacency pair. In two-party conversations, this suggests the following rule: 'If one party asks a question, when the question is complete, the other party properly speaks and properly offers an answer to the question, and says no more than that' (*LC*1: 264). Moreover, once a recognizable 'answer' has been provided, the person who asked the question has what Sacks calls 'a reserved right to speak' (*LC*1: 264). Since this right *can* be used to ask a further question, we can have an indefinitely long chain of the form: Q-A-Q-A-Q etc. (*LC*1: 49, 102, 264).

Sacks illustrates this 'chaining rule' through a classic Yiddish joke. A young man (A) finds himself on a train sitting next to an older man (B). This conversation then ensues:

6.6 [*LC*1, 49–50, modified]
A: Can you tell me the time?
B: No.
A: What do you mean no?
B: If I tell you the time we will have to get into a conversation. You'll ask me where I'm going. It will turn out we're going to the same place. I'll have to ask you for dinner. I have a young marriageable daughter, and I don't want my daughter to marry someone who doesn't wear a watch.

B's wariness about answering a question shows the power of the 'chaining rule' and explain why, in other circumstances, as we saw in chapter 1, questions can be effective 'pick-up devices' (*LC*1: 49). The chaining rule operates most commonly in particular kinds of professional–client settings such as doctor–patient consultations (Heath 1986), counselling interviews (Peräkylä and Silverman 1991b; Peräkylä 1995) and job selection interviews (Button 1992), where long strings of talk may be organized in the Q-A-Q-A format.

However, as we have seen, Sacks is very aware of the dangers of a purely mechanistic reading of anything he calls a rule. This leads to three notes of caution. First, obviously, because questioners can ask a further question, this does not mean that they will actually do so. Second, as we saw in 6.5, adjacency need not mean that the answer will be produced in the very next turn. Finally, relatedly, when questions produce further questions, this can sometimes turn the chaining rule around. So, as in the case of 'You know what Mommy?', children set up a situation where they revert to an answering role as a result of the predictable 'Mommy's' response of 'What?'

Moreover, Sacks notes that we should not rush to the assumption that the conversation analyst can straightforwardly identify 'questions' and 'answers'. Certainly, what is a question can usually be readily identified by a particular grammatical form and intonation. But to establish whether an object is an 'answer' we have to examine closely how speakers treat it (*LC1*: 49). We see this most clearly in the way in which psychiatrists and family therapists treat any response from a silence to a minimal utterance (like 'mm') to an extensive reply as properly (or not) an 'answer' (Peräkylä 1995: 287–328).

Moreover, once a sequence of questions has started, Sacks notes that subsequent turns by the initial questioner are likely to be heard as questions as well unless they have a very clear non-question form. In this situation: 'the characteristic of a question is to be found by its occurrence in a list that is hearable as being "a list of questions"'; in this case 'it would be difficult to warrant an argument which counted [questions] as singly independent objects' (*LC1*: 373).

Once more, Sacks elegantly makes a more general point. Categories should not, as in most social science, be regarded as 'singly independent objects'. Instead, even the most apparently obvious categories, such as 'questions' and 'answers', should be viewed as accomplishments of members' local, sequential interpretation.

In the next two sections of the chapter, I will illustrate this point in relation to two issues to which Sacks gave a great deal of attention: telephone calls and storytelling.

Telephone Calls

As already noted, Sacks used data from telephone conversations in his Ph.D. dissertation. As we saw in chapter 5, this data showed how counsellors and clients might analyse a person's situation as meaning that they had 'no one to turn to'.

One of the nice things about telephone conversations is that (at least before the advent of video links) they provide an opportunity for people to make sense of each other's talk without recourse to visual cues because non-verbal forms of communication – apart from the telephone bell – are absent. Somehow, despite the absence of such cues, speakers manage an orderly sequence in which both parties know when to speak. This meant that Sacks could happily use telephone calls to address the sequential organization of conversation without needing to make reference to anything apart from purely audio material.

I discuss below the four basic questions that Sacks raised about the organization of telephone conversations, namely:

1 Who speaks first?
2 Why is 'answerer' not necessarily 'called'?
3 Who introduces first topic?
4 How is the closing of the call organized?

1 Who speaks first?

In certain environments, like law courts and committees, there are rules about who may speak first. However, in 'ordinary' conversations, at least in Western societies, there is no general rule to say who speaks first. But telephone conversations are an exception. As Sacks notes: 'there is a rule for telephone conversation which is *"Answerer speaks first"'* (*LC2*: 542).

Sacks illustrates this point in his fall 1967 lectures (*LC1*: 631–2) by reference to a paper by Emanuel Schegloff then awaiting publication. Here Schegloff had argued, like Sacks, that 'a first rule of telephone conversations which might be called "a distribution rule for first utterances" is: *the answerer speaks first*' (1968, see Gumperz and Hymes 1972: 351, original emphasis).

Schegloff's study is based on data drawn from the first five seconds of around 500 telephone calls to and from an American police station. He begins by noting that the basic rule for two-party conversation, that one party speaks at a time (that is, providing for a sequence A-B-A-B where A and B are the parties), 'does not provide for the allocation of the roles "a" and "b"' (p. 350). In telephone calls, the issue of who speaks first is resolved by the 'distribution rule' above.

In order to see the force of the 'distribution rule', consider the confusion that occurs when a call is made and the phone is picked up, but nothing is said by the receiver of the call. Schegloff cites an anecdote by a woman who adopted this strategy of silence after she began receiving obscene telephone calls. Her friends were constantly irritated by this practice, thus indicating the force of the rule 'the answerer speaks first'. Moreover, her tactic was successful. As Schegloff notes: 'However obscene her caller might be, he would not talk until she had said "hello", thereby obeying the requirements of the distribution rule' (p. 355).

On examining his material further, Schegloff discovered only one case (out of 500) which did not fit the rule 'answerer speaks first'. Using 'deviant case analysis' (see chapter 4), he reworked all his data to find rules which would account for this apparently deviant case. He concluded that this could be done by seeing the distribution rule as 'a derivative of more general rules'(p. 356).

Schegloff argued that a person who responds to a telephone bell with 'hello' is responding to a *summons*. A summons is any attention-getting device (a telephone bell, a term of address – John? – or a gesture, like a tap on the shoulder or raising your hand). Like the other adjacency pairs discussed earlier, a summons tends to constrain the form of the next turn (that is, it suggests that it will be an 'answer').

Schegloff is now able to explain his deviant case as follows: summons (phone rings) – no answer; further summons (caller says 'Hello'). The normal form of a telephone call is: summons (phone rings) – answer (recipient says 'Hello'). In the deviant case, the absence of an answer is treated as the absence of a reply to a summons. So the caller's use of 'Hello' replaces the summons of the telephone bell. The failure of the summoned person to speak first is heard as an uncompleted SA sequence. Consequently, the caller's speaking first makes sense because further interaction is conditional upon the successful completion of the SA sequence.

2 Why is 'answerer' not necessarily 'called'?

As we all know, when we make a call we sometimes get a wrong number or find that the person who answers the phone is not the person we called. This obvious point explains why 'answerer' is not necessarily 'called'. Sacks shows how these unremarkable circumstances are associated with further features that make telephone calls different from most face-to-face conversations. This is the example he uses:

6.7 [*LC2*: 546–7]
1   Lana: Hello:,
2   Gene: I:s, Maggie there.
3   Lana: 'hh Uh who is calling,
4   Gene: Uh this's Gene:. Novaki.
5   (0.3)
6   Lana: Uh just a mom'nt,

The feature of this call that Sacks emphasizes is to be found in the absence of a greeting in line 2. To see this feature, notice that Lana says 'hello' in line 1. Now 'hellos' are usually greetings and greetings are adjacency pairs. So why does not Gene return Lana's greeting in line 2?

An initial answer to this question is that, in telephone calls, the identities of caller and called cannot be certainly known prior to a greeting. For this reason, callers may scan a 'hello' to see if they are talking to the one they called, using a 'voice-recognition test' (*LC2*: 161, 546). As Sacks points out, this 'raises a possible exception to the "return a greeting with a greeting" rule in the case of telephone conversations. Caller need not do a greeting return if answerer is not equivalent to called' (*LC2*: 543).

However, we should not assume that Lana's 'hello' is hearable as a 'greeting'. Schegloff's earlier analysis suggests that in the context of a first turn of a telephone conversation, Lana's 'hello' is not heard as a first-placed greeting but as a response to the summons of the telephone bell, that is, as a second-placed object. For these reasons, a failure to return 'hello' at the start of a telephone call need not be a recognizable 'absence'.

Even if 'answerer' turns out not to be 'called', this does not mean that she has no obligations. As Sacks notes, answerers do not normally answer questions like 'Is Maggie there?' by saying 'no' and hanging up. Equally, when callers get asked their name, as happens here, they have to select a name which will appropriately identify them ('Gene Novaki', 'Gene', 'Mr Novaki', 'the gardener', etc.). As Sacks notes, Gene's hesitation at the start of line 4 can be seen to arise because of the selection that needs to be made, not because Gene does not know his name (*LC2*: 547).

3 *Who introduces first topic?*

Although answerers are expected to speak first, it is callers who are expected to provide the first topic. Answerers, after all, do not normally know who is making the call, whereas callers can usually identify answerers and answerers will assume that callers have initiated a call in order to raise a topic.

So first topics are usually raised by the caller, as in lines 4–5 of this instance:

6.8 [*LC2*: 158]
1   Jeanette: Hello,

2	Estelle:	Jeanette,
3	Jeanette:	Yeah,
4	Estelle:	Well I just thought I'd–re–better report to you
5		what's happen' at <u>Bu</u>llocks toda::y?

However, Sacks shows that the issue of 'first topic' is also responsive to at least three other issues. In the case of telling bad news, a caller may want to avoid a 'how are you?' sequence which might well elicit a response of 'fine'. They may therefore use the called's name immediately after the called person says 'hello'. When they get a 'yeah', they can go into first topic without a long greeting exchange (*LC2*: 159–60).

Secondly, callers are attentive to the way in which first topics are heard as special or important. So when you say you are 'calling for no reason', you can postpone first topic indefinitely by showing that you do not have a 'first topic' item (*LC2*: 165).

Finally, it sometimes happens that someone calls you and you have a piece of news that constitutes a 'reason for a call' but you have neglected to call. How do we handle our failed obligation in these circumstances and get round the rule that says 'caller raises first topic'? One solution is to convert ourselves from answerers to hypothetical callers. We can do this by using some formula like: 'Oh, I've been trying to reach you.' Having reallocated our roles, we are now free to introduce the first topic (*LC2*: 163, 552).

4 How is the closing of the call organized?

Having talked about a first (and other) topic(s), how do telephone calls reach their end? More technically, how do the speakers arrive at a point 'where one speaker's completion will not occasion another speaker's talk, and that will not be heard as some speaker's silence' (Schegloff and Sacks 1974: 237).

Clearly, we can see that end happen by the parties exchanging 'goodbyes' where completion of the pair demonstrates that last speaker has understood what the prior turn was aimed at and goes along with it (p. 240). But 'goodbye' is only a 'terminator' which follows *earlier* closing work. So how does a speaker find out where to put that first 'goodbye' (*LC2*: 364)?

One solution is provided where another speaker has just said 'okay.' or 'we-ell.' with a downward intonation. Such utterances may be heard to convey a 'pre-closing' invitation and may be used by any speaker in any conversation (Schegloff and Sacks 1974: 246).

However, in telephone calls, rights and obligations are rather different. Sometimes the called person may say something that will be heard as a pre-closing invitation (such as 'this is costing you a lot of money' (p. 250). But, in principle, having initiated the call, Sacks suggests that it is caller's business to invite a close (*LC2*: 364). This can get done by referring to the interests of the called party ('well I'll letchu go') or by reference to previous activities cited by the called party at the beginning of the conversation (watching TV, eating, having people over) (Schegloff and Sacks 1974: 250). The called person's prior mention of such activities gives the caller a 'ticket' (*LC2*: 364) which can be saved up and later used to show that the proposal to close is actually being done in the interests of the called person.

This account of pre-closing invitations nicely underlines Sacks's insistence that conversation depends upon cooperatively organized, sequential work. 'Pre-closing' involves reference to the needs of the other. And what is proposed is only an 'invitation', which can be declined. Of course, this is not to deny that telephone speakers may sometimes put the phone down on each other. But it is to note how strongly this will be heard as a 'breach' which requires later explanations and apologies.

Sales calls may be thought to be an exception to hearing a breach in an abruptly put-down phone. However, I remember the salesman who called me back after such an incident and, no doubt appealing to the absence of a proper pre-closing invitation, told me that I had 'no right' to do that! Moreover, note that even the exasperated recipient of an unwanted call will usually preface putting down the phone by an announcement ('I'm going to put the phone down now') which, while suggesting that when the phone line goes down this is deliberate rather than accidental, also may allow the other party to say 'wait just one moment.'

Storytelling

At first sight, storytelling might be thought to be the work of one party – the teller. However, just like telephone conversations, the telling of a story requires collaboration. Given the mechanisms for the exchange of turns, cooperation between teller and recipient is required if a story is to be extended through various possible completion points.

For instance, to tell a story may involve a 'preface' (*LC2*: 10,

18–19) which both provides for the multi-turn nature of the talk and allows its recipient to know when it is to be completed. But equally the recipient will need to offer minimal 'response tokens' (such as 'mm') which serve to indicate that they are listening but are passing their turn and inviting the other to continue (see the discussion of response tokens below).

Sacks's account of the cooperative organization of storytelling is discussed below in relation to four issues:

1 obtaining and retaining the 'floor';
2 'tying' mechanisms;
3 using 'response tokens' (like 'mm mm');
4 'heckling' stories.

1 Obtaining and retaining the 'floor'

There are various mechanisms through which persons obtain the right to speak. For instance, children may use the question 'you know what, Mommy?', and anybody may claim a speaking right by saying something such as 'your clothes are on fire' which, by drawing attention to some matter of presumed immediate importance to the hearer, may constitute a 'ticket' to speak (*LC1*: 256–7, 263–5).

However, because stories go on over more than a single turn of talk, they create particular issues in retaining the 'floor'. Indeed, 'floor' considerations are central to the identification of a story as 'an attempt to control the floor over an extended series of utterances' (*LC2*: 18). If you want to tell a long story, involving multi-unit turns, you face problems (*LC1*: 682). In particular, you want people just to *listen* without attending to how they can be next speaker, given that the built-in motivation for hearers – that they may be next speaker – is missing (*LC1*: 683–4). Given the various mechanisms for speaker transition (*LC2*: 223–6 and pp. 104–5 above), how then do you produce a multi-utterance turn?

As Sacks tells us, the storyteller's problem is how to get selected as speaker after next. Like the child's 'You know what?', a story is 'an attempt to control a third slot in talk, from a first' (*LC2*: 18). One way of doing this is to ask a question such as 'You want to hear a joke?' or 'You know what happened to me last night?' Another way is to make an announcement like 'Something terrible happened to me today' or 'I heard a good joke' (*LC1*: 680–1).

Utterances like these serve two functions. First, they are heard as prefaces (*LC2*: 19) which alert their hearer to an upcoming story. Second, such prefaces, like the child's question, are routinely received by 'what?' As in that case, the first speaker retains the floor by being *required* to continue (*LC2*: 226).

Any response to such a preface (even 'big deal' to an announcement) will do as a take-off point, as Sacks shows in the following example:

6.9 [*LC1*: 681]
A: I was at the po<u>lice</u> station this morning.
B: Big deal.
A: 'Big deal' yeah. Somebody stole all my radio equipment outta my car.

This example shows how 'newsworthiness' is a consideration in storytelling both through how A constructs his announcement (as potentially newsworthy) and how 'Big deal' works to deny that. Nevertheless, A can still continue by demonstrating other aspects which make his story newsworthy. However, when hearers say either that they already know that or that you already told them, you no longer have a story to tell unless you offer an alternative preface announcing a story that will be heard to be 'tellable' (*LC2*: 13).

Such announcements have a function for hearers as well as tellers of stories. In particular, they allow hearers to work out the completion point of the story (*LC1*: 682) and, therefore, the appropriate place for an appreciation. For instance, as Sacks notes: '"I have something terrible to tell you" ... [serves] not just to arouse interest but to instruct hearers to use that term to monitor the story – when they've heard something that ['terrible'] could name, the story will be over' (*LC2*: 228). With the prior guidance of the story preface (something 'terrible' or 'funny'), a hearer can both work out when the story has ended and do an appreciation of it in the very terms provided by the teller (*LC2*: 11).

Sometimes these terms can be very finely shaded. For instance, if you want your story to be treated lightly but not as a joke, how do you convey this to the hearer? One way to do this is to laugh while telling your story. Note the laughter by Portia in the following extract:

6.10 [*LC2*: 275]
Agnes: I bet it's a dream, with the swimming pool enclosed huh?
Portia: Oh God, we hehh! we swam in the nude Sunday night until about
            two o'clock.

Sacks suggests that Portia's laughter conveys that she took these reported events 'lightly'. Placed here, it thus serves to inform Agnes in advance how Portia took the reported event. For instance, without it, Agnes might have laughed afterwards and, if Portia had joined in, Agnes would not have known if Portia really felt the event was funny or was just doing an appreciation of Agnes's response.

Laughter thus can work as a way of attuning someone to know how to hear someone's story. As an attuning device, laughter is, then, one of the 'ways for the teller ... to guide the recipient in figuring out what's happening and also in figuring out things about the teller's participation' (*LC2*: 275).

2 'Tying' mechanisms

We have just seen how 'appreciations' claim an understanding of a story. 'Oh really' or 'I know just what you mean' work in this way. However, a far stronger kind of appreciation is displayed when the hearer uses the topics or characters of a first story to construct a further story. Such 'second stories' *exhibit* an understanding of a first story which is only *claimed* by responses like 'I see' (*LC2*: 6–8, 252).

Of course, this kind of exhibited understanding also allows a hearer to tell her own story. Sacks refers to 'second stories' as an instance of the kind of 'tying' mechanisms through which, in multi-party conversations, next speaker can self-select by 'tying' her utterance to a previous turn. Examples of such tying include the use of:

- a pronoun (such as 'they') tied to persons named in a prior turn (*LC1*: 717);
- 'that' to refer to a prior topic (*LC1*: 372);
- 'anyway' to tie talk to an earlier topic not present in the previous turn (*LC2*: 567–8);
- 'I still say though' – marking that I talked before, that someone else disagreed and that, despite that, I am reasserting my position (*LC2*: 557).

In all these cases, Sacks shows us how movement between topics in conversation is rarely abrupt but involves stepwise transitions. As he puts it:

> It's a general feature for topical organization in conversation that the best way to move from topic to topic is not by a topic close followed by a topic beginning, but by what we call a *stepwise* move. Such a move involves connecting what we've just been talking about to what we're now talking about, although they are different. (*LC2*: 566)

This stepwise transition of topics underlines a wider point. 'Tying' rules are just one instance of how conversation is sequentially organized and a context is locally produced. So a first speaker creates a context for a second. And a second speaker renews that context by providing a reading of the first turn and projecting a meaning for the next speaker's turn (*LC1*: 372).

Such sequential organization provides for a highly complex 'indefinite nesting of a conversation' out of 'very simple pairs of rules' (*LC1*: 372). It also means that anything a speaker says will be monitored for how it displays some understanding of a prior turn. As Sacks says about second and later turns: 'you can't but show that in fact you did understand, i.e. you can't but tie an utterance, and thereby show that you understood the last (or that you didn't understand [it])' (*LC1*: 720).

In this respect, tying – or 'positioning' (*LC2*: 557) – is not just something done by a present speaker but by all hearers. So tying shows how members attend to 'order at all points'. No wonder that Sacks remarks that 'that's an absolutely fabulous machinery' (*LC1*: 720).

3 Using 'response tokens'

Because speakers are dealing with a 'machinery' that is intersubjective, any attempt to explain or describe an utterance in psychological terms becomes, for Sacks, a 'lay' rather than an 'analytic' enterprise. A case in point is an utterance like 'uh' or 'uh huh'. Here, rather than try to read the speaker's mind, conversation analysis wants to ask: what sequential function does such a turn serve? To answer this question we are forced to examine how any conversation unfolds.

To understand this machinery further we might distinguish between how 'uh' and 'uh huh' are often used. One function that 'uh' can have is to get the floor in a multi-party conversation. So you say 'uh' close to or precisely on the end of an utterance. Then, if a silence follows, you've got the floor. As Sacks puts it: 'One doesn't ... produce "uh" because one is hesitating with what one has to say, but ... to get the floor so as to be able to say what one isn't prepared to say [straight off]' (*LC2*: 497).

By contrast to 'uh', 'mm' and 'uh huh' are part of a class of 'response tokens' that display particular understanding of a prior turn. Response tokens are not, however, just used to stake a claim for the floor. They can also signal that someone is saying: 'The story is not yet over. I know that' (*LC2*: 9). In this way, the previous speaker is informed that they can continue with whatever they were talking about (*LC2*: 410). Indeed, in this case, by declining a possible turn, response tokens can *require* a speaker to produce more, even when they are not claiming an extension of their turn – think of 'mm mm' or 'uh huh' used by counsellors and the like (*LC2*: 410–11).

Above all, as Sacks notes, response tokens can be subtly recipient designed by anticipating a possible pause and ensuring no gap and no overlap between speakers. In this way, utterances like 'mm' show that someone is listening and has identified a possible completion point, that is, a unit like a clause, a phrase or an intonation sequence. As Sacks notes, such units serve as 'grammatical stopping points within larger units' (*LC1*: 746).

Response tokens are, then, obviously non-trivial, tying terms. But the understanding they show is more ambiguous than, say, laughter or 'He did?' Hence the recipient of a response token needs to look at the token producer's next utterance to see the analysis of their utterance that 'uh huh' is doing. At the same time, a response token can 'go wrong' when the previous utterance has projected another sort of response (such as laughter, 'Oh', etc.) (*LC1*: 747).

4 'Heckling' stories

The foregoing shows how storytellers need some response to establish and to sustain their claim to the floor. So anything that the storyteller says is available as a resource for hearers. As Sacks shows in the extract below, speakers can, if they want, use a story's announcement to 'heckle':

6.11 [*LC2*: 284]
Ken: I mean I'm thinking about what someday I'm going to be, and stuff
        like // that
Roger: heh Wh(hh)en I grow up! heh hhh hheh hhh hh

Roger's response to Ken's attempted storytelling listens 'to what's being said in a way other than the teller intends' (*LC2*: 286). In this respect, it is similar to B's 'big deal' in response to A's story announcement on p. 116 above. Now Ken, like A, will have to redesign his turn if he wants to continue his topic.

However, storytellers like Ken and A know that heckling is always a possibility. As a consequence, Sacks says that this implies that perhaps tellers 'design their stories so as not to invite heckling, or to be in some way invulnerable to heckling as a possibility' (*LC2*: 287). Sacks does not give any examples of this, but story announcements with embedded statements like 'this sounds crazy but ...' or 'you may have heard this one before' seem good instances of an anti-heckling device.

Of course, heckling is not the only option for a hearer who doesn't see the point of a story. Very commonly, hearers hold off asking a teller what something means, expecting to find out later. This is not to satisfy some abstract ethical principle like 'fair play' or rule of good taste such as 'politeness'. Rather, in conversation, we do not always expect to find out what things mean right at the start. Sacks calls this 'a delay-interpretation rule for a hearer ... [which] wasn't an operation of interpreting the thing as the words come out, but one in which there would be some storage' (*LC2*: 315).

However, as we have seen, if a storyteller *can* provide an acceptable announcement of how her story is to be heard (say, as something 'serious', as a joke), so much the better for all parties.

Some Implications

Sacks's analysis of both storytelling and telephone calls reveals the mutual monitoring of each other's turns which is basic to the sequential organization of conversation. This organization shows the inadequacies of an analyst's attempt to treat any utterance as an expression of someone's thoughts. By contrast, in hearing how what they have just said is heard, speakers discover from recipients' responses what they were taken to have intended to mean.

In notes attached to the transcripts of his lectures, Sacks sometimes remarked on how he had simplified some of what he had said for his student audience. His systematic statement of these issues is to be found in a later joint paper (Sacks, Schegloff and Jefferson 1974). A brief presentation of this paper will serve as a summary of the significance of the foregoing.

The concepts and examples we have been discussing derive their import from the sequential organization of conversation to be found in the structure of turn-taking. The character of any turn is thus only to be understood from its presence in a series of turns:

> Turns display gross organizational features that reflect their occurrence in a series. They regularly have a three-part structure: one which addresses the relation of a turn to a prior, one involved with what is occupying the turn, and one which addresses the relation of the turn to a succeeding one. (p. 722)

Earlier in this chapter, we encountered examples of each part of this three-part structure:

1 How the speaker makes a turn relate to a previous turn (for instance by response tokens or by an appreciation).
2 What the turn interactionally accomplishes (for instance, as a story, serious or light, or as a joke).
3 How the turn relates to a succeeding turn (for instance, as the first part of an adjacency pair such as a question, request, summons, etc.).

In conclusion, Sacks, Schegloff and Jefferson note three *consequences* of their model of turn-taking:

1 *Needing to listen* The turn-taking system provides an 'intrinsic motivation' for listening to all utterances in a conversation. Interest or politeness alone is not sufficient to explain such attention. Rather, every participant must listen to and analyse each utterance in case she or he is selected as next speaker.
2 *Understanding* Turn-taking organization controls some of the ways in which utterances are understood. So, for instance, it allows 'How are you?', as a first turn, to be usually understood not as an enquiry but as a greeting.
3 *Displaying understanding* When someone offers the 'appropriate' form of reply (such as an answer to a question, or an apology to a complaint), she or he displays an understanding of the interactional force of the first utterance. The turn-taking system is thus the means whereby actors display to one another that they are engaged in *social* action responsive to the needs of others.

Before I offer a conclusion to this chapter, I want to emphasize the social or intersubjective character of the turn-taking system through a brief discussion of two further features of conversational organization: 'repair' and 'preference organization'.

Repair

In our earlier discussion of storytelling, we saw how the topical orientation of conversation linked to what Sacks calls 'tying' (or 'positioning') structures (*LC1*: 540). Such structures mean that 'Speakers specifically *place* almost all of their utterances ... they put them into such a position as has what's just been happening provide an obvious explanation for why this was said now' (*LC2*: 352, emphasis added).

Through such positioning, they can, if necessary, introduce an utterance as 'off-topic' (for instance, through saying 'by the way'). In this way, they tie their talk to a previous turn precisely by showing that they appreciate that they are now going to talk about something different.

But how does a second speaker demonstrate that they have not understood or even heard a first turn? Sacks describes 'a local cleansing' mechanism to be used in such cases (*LC2*: 560). This mechanism puts a 'remedial question' like 'why? how? what? where? when?' immediately after what is heard as a problematic turn. Indeed, unless such an attempted 'repair' is placed in the very next position, then the speaker may take it that what he or she said 'was heard, and was clear' (*LC2*: 352).

'Repair mechanisms' will be used in other circumstances than 'misunderstandings'. For instance, where more than one party is speaking at a time, a speaker may stop speaking before a normally possible completion point of a turn. Again, when turn transfer does not occur at the appropriate place, the current speaker may repair the failure of the sequence by speaking again. Finally, where repairs by other than the current speaker are required (for instance because another party has been misidentified), the next speaker typically waits until the completion of a turn. Thus the turn-taking system's allocation of rights to a turn is respected even when a repair is found necessary.

Turn-taking and repair can now be seen to be embedded in each other:

> The compatibility of the model of turn-taking with the facts of repair is thus of a dual character: the turn-taking system lends itself to, and

incorporates devices for, repair of its troubles; and the turn-taking system is a basic organizational device for the repair of any other troubles in conversation. The turn-taking system and the organization of repair are thus 'made for each other' in a double sense. (Sacks, Schegloff and Jefferson 1974: 723)

Preference Organization

This turn-taking system also means that first turns can be constructed so as to imply 'preferred' kinds of second turns. Thus Sacks notes that questioners can create preferred answers – for instance, by asking a question like 'so you're quite happy now?' which embeds an expectation that the answer will probably be 'yes'.

For this very reason, basic books on survey research advise against designing questions which imply an expected answer. However, Sacks is not concerned with remedying what we do but understanding the complexity of our communication. On that track, he observes that preferred answers, because they meet this inferred expectation, are short, while dispreferred ones add an account. So preferred answers take on a form which Sacks describes as 'Yes–period'. And dispreferred answers are of a 'No–plus' form, that is, they provide an account (*LC2*: 414). This means that 'if a question is built in such a way as to exhibit a preference as between "yes" and "no" ... then the answerers will pick that choice' (Sacks 1987: 57) and will delay any other elements.

In the following example, Sacks notes how A builds up a preference for a 'yes' answer:

6.12 [Sacks 1987: 57]
A: And it– apparently left her quite permanently damaged (I suppose).
B: Apparently. Uh he is still hopeful.

Note here how B spots this preference by initially agreeing – although skilfully couching that initial agreement by using A's term 'apparently'. This foreshadows the delayed disagreement ('he is still hopeful').

In the next extract, A's use of 'really' establishes that a 'no' answer is expected:

6.13 [Sacks 1987: 57]
A: Well is this really whatchu wanted?

B: Uh ... not originally? <u>No</u>. But it's uh ... promotion? en it's <u>very</u>
    interesting,

Note here how B's turn meets this expectation by its initial agreement ('Uh ... not originally?'). As in the previous extract, B delays
the disagreement components of his turn.

As well as such delays, Sacks notes that we find 'well' prefaces,
warrants and 'excepts' in dispreferred turns, as in these two
examples:

6.14 [Sacks 1987: 63]
A: You <u>are</u> afraid of your father
B: Oh yes. Definitely. I–I am. To a certain <u>extent</u>.

6.15 [Sacks 1987: 63]
A: 'N they haven't heard a <u>word</u> huh?
B: Not a word, <u>uh</u>-uh. Not– Not a word. Not at all. <u>Except</u> – Neville's
    mother got a call

Two further points need to be made about this organization of
preference. First, because it derives from a turn-taking system
based on the continual display of mutual understanding, all
speakers have a vested interest in avoiding conversational
'troubles'. So not only do answerers show that they understand the
preference embedded in a question, but questioners, who monitor
an upcoming disagreement, reformulate their question in the
direction of possible agreement (1987: 65).

The second point is that we must not confuse conversational
preference with any kind of psychological preference. So preference organization does not relate to what people want but to what
the logic of the turn-taking system implies. As Sacks puts it: 'it is
not that "people try to do it" ... [rather] there is an *apparatus* that
has them being able to do that' (p. 65).

Conclusion

I believe that Sacks was properly amazed by the beauty of the conversational apparatus he had unearthed. In conclusion, I will
suggest three aspects of the way in which he helps us to think
about this apparatus: as an 'economy' of 'omnipresent' and
'observable' objects.

An economy

As we saw in the preceding section, Sacks drags us away from our temptation to see conversation as an inner process concerned with the communication of thoughts. This anti-psychologistic thrust is seen in his use of the term 'apparatus' to describe the turn-taking system (see chapter 4).

However, Sacks and his colleagues also used the metaphor of an 'economy' to describe this system: 'For socially organized activities, the presence of "turns" suggests an economy, with turns for something being valued – and with means for allocating them, which affect their relative distribution, as in economies' (Sacks, Schegloff and Jefferson 1974: 696).

This concept of an economy powerfully directs us away from our temptation to treat conversation as a trivial outpouring of our individual experiences. Instead, like goods and services, turns-at-talk depend on a system for their distribution. Moreover, such turns have a value, seen in the potential 'profits' of obtaining the floor, and potential 'losses' (for example, of remembering what you wanted to say) in failing to get a turn at a particular point. In this way, the metaphor of 'economy' reminds us of the power and factual status of the turn-taking system.

Omnipresence

The power of omnipresence is reflected in the way in which speakers attend to the conversational rules we have discussed in all social contexts. Even the apparent boundaries of different cultures seem to matter little in this regard. We see this in a joint paper that Sacks wrote with the anthropologist, Michael Moerman. Moerman and Sacks (1971) note basic similarities between Thai and American-English speakers. In Thai, just as much as in American English, one speaker talks at a time with no gaps or overlaps. Equally, in both 'cultures' this is accomplished by speakers noticing and correcting violations, collaboratively locating transition points, collaboratively locating next speaker and listening for completions, turn transitions, insults, etc. As these authors put it, in both Thai and American English:

> participants must continually, there and then – without recourse to follow-up tests, mutual examination of memoirs, surprise quizzes and

other ways of checking on understanding – demonstrate to one another that they understood or failed to understand the talk they are party to. (Moerman and Sacks 1971: 10).

As in Sacks's lectures, this paper reminds us that we should not be surprised about how quickly people can do all these things: 'The instant availability of elaborate rules of grammar shows that our naive notion of how little the human brain can do quickly is wrong' (p. 11). However, this 'instant availability' and omnipresence should not be taken to mean that conversational rules are coercive. Instead, as Sacks notes, such rules achieve their relevance by being attended to and used:

> Somebody once said to me that they found people who violated the A-B-A-B rules, as if that ought to be something enormously shocking ... That is, as if, in fact, A-B-A-B would characterize any two-party conversation as a natural law, rather than it was something that persons attended to and used in various ways, and something that could tell people that, and *when*, it's their turn to speak. (*LC1*: 524)

Observability

I have repeatedly stressed, both here and in chapter 4, Sacks's claim to reveal members' observable activities rather than to build a self-enclosed system of rules and categories. This means that the 'orderliness' he describes is an orderliness which members rely upon and use: 'insofar as the materials we worked with exhibited orderliness, they did so not only to us, indeed not in the first place for us, but for the co-participants who had produced them' (Schegloff and Sacks 1974: 234).

The upshot of this is that 'problems' have to be observable problems for members in order to be interesting for analysts. But the 'ready observability' to which Sacks refers below implies something deep and profound:

> omnipresence and ready observability need not imply *banality*, and, therefore, silence. Nor should they only set off a search for exceptions or variation. Rather, we need to see that with some such mundane occurrences we are picking up things which are *so overwhelmingly true* that if we are to understand that sector of the world, they are something we will have to come to terms with. (1987: 56, emphasis added)

'Coming to terms with' this omnipresence gives us our research task. For Schegloff and Sacks, we must seek to achieve nothing less than 'a naturalistic observational discipline that could deal with the details of social action(s) rigorously, empirically and formally' (1974: 233). As I try to show in chapter 8, since Sacks's death in 1975, conversation analysis has become that discipline.

7

Using Membership Categorization Analysis

The status of membership categorization analysis within Sacks's project (or, indeed, as properly ethnomethodological) is still a subject of fierce debate. For instance, in his introduction to volume 1 of Sacks's *Lectures on Conversation*, Schegloff argues that MCD analysis, when separated from sequential considerations, is incipiently 'promiscuous' (*LC1*: xlii). This is because such analysis depends on the investigator's authority rather than on what it can be shown that participants are attending to, and hence inevitably must lapse into purely commonsense observations. As Schegloff puts it:

> The observation that 'crying is bound to "baby"' is . . . not a finding; it is merely the claimed explication of a bit of commonsense knowledge. As such it is just a claim, and cannot be simply asserted on the analyst's authority. It has to be warranted somehow, either by a test of it or by requiring it to yield some further pay-off to analysis. (*LC1*: xlii)

For this reason, Schegloff downgrades the significance of Sacks's work on MCDs and, indeed, argues that, by the late 1960s, Sacks had more or less moved away from it for these very reasons.

However, the situation seems to me to be rather more ambiguous. For instance, as Schegloff himself shows, Sacks's analysis of 'the baby cried' story does *not* simply depend upon the analyst's authority. In fact, Sacks constructs a test of the category-boundedness of 'crying'(*LC1*: 241), and in the teenage therapy group data, he tests his claim that 'therapist/patient' is 'omni-relevant' (*LC1*: 315).

So what is the problem if Sacks's use of categorization analysis recognized, as Schegloff puts it, that 'commonsense knowledge cannot properly be invoked as itself providing an account, rather than providing the elements of something to be accounted for' (*LC1*: xlii)? Schegloff seems to worry that, despite these contrary instances, Sacks was sometimes drawn in a reductive, common-sense direction. In particular, he refers to the 'culturalist tenor' of some of the spring 1966 lectures (on 'the baby cried' and 'children's games') where, he claims, 'culture' appears to be used in an 'anthropological sense in which it refers to the categories through which "reality" is grasped' (*LC1*: xliv).

Along these lines, Schegloff argues that Sacks became less interested in MCDs, even 'abandoned' their use because he recognized the danger that they might lead to purely commonsensical (or 'culturalist') observations. As he puts it:

> In my view, Sacks abandoned the use of 'category-bound activities' because of an incipient 'promiscuous' use of them, i.e. an unelaborated invocation of some vernacularly based assertion (i.e. that some activity was bound to some category) as an element of an account on the investigator's authority without deriving from it any analytic pay-off other than the claimed account for the data which motivated its introduction in the first place. (*LC1*: xlii)

In this review of contemporary MCD studies, I will argue that such 'promiscuity' is only a risk and is not inevitable, particularly where analysis of membership categorization is embedded in an address of sequential organization. Moreover, it is arguable how far Sacks changed the direction of his later work. As Watson suggests: 'The argument that Sacks's object of study shifted from categorization to utterance sequences shows an overly-selective attention [to] the empirical topics of Sacks's work rather than its generic conceptual commitments' (Watson n.d.: 2).

By contrast to Schegloff, Watson argues that four features remained constant in Sacks's position:

1 Sacks was always concerned with social *activities*: 'categorization was to be analysed as a culturally methodic (procedural) activity rather than in terms of an inert cultural grid' (p. 3).
2 For Sacks, categories came to have meaning in specific *contexts*: 'he did not see categories as "storehouses" of decontextualized meaning' (p. 4).
3 Sacks made it clear that category use did not reflect psychological processes (such as information processing) but depended upon 'cultural resources [which are] public, shared and transparent' (p. 4).

4 Above all, the issue for Sacks was not the *content* of categories but the procedures through which they are invoked and understood.

Moreover, Watson suggests that Sacks's work on the sequential organization of conversation (see chapter 6) is not separated off from MCD analysis. So, in Watson's version of Sacks, 'categorial organization is intrinsic to ... turn ordering' (n.d.: 16). In particular, Watson refers to Sacks's observation that 'caller–called' are 'identities that the conversation itself makes relevant' (*LC2*: 361). Moreover, when such categories are invoked, this limits, via the economy rule (chapter 5, p. 79 above), the relevance of other possible categories. This is what, for Sacks, makes the social organization of conversation autonomous from other social identities unless these are actually invoked (see his critique of Albert's work on the Burundi in chapter 3).

Moreover, Watson argues, such turn-generated categories as caller–called fit with much of Sacks's account of categorization:

> For a start, these categories are identities for persons. Secondly, he [Sacks] conceives of these identities as the loci of a set of rights and obligations ... [which] yield several organizational forms to the conversation which we might categorize in terms of category-bound activities and, in terms of the co-selection of categories, as relational pairs or membership categorization devices. (n.d.: 21)

In particular, Watson notes the following MCD features of caller–called (p. 28):

1 Category-bound rights and obligations are most obvious at the opening and closing phases of a conversation – in this way, called speaks first; caller is category-bound to initiate a pre-closing sequence.
2 Both caller and called attend to 'the reason for the call' as giving themselves a set of category-bound rights and obligations relative to the other needs or time constraints of each of them (so each may ask: 'are you busy?').
3 Participants may attend to a differentiation between 'called' and 'answerer' (with such mediating categories as butler, switchboard operator). As Watson puts it: 'Incumbents of mediating categories have, as part of their category-bound obligations, the task of "translating", for this specific conversation, the extrinsic categories into the integral ones "caller"–"called".'

Watson concludes that MCD analysis should not be relegated to a minor or even negative status within Sacks's work. So members' use of categories nicely demonstrates the crucial claim that conversational organization is at once ' 'context-free' and 'context-sensitive' (Sacks, Schegloff and Jefferson 1974). Indeed, Watson even suggests that CA needs MCD analysis since 'the procedural apparatus Sacks formulated in his early work concerning MCDs can work to explicate the operation of turn-generated categories' (n.d.: 30).

Complementarity (and not Armed Camps)

Up to now, I have suggested that there are grounds for supporting Watson's argument about the potential complementarity of membership categorization and conversation analysis. However, just as I resisted Schegloff's critique of the 'promiscuity' of MCD analysis, so too do I resist Watson's (1996) suggestion that 'sequential analysis' tacitly draws on membership categorization without explicating it.

Watson tries to support his argument by examining how CA studies identify speakers in transcripts of institutional talk. He notes correctly that when we read from left to right, we are predisposed to reading a transcript in terms of the identity given on the left. In this way, he claims, CA tacitly builds our sense of social structure into its analyses. For instance, Watson cites this extract:

[Frankel 1990: 149,simplified]
Dr: Did y'feel sick.
        (0.6)
Pt: A little bit. [Yes
Dr: [Mmh hmh.
Dr: Right. hh Now c'n yih tell me–

He argues that, without the identities provided, we might, perhaps, read such an extract marked Dr (doctor) and Pt (patient) as, say, 'troubles talk' between strangers grounded in the 'chaining rule' for questions and answers (Q-A-Q in the extract above).

However, I suggest that the second question here 'Now c'n yih tell me–' looks a little odd in the context of talk between strangers. This is not to say it could *never* occur in such talk but rather that it (or some variant) is routinely warranted by the investigatory rather than empathic stance that professionals properly take towards clients' troubles. That is why this question works as a likely example of professional–client talk in a way in which, as Sacks noted, a third-position utterance like 'Yeah. I feel sick myself sometimes too' would not.

Since CA-informed studies of institutional talk usually show how, in ways like this, participants invoke institutional identities (see Drew and Heritage 1992; Schegloff 1991; Heritage 1997), Watson's argument, in my view, falls. However, given what Sacks teaches us about the implications of choosing particular identities, this in no way detracts from Watson's argument about the complementarity of CA and MCD analysis. So rather than fight mock battles between theorists who constitute themselves as members of armed camps, this chapter seeks to reveal the richness of studies based on categorization analysis while rejecting the claim that such studies either replace CA or are replaced by it.

In fact, a significant corpus of studies has emerged over the years, stemming from Sacks's pioneering observations about categorization devices (for example, Watson 1978; Cuff 1980; McHoul 1982; Baker 1984; Silverman and Peräkylä 1990). In this chapter, I do not offer a general review of these studies. This is beyond the confines of this volume and such reviews are available elsewhere in a book (Jayyusi 1984), an edited collection (Hester and Eglin 1996) and a journal article (Eglin and Hester 1992). Instead, I focus on a selection of studies which advance my argument about the unity of Sacks's work.

On Locations

Schegloff (1972: 80) suggests that Sacks's work on how we select identifications of *persons* can be extended to how we select formulations for locations. For instance, how do we describe where we are now – as in a particular room, house, street, town, etc.? Note the children's game of writing on exercise books not just their name but their 'address' including such items as 'Earth', 'the solar system', the universe'! As he puts it, the analyst's interest in locational formulations is that:

> For any location to which reference is made, there is a set of terms each of which, by a correspondence test, is a correct way to refer to it. On any

actual occasion of use, however, not any member of the set is 'right'. How is it that on particular occasions of use some term from the set is selected and other terms are rejected? (Schegloff 1972: 81)

One rule seems to be: do not refer to locations at which all parties are *co-present*. For instance, in a collection of calls to a police department, none referred to the name of the city in which the call was made and the police department was situated (p. 83).

A second rule is that people who live or work in a place 'may be expected to recognize place names in or near it' (p. 92). For instance, Schegloff refers to someone asking him 'Are you going to Columbia' prior to asking directions to the university (p. 89). In this way, asking for or providing a location is an activity rich in membership category implications because we can inspect it 'to see what sort of person [the speaker] must be to have produced it' (p. 94).

Thirdly, Schegloff distinguishes between location formulations such as street address, which he calls geographical (G), and location formulations which relate to members (Rm) – such as 'John's place' and 'Al's house' or even 'the supermarket' – where this is the place to which we both go (p. 97). He then suggests that, providing that the recipient is not a stranger, 'the preference rule appears to be: use an Rm formulation if you can' (p. 100).

All this implies for Schegloff that members use 'a common sense geography' to report relevant locations. For instance, in conversations between Americans about foreign travel 'it appears one goes "to South America" not "Peru", just as one goes "to Europe" not "France". If one says one went to France, one is asked "where else?", rather than "where in France, did you visit?" Persons who went "just to France" may have to account for it' (p. 86).

However, consonant with Schegloff's later critique of purely commonsense observations, there are problems with the idea of 'a common sense geography'. First, what counts as 'common sense' will surely be very dependent on historical patterns of travel and means of transport (twenty-five years after Schegloff's paper was published, when going to Europe is perhaps no longer such a big deal, does one still have to account for going 'just to France'?). Second, more importantly, spoken location formulations seem likely to be dependent on indexical (or context-bound) properties inherent in the sequential organization of the talk in which they occur. As Schegloff himself implies, how do we translate 'downstairs', 'in front' and 'across the street' into meaningful objects (p. 88)?

The same issues arise if, for instance, reporting a location when someone wants to know where to pick you up is compared to the same activity as the second part of a classroom question-answer-evaluation sequence (Mehan 1979). Perhaps this is one of the reasons why Schegloff was later to reject certain aspects of MCD analysis as 'promiscuous' when separated from sequential considerations?

Even in 1972, he was clearly foreshadowing these issues. In the conclusion to his paper on location, he reminds us of the ineffable indexicality of such matters:

> on each occasion in conversation on which a formulation of location is used, attention is exhibited to the particulars of the occasion. In selecting a 'right' formulation, attention is exhibited to 'where-we-know-we-are', to 'who-we-know-we-are', to 'what-we-are-doing-at-this-point-in-the-conversation'. (Schegloff 1972: p. 115)

It is worth pointing out that recognizing the indexicality of location formulations is very different from saying that such formulations are dependent on social context. As Schegloff suggests: 'To say that *interaction* is context-sensitive is to say that *interactants* are context-sensitive.' It follows that, rather than try to engage in conventional social science tasks (such as relating location formulations to 'contexts'), we must investigate 'how participants analyze context and use the product of their analysis in producing their interaction' (p. 115).

The upshot of this seems to be twofold. First, 'location formulations' are undoubtedly an important, investigable matter. However, second, investigation should be directed to how members, in the contingencies of their interaction, actually 'do' location rather than to the attempt to formulate analysts' rules.

Alec McHoul and Rod Watson have pursued the topic of location by an analysis of a brief extract from a geography lesson at an Australian high school. They ask: 'how is commonsense geographical knowledge transformed into subject knowledge and how do such methodical features of the co-participants' talk provide for this?' (1984: 283). They trace this movement from 'commonsense' to 'subject' knowledge through the ways participants select and come to agree about 'place references'. Part of the extract they analyse is reproduced here. In it T refers to a teacher, CBD to the 'central business district' and Lois is a student:

[McHoul and Watson 1984: 287, simplified]

```
1    T:      Perhaps a court house is likely to be centred very
2            close–t'the CBD then again there're other types of
3            public buildings
4            (0.7)
5    T:      ee gee (0.3) e:r fire station–which possibly should
6            be– located in the suburbs–so you'd be wrong if
7            y'had all y'public buildings in the CBD–y'd probably
8            be wrong if y'had e::::::r a great dispersal of
9            y'public buildings
10   Lois:   The university also would be away from the s::: city
11           centre (a bit) too
12   T:      Why's that Lois?
13   Lois:   Oh th's just more space out there I s'pose
14           (1.0)
15   Lois:   Ahm
16           (3.4)
17   Lois:   Ah wouldn't be too far away but it would be right in
18           among all the court houses 'n (0.2) churches 'n
19           things like that
```

McHoul and Watson argue that, in lines 1–3, the teacher establishes a location device with 'court house' as a category drawn from the MCD 'public buildings'. Given court house's positioning with this MCD, the teacher suggests being 'central' as category-bound to it (that is, a category-bound activity, or CBA).

However, McHoul and Watson remind us that Sacks suggested that not all CBAs cover all categories in any MCD. In particular, in 'positioned category devices' (see chapter 5 above), each category may be *ranked* in relation to the appropriate CBA. In this regard, they argue, 'fire station' (line 5) is used by the teacher to suggest that that the MCD 'public buildings' can include CBAs ranked in the range from 'probably central' (court houses) to 'possibly suburban' (fire stations).

Lois shows her understanding of this structure by offering a further category ('university', line 10) from the same MCD ('public buildings') ranked in the same way as 'fire station'. Moreover, in line 18, she provides another category ('churches') which she ranks with court house.

Following Schegloff's (1972) insistence that there is no 'right' formulation of location, McHoul and Watson remind us that categories such as 'court house' are not automatically tied to 'central' but depend, on every occasion, on members' interpretive work. Their analysis, then, distances itself from any claims about the cultural meaning of location terms. Instead, it sets out to be an analysis of what they call 'commonsense geography (or urban ecology)' (1984: 291). As Garfinkel (1967) shows, such a commonsense geography inevitably depends upon the employment of such members' resources as 'ad hocing' and 'the documentary method of interpretation'.

In the classroom, these resources are used by teacher and pupil to produce a recognizable 'geography lesson'. As Paul Drew points out, through the descriptions that members provide, 'interactional tasks' (like a lesson) are accomplished (Drew 1978: 3–4). Sometimes, however, these tasks may be more obviously politicized and so the issue of location descriptions becomes more politically 'loaded' than in either the classroom example or Schegloff's discussion of street directions.

For instance, in British public hearings into 'Violence and Civil Disorder in Northern Ireland' in 1969, Drew shows how witnesses' descriptions of locations appealed to 'the normally organized religious geography of Belfast' (1978: 4). So, for instance, when witnesses refer to the Shankill Road, they will be heard to use a category drawn from the MCD 'Protestant areas' and associated with various category-bound activities (Orange Order, marching, wearing bowler hats, etc.).

Moreover, this is not an analyst's surmise. As Drew shows, a lawyer at the hearings used such location devices (among other items) as 'indicative of an invasion of Catholic areas by Protestants' (p. 11). In turn, this formulation is not a passive, culturally determined reading. Rather, it actively constructs a category-bound set of activities with clear political implications – in this case what Drew calls an 'accusation'. We can see the force of Drew's point if we compare, for instance, the word 'invasion' used here with the possible alternative description 'peaceful march'.

Similarly, Georgia Lepper's (1995) study of a 'duty rota logbook' compiled at a British further education college shows how the entries are organized as accusations which encourage further disciplinary action. In one case, for instance, a student's activities are defined as follows: 'spends her time in the refectory and not in the Library'. When this location category is combined with the description 'she is rude and aggressive', the reader is provided with a set of CBAs which imply the MCD 'trouble-maker'. Such a membership category powerfully encourages some disciplinary outcome while prospectively exonerating college staff from any possible counter-charge, for example 'harassment' (pp. 197–9).

On 'Reliable' Accounts

Lepper's close attention to the procedures through which moral characters are constructed fits very neatly with Dorothy Smith's work on a tale about a student's 'mental illness'. Although, unlike Lepper, Smith does not explicitly make use of Sacks's analysis of membership categorization, the title of her paper ('"K is mentally ill": the anatomy of a factual account') suggests that she is concerned with precisely these issues.

Smith's data consists of an account of how Angela came to see her friend K as 'mentally ill'. In this account, we are taken slowly and delicately from Angela's initial praise of K's good 'normal' qualities, through initial doubts about her sanity, to sad and reluctant certainty and, ultimately, to K's referral to a psychiatrist.

Smith (1978) asks us to consider how Angela (and her interviewer) invite the reader to collaborate with them in their version of K as 'mentally ill'. For reasons of space, I present below only a few of the issues to which Smith draws our attention. In each case, I have added, in square brackets, an MCD reading of Smith's analysis:

1 Angela is a defined as K's 'friend' both by the interviewer and by Angela herself. In this way, we are precluded from doubting Angela's motives (p. 35). [Within the standardized relational pair (friend:friend) mutual help and support is to be expected.]
2 Side by side with Angela's descriptions of K's activities are adjectives like 'odd' and 'wrong' which serve as instructions as to how to read the import of these descriptions (p. 33). [Angela constructs K's activities as CBAs bound to particular 'deviant' categories.]
3 A series of 'independent' witnesses are cited (mutual friends, Angela's family, a psychiatrist) who all read K's behaviour in the same way as Angela (pp. 36–7). [Angela appeals to two collections of members bound to offer care or support: collection R (friends and family) and collection K (professionals and their clients).]
4 Activities which can appear 'routine' in 'appropriate' contexts (such as 'tip-toeing' and 'whispering') can be constructed as

deviant when stripped of their social context and/or made to appear to be 'obsessional' (p. 45). [Angela constructs K's activities as CBAs bound to particular 'deviant' categories.]

Smith's focus on how context-stripping makes accounts become more or less 'reliable' is developed by Harvey Molotch and Deirdre Boden (1985). They argue that a problem resolved in all talk is that, while accounts are context-bound, a determinate account has 'somehow' to be achieved (see Garfinkel 1967). Molotch and Boden apply this insight to the interrogation of President Nixon's counsel (John Dean) by a pro-Nixon Senator (Senator Gurney) during the 1973 Watergate hearings in the US Congress.

Dean had made public charges about the involvement of the White House in the Watergate 'cover-up'. Gurney's strategy is to define Dean as someone who avoids 'facts' and just relies on 'impressions'. This is seen in the following extract: (G = Senator Gurney; D = John Dean; for transcription conventions, see appendix 1 below):

[Molotch and Boden 1985: 280, adapted]
G: Did you dis<u>cuss</u> any aspects of the <u>Water</u>gate at that meeting with the President? For example, did you <u>tell</u> him anything about (1.4) what <u>Halde</u>man <u>knew</u> of or what Ehrlichman knew?
D: Well, given the– given the fact that he <u>told</u> me I've done a good job I assumed he had been very pleased with what ha– what had been going on . . .
G: Did you discuss what Magruder knew about Watergate and what involvement <u>he</u> had?
D: No, I didn't. I didn't get into any – I did not give him a report at that point in time
G: Did you discuss <u>cover</u>-up money <u>money</u> that was being raised and paid?
D: No, sir. . ..
G: Well now how can you say that the President knew all about these <u>things</u> from a <u>simple</u> observation by him that 'Bob tells me you are doing a good job'?

As Molotch and Boden show, Gurney's strategy is to insist on literal accounts of 'facts' not 'impressionistic' ones. Throughout this extract, for instance, Gurney demands that Dean state that he actually discussed the cover-up with Nixon. When Dean is unable to do this, Gurney imposes limits on Dean's ability to appeal to a context (Dean's 'assumptions') which might show that Dean's inferences were correct.

However, as Gurney knows, all accounts can be defeated by demonstrating that *at some point* they are not 'really objective' since they depend upon knowing the context. Hence: 'Demands for "just the facts", the simple answers, the forced-choice response, preclude the "whole story" that contains another's truth ... [consequently] individuals can participate in their own demise through the interactional work they do' (1985: 285).

The parallels between these studies of 'reliable' accounts with the earlier studies of 'location' should by now be fairly obvious. Molotch and Boden's interrogator, Smith's 'friend', Lepper's logbook keeper, Drew's witnesses and McHoul and Watson's teacher and pupil all construct accounts which imply particular 'readings' of activities and of categories of people and their locations. So we learn from these studies, as Sacks showed his students, how 'descriptions' are collaboratively organized as speakers and hearers locally mobilize particular ways of interlocking categories and activities.

'Owning' Knowledge

As I stressed in chapter 5, Sacks's account of membership categorization is not to be confused with the familiar (anthropological/ sociological) concept of 'culture'. This means much more than, say, cognitive anthropology's insistence on the priority of actors' own ('emic') categories (see Gumperz and Hymes 1972). Rather it demands that these categories must be studied *in use* and that analysts' claims must be grounded in demonstrable features of that use.

This is because membership categorization only amounts to anything if it can be shown to be a lay members' method, assembled and managed in members' dealings with each other and the physical world. In this respect, for instance, activities become 'category-bound' not through some social scientist's assertion but through the way members actually invoke particular categories. Ultimately, then, members 'own' categories.

A poignant example of this is to be found in Michael Moerman's study of a Thai lowland tribe called the Lue. As a cognitive anthropologist, Michael Moerman was interested in learning how this people categorized their world, that is, their 'emic' categories.

However, as we shall see, his initial methods led him towards a set of analyst's ('etic') categories with an unknown relation to how members actually categorized their world.

Like most anthropologists and Chicago School ethnographers (see chapter 3), Moerman used native informants. His aim was to elicit from them what 'being a Lue' meant to them. So he started to ask tribespeople questions like 'How do you recognize a member of your tribe?' Moerman (1974) reports that his respondents quickly became adept at providing a whole list of traits which he called 'ethnic identification devices'. These included beliefs and actions which they regarded as unique to the Lue people (such as their approach to trading with their neighbours). The final list of such traits seemed to describe the tribe and to distinguish it from its neighbours.

However, Moerman was troubled about what sense to read into the Lue's own accounts. His questions often related to issues which were either obvious or irrelevant to the respondents. As he puts it: 'To the extent that answering an ethnographer's question is an unusual situation for natives, one cannot reason from a native's answer to his *normal* categories or ascriptions' (p. 66, emphasis added).

So Moerman started to see that ethnic identifications were not used all the time by these people any more than we use them to refer to ourselves in a Western culture. This meant that if you wanted to understand this people, it was not particularly useful to elicit from them what would necessarily be an abstract account of their tribe's characteristics. So instead, Moerman started to examine what went on in everyday situations through observation.

However, it was not so straightforward to switch to observational methods. Even when ethnographers are silent and merely observe, their presence indicates to people that matters relevant to 'identity' should be highlighted. Consequently, people may pay particular attention to what both the observer and they themselves take to be relevant categorization schemes – like ethnic or kinship labels. In this way, the ethnographer may have 'altered the local priorities among the native category sets which it is his task to describe' (p. 67).

What, then, was to be done? A clue is given by the initially opaque subheadings of Moerman's article:

Who are the Lue?
Why are the Lue?
When are the Lue?

Moerman argues that there are three reasons why we should *not* ask: 'Who are the Lue?' First, it would generate an inventory of traits. Like all such inventories it could be endless because we could always be accused of having left something out. Second, lists are retrospective. Once we have decided that the Lue *are* a tribe, then we have no difficulty in 'discovering' a list of traits to support our case. Third, the identification of the Lue as a tribe depends, in part, on their successful presentation of themselves as a tribe. As Moerman says: 'The question is not "Who are the Lue?" but rather when, how and why the identification "Lue" is preferred' (p. 62).

Moerman adds that this does *not* mean that the Lue are not really a tribe or that they fooled him into thinking they were one. Rather their ethnic identity arises in the fact that people in the area use ethnic identification labels some of the time when they are talking about each other.

Of course, some of the time is not all the time. Hence the task of the ethnographer should be to observe when and *if* ethnic identification labels are used by the participants being studied. Moerman neatly summarizes his argument as follows:

> Anthropology [has an] apparent inability to distinguish between warm ... human bodies and one kind of identification device which some of those bodies sometimes use. Ethnic identification devices – with their important potential of making each ethnic set of living persons a joint enterprise with countless generations of unexamined history – seem to be universal. Social scientists should therefore describe and analyse the ways in which they are used, and not merely – as natives do – use them as explanations. (pp. 67–8)

So Moerman had moved his research question away from 'Who are the Lue?' From now on, the issue was no longer who the Lue essentially are but when, among people living in these Thai villages, ethnic identification labels are invoked and the consequences of invoking them.

Curiously enough, Moerman concluded that when you looked at the matter this way, the apparent differences between the Lue and ourselves were considerably reduced. For instance, turn-taking in conversations works in much the same way among Lue speakers and English speakers. Only an ethnocentric Westerner might have assumed otherwise, behaving like a tourist craving for out-of-the-way sights.

Moerman's intellectual journey provided Wes Sharrock (1974) with the metaphor 'Owning knowledge'. Following Garfinkel

(1967), Sharrock argues that when social scientists use concepts like 'tribe' or 'culture' as a description of some activity, they are engaged in the same back-and-forth movement between 'appearances' and 'reality' that all members use. By contrast, as in Moerman's conclusion, Sharrock proposes that:

> there is no reason to suppose any special connection between collectivity and corpus [of knowledge] and that any set of activities might be understood in relation to any corpus ... [this] distract[s] attention from a prospectively interesting question: how do we come, in the very first place, to conceive of a corpus as a *collectivity's* corpus. (1974: 45)

In this regard, Moerman's analysis of how 'tribe' is constructed and Dorothy Smith's account of the implications of describing K as 'mentally ill' precisely address how a corpus of knowledge (about the Lue or about K) is actively translated into some collectivity (a 'tribe', 'mentally ill people'). Following Sacks, once we describe category-bound activities, we imply the categories of persons involved (and vice versa). As Sharrock argues:

> The assignment of a name to a corpus sets up the way in which further description is to be done. The name is not, then, *merely* descriptive in that once it has been assigned it becomes a device-for-describing: that is, the name is not to be revised in the light of events but is, rather, to be invoked in the description of whatever events occur. (1974: 49)

By drawing our attention to the issue of 'owning knowledge', Sharrock reveals the interpretive work of anthropologists who describe 'tribes', and interviewers who treat respondents' answers in relation to some assumed corpus of knowledge like 'mental illness'. A discussion of one further interview study will underline Sharrock and Smith's arguments.

Carolyn Baker conducted a comparative study of interviews with teenagers in Canada and Australia. Her initial concern was to use the interviews to learn about how adolescents see themselves relative to children and adults. However, she soon realized that the participants themselves were constructing a version of adolescent–adult relations for each other. As she puts it:

> at the same time as these passages contain comment about adolescent–adult talk, they are instances *themselves* of adolescent–adult talk. They are conversations between a researcher who could commonsensically be understood to be an adult, and persons who could similarly be describable as adolescents, given their age. (1982: 111)

Baker's observations fit neatly with how Dorothy Smith posed the issue of treating interview accounts as descriptive of 'mental illness'. However, unlike Smith, Baker explicitly discusses the membership-categorization work involved in a constituting a corpus of knowledge. To show how she proceeds, let us take one extract from one of her interviews. The respondent is Pam, aged fourteen:

[Baker 1984: 316]   (P = Pam; I = interviewer)
```
1  I:   Are there any ways in which you consider yourself to
2       still be partly a child?
3  P:   Well, I like to watch TV and, uh,
4  I:   Well, adults do that
5  P:   Yeah, I still read the comics ((laugh))
6  I:   Adults do that
7  P:   That's about, only thing I can think of
```

Note how I assigns P to a place between childhood and adulthood (lines 1–2) and how P enters into the discussion in these terms. Moreover, as Baker notes (1984: 317), in lines 4 and 6, I treats as invalid P's nominated instances of 'childish' behaviour. By showing that a valid response would involve depicting something exclusive to children, I proceeds on the basis that, although child–adolescent overlap can properly arise (being 'partly a child'), child-adult overlap constitutes an unacceptable answer. The interview continues as follows:

[Baker 1984: 317]
```
8   I:   Do you notice any leftovers of childhood in your
9        personality?
10  P:   Well, my food tastes have all changed differently, like I
11       used to hate lots of things, now I like most, almost
12       everything. I used to really hate vegetables, and now I'd
13       rather have vegetables than anything else! And um, when I
14       was a child, I used to really be worried about what I
15       looked like and that an now I don't, I don't really care.
16       If peop//
17  I:   // You really don't care?
18  P:   Pe, I don't care what people think, I just, think well I
19       like this, and if no one else does, that's too bad
20  I:   At what point were you, so terrible self conscious about
21       your appearance?
```

Baker draws our attention to the way in which I picks up and pursues the topic of P's feelings about her appearance, while paying no attention to what P says about vegetables. In this way, she shows Pam that her tastes in food are not entirely compatible with I's attempt to depict overlaps between childhood and adolescence. As Baker suggests:

> by doing this, (I) shows Pam how adolescence should be done in the interview. While Pam's 'vegetable eating' is passed by, her 'not caring' about her appearance becomes the basis for an identity rich puzzle and solution whose pursuit by the interviewer binds this activity to her category 'adolescence'. (1984: 317–18)

Anssi Peräkylä (personal correspondence) has also pointed out that I's first questions, in both extracts, treat P as a subject who might be puzzled by her identity. This can amount to treating P as a *non-child* (because children are not supposed to have that kind of self-consciousness about their identity) and simultaneously as a *non-adult* (because adults are not supposed to be puzzled about who they are). So, straight off, I constitutes P as neither child nor adult (that is, as an 'adolescent').

It will be recalled that membership categorization devices are used by members to group together collections of 'similar' identities or categories. Any category is a potential member of more than one MCD. One MCD that can be heard in these attempts to position people as 'children', 'adolescents' or 'adults' is 'stage of life'. Now MCDs like 'stage of life' have three features noted by Sacks:

1 Like all MCDs, they are associated with category-bound activities. So, in categorizing someone as a child within a stage-of-life MCD, certain activities are predictable (being irresponsible, having 'fads', etc.). Similarly, in defining an activity (irresponsibility, faddishness) one also implies the kind of categories of people who might engage in it (such as children).
2 In a stage-of-life MCD, unlike some other MCDs, the members of the collection are differentially positioned so that, in this case, adult is higher than adolescent, adolescent is higher than child and thus adult is higher than child.
3 It follows that if an adult (A) or an adolescent (B) engages in a category-bound activity appropriate to a child (C) then 'a member of either A or B who does that activity may be seen to be degrading himself, and may be said to be "acting like a child". Alternatively, if some candidate activity is proposedly

bound to A, a member of C who does it is subject to be said to be acting like an A, where that assertion constitutes "praising" ' (Sacks quoted by Baker 1984: 302).

All of these features are present in the brief interview extracts above. First, in the exchanges between line 1 and 7, I requests and P attempts to provide a set of activities hearable as bound to the category 'still partly a child'. I's comments at lines 4 and 6 now may be heard as attending to the unclear category-bounding of activities such as 'watching TV' or 'reading comics'. Similarly, I's pursuit of P's comment about her looks makes sense in terms of the association between the way in which the activity 'being concerned about one's appearance' is category-bound to the category 'adolescent'.

Second, the hierarchical relationship between each of these stage-of-life categories is attended to by both speakers. I uses the term 'leftovers' to describe elements left behind from childhood, while P describes her 'non-childlike' self in terms of greater independence and maturity. By reporting her activities in this way, P can be heard to be acting more like an adult than a child.

Most stage-of-life categories are mutually exclusive, that is, you are either an 'adult' or a 'child' but, usually, cannot be both at the same time. Hence to refer to an 'adult's' behaviour as 'childish' is hearable as quite a powerful charge. People recognizable as 'adolescents' may, therefore, want to set up a mutually exclusive framework between such categories. In the extract above, notice how Pam makes a sharp distinction between the past ('when I was a child') and the present (when she has more 'adult' qualities). At the same time, as Baker notes: '"adolescence" can be made to overlap with "childhood" or "adulthood" by discovering "childness" or "adultness" in the "adolescent"' (1984: 303).

The interviewer's question about 'leftovers' (at line 8) depends precisely on the availability of this sense of overlap. Indeed, people can use both 'childness' and 'adultness' as simultaneous descriptions of the 'adolescent'. Indeed, as Baker notes, 'this is a classic "problem of adolescence"' (p. 304) to be found in everyday life just as much as in this interview.

On Pronouns

Although Baker's data turns on the ambiguity of the nouns 'children' and 'adolescent', the pronouns used by Pam and her interviewer ('you' and 'I') are treated by both as unambiguous. However, this is by no means always the case. Take this extract from a telephone call to a suicide prevention centre:

[Watson 1987: 269]   (Co = counsellor; Cl = client)
1   Co: Well everybody needs help sometime Mrs. R, in different
2   degrees.
3   Cl: I know they do I know that.
4   Co: You know you have to ask for it sometimes.
5   Cl: I know that ... have you, yes well I am not going on my
6   knees to ask for 'elp no more.

In this extract, both Co and Cl can be seen to play with the pronoun 'you'. Note how Co only uses it in line 4 after Cl has appeared to accept (line 3) Co's observation which avoids 'you' in favour of 'everybody' (lines 1–2). Co's 'everybody' is used in the cautious context of delivering a maxim – with which, as we have seen, it is difficult to disagree. However, as Watson points out, this now gives Cl the opportunity to distance herself (lines 5–6) from the 'everybody' in line 1.

As Watson notes, this suggests the weaknesses of a purely grammatical model of pronoun use. In this model: 'choosing between pronouns is ... choosing between mutually-exclusive linguistic alternatives' (1987: 262).

Watson's extract demonstrates that 'exclusiveness' or 'ambiguity' are not determined by grammar or logic but are matters that members decide. As Sacks says: 'in the ambiguity of "you", one has the this-and-that format; that is to say, is it "you" (you alone) or "you" (you and others). When a person hears "you", they then go through a procedure of deciding what it refers to' (*LC1*: 165). In this procedure, Sacks suggests, members ask themselves a series of questions such as: Is it definitely 'me'? If not, is there some group of people ('plurality') for which 'you' would be correct? Does this plurality include me?

The active achievement of the meaning of the reference 'you' is nicely shown in the extract below, taken from a pre-HIV test counselling interview. As we shall see, in some respects, it has the reverse organization of the previous extract in that 'you' is initially unambiguous but is subsequently made ambiguous by the later introduction of the category 'everybody':

[Silverman 1997a: 74]   (C = counsellor; P = patient)

```
 1  C:  [.hhh Uhm .hhh d'you know if any of your: your er
 2      partners have been drug users.=Intra[venous drug=
 3  P:                                      [No:.
 4  C:  =[users is our main [uhm you- you've never used=
 5  P:   [They haven't.    [Mm
 6  C:  =needles for yourself [(either.=No). .hh I ask=
 7  P:                        [No:
 8  C:  =everybody those questions.=I haven't saved them
 9      [up for you. .hhhh Obviously when we're talking=
10  P:  [(That's okay yeah).
11  C:  =about HIV .hhhh uhm (.) the intravenous drug using
12      population are a population that are at ri:sk.
13  P:  Yea[:h.
14  C:     [Because (.) if they share needles (.) then they're
15      sharing (.) infection with the blood on the needles
16      obvious[ly.
17  P:         [Mm h[m
18  C:              [.hhhhhh Uhm (0.5) d'you know if any of your
19      partners have been bisexual.
20  P:  No they haven't.=
```

The task of pre-test counselling involves asking clients to assess the nature of their risk of having been exposed to HIV. In this passage, both parties have to cope with the implications of discussing potentially delicate aspects of the status of P's sexual contacts, relating to drug-using partners. As Schegloff (1980) points out, various types of action projection can serve to mark out and request formal permission for potentially delicate or risqué actions. Here, however, we find a *retrospective* justification of C's line of questioning ('Intravenous drug users is our main ... I ask everybody those questions.=I haven't saved them up for you').

This retrospective justification for asking such a question serves neatly to counter the category-bound implications of the activity of asking someone if they have had sex with drug users. Without the elaboration, the implication might be that C had reason to suspect that P might be the sort of person who would engage in such an activity.

The elaboration seems to be about to make clear that the question has not been generated by anything that P has said or done – other than presenting herself at a clinic in which 'intravenous drug users is our main' (client population?). This is underlined by C's observation 'I haven't saved them up for you.'

P's agreement tokens on line 10 ('That's okay yeah') show her acceptance of C's elaboration and thus mark her continued recipiency for this line of questioning. However, even at the beginning of this extract, C has constructed a *preface* to her question. Notice how C begins her question at line 1 by 'd'you know'. We can see the power of this preface by imagining an alternative way of posing the question:

*C: Have any of your partners been drug users

Putting the question this way would imply that P is the kind of person who *knowingly* might associate with drug users. So this form of the question can be a category-bound activity, where its recipient is to be heard in the category of a-person-who-might-consort-with-drug-users. C's preface is a neat device to overcome this hearing. It allows P, if necessary, to reveal that she had subsequently discovered that a partner was a drug user, without any kind of implication that she would knowingly associate with that category of person. Exactly the same 'd'you know' device is used at the end of this extract (lines 18–19) by C to ask a further question (about bisexual partners).

One further feature of this extract is worth developing. In line 4, note C's use of 'our' in her comment 'intravenous drug users is our main' (client population?). The use of such a plural pronoun nicely indicates C's institutional or corporate identity (presumably as part of a clinic 'team'). In turn, the plural pronoun 'they' is routinely used by people assuming client identities in order to refer to staff. In both cases, people are being categorized as part of a duplicatively organized device (for instance, as a 'team'). As Sacks puts it: '"we" and "they" are not only plural references, but also, among other things, "organizational references"' (*LC2*: 391).

An example of the use of 'we' in an organizational sense occurs in the following extract from Watson's telephone counselling data:

[Watson 1987: 271]
1   Cl: now a: a blue Ford came for her, and I think she phoned
2   you before she came, would you have any record of it, you
3   know?
4   Co: er, well, I'm sorry but we can't just divulge any
5   information at all.
6   Cl: You can't do anything.
7   Co: I'm sorry I can't no.

As Watson comments on Co's use of 'we' in line 4: '[it] disavow[s] any assertion ... that s/he has made a given decision in a "personal capacity" [instead it asserts that Co] has made the decision "purely" in his/her capacity as one of the centre's counsellors' (1987: 271).

Although Cl's subsequent use of 'you' (line 6) retains its (in-principle) ambiguity, both this 'you' and Co's 'I' (line 7) can be heard to attend to the organizational constraints implied by Co's earlier 'we can't just'. Indeed, as Watson points out, in the context of this, Co's use of 'I' in line 7 can be heard to provide for 'such potential imputations as ... "it's not my personal choice" or "it's more than my job's worth to divulge such information" and so on, should an accusation, complaint or whatever ensue from the turning down of a request' (p. 272).

So Watson shows how such 'plural references' may be used and acted upon by hearers as they are asked to attend to the organizational auspices under which someone is speaking. In my pre-test HIV counselling data (Silverman 1997a), counsellors tended to package their advice to clients in the voice of the organizational 'we'. In this extract from a US health clinic, C is giving advice to a male client about using condoms as a means of safer sex:

```
        [Silverman 1997a: 174]
1       (10.6)
2   C:  we recommend tha'chu use co:ndoms
3       (1.0)
4   C:  ah:: if you are not su:re about your partner's: (0.2)
5       status.
6       (.)
```

Although C's 'u' (line 2) apparently addresses his advice personally to the client, C constructs what she is saying as 'organizationally constructed' advice ('we recommend tha'chu use co:ndoms'). As such, it is hearable as information-about-the-advice-we-give-in-this-clinic. This is what I have called an 'advice as information sequence' or AIS (pp. 154–81). In this context, C's use of 'u' retains its ambiguity as hearable as either this particular client or as an 'indefinite reference' (Peyrot 1987) to 'our' clients in general.

But why should AIDS counsellors construct their advice in the AIS format? One answer can be found in the absence of any uptake from the client in the extract above in the possible turn-transition points on lines 3 and 6. As I have shown in my analysis of that data (Silverman 1997a: 134–53), advice-giving which does not appeal to such organizational requirements usually needs a strong uptake from its recipient if it is to continue. Conversely, if a set of turns is hearable as perhaps organizationally constrained information delivery, then the turns can follow one another without any difficulty, given only an occasional response token from the other party. So the AIS works by shielding both C and the client from the implications of the non-uptake of advice.

One further feature of the extract above underlines how it is set up as hearably non-personalized, organizationally constrained advice. Note how C follows her condom recommendation by 'if you are not su:re about your partner's: (0.2) status' (lines 4–5). When C invokes the category 'being sure about your partner's status, this links her advice to a category that may not turn out to be relevant to the client (maybe the client's partner has just tested HIV-negative).

This possibility means that what C is saying about condoms is hearable as the advice C 'would give' *if* certain things were to be so (that is, as conditional advice). Such a tentative formulation of a situation which might be appropriate to someone but not necessarily the client has been identified in HIV counselling as a 'proposal of the situation' or POTS device (Kinnell and Maynard 1996). When wedded to an AIS sequence (such as C's use of the voice of 'we' as well as an 'if' clause), the client's non-response need not be so damaging as minimal responses to unambiguously 'personal' advice.

In this final extract, the AIS and the POTS device are once more combined. In this extract a counsellor at the same US clinic is discussing the medical needs of someone who tests HIV-positive with a male client:

[Silverman 1997a: 171]

```
1      (1.0)
2  C:  a::nd (1.5) u::m some– okay, if a person (.) should
3      happen to test an'ibody po:sitive .hhh we would
4      strongly encourage them to seek out a a physician (.)
5      particularly physicians who work in infectious disease
6      .hhh u:m because they seem to: (1.0) uh:: be m:ore on top
7      of what's happening in the world of: viral infections and
8      things like that. (0.4)
9  P:  mm hmm=
```

```
10  C:  =and medications .hhhh we would also encourage a person
11       certainly to take a look at some of their behavior
12       patterns .hhh u:m encouraging them to: .hhh look at
13       things that might have in fact (0.5) caused them to
14       (feel) infected in the first place whether that be sexual
15       practices that were not particularly safe? (0.7) o:r
16       (0.6) u:m (0.5) drug use: (0.4) °or (0.7) um° (1.0) well
17       those two basically (0.4) °I m'n not much you can do
18       about transfusions.°
19       (1.5)
```

Let us look at C's first turn. As in the previous extract, C's advice commences with an 'if' given in regard to a category (testing antibody-positive) with only a possible relevance to the advice recipient, that is, a POTS sequence. Moreover, once again, the 'advice' is not personalized but addressed to 'a person' (line 2) and 'them' (line 4), in the same manner as C's use of 'u' in the previous extract was ambiguous. Similarly, just as the earlier counsellor says 'we recommend', her colleague says 'we would strongly encourage' (lines 3–4).

Once more, we have a C packaging what she is saying as, at best, ambiguous advice-giving, hearable as information-about-the-advice-that-would-be-given. The evidence that both parties monitor C's talk in this way is found in the lack of local problems created by P's minimal uptake – no response at the candidate completion point of the 'advice' during the micro-pause after 'seek out a physician' (line 4) and the presence of only a response token ('mm hmm') on line 9.

Now C takes a second turn without any noticeable hesitations or repairs in the design of her utterance. In this second turn, she introduces fresh topics (safer sex, drug use, transfusions) but they are all referred back to the category 'testing positive' and packaged via the same pro-terms ('person', 'their' and 'them'). Despite the presence of two slots where P might have taken a turn (after 'drug use', line 16, and after 'transfusions', line 18), not even a response token is contributed.

These last two sequences have shown that the AIS is a powerful device which manages the potentially difficult interactional problems of advice-giving and advice reception about presumably delicate topics. It constitutes the professional as a mere reporter on the-advice-we-give-in-this-clinic rather than as a potentially intrusive personal advice-giver. It allows the client to be defined as an acceptably passive recipient of information about the kinds of things that other people get told (or that she may get told in future). Finally, and most significantly, it overcomes the potentially damaging local implications of minimal client uptake which would arise if Cs could be heard to be giving clear-cut advice.

Concluding Remarks

As I noted earlier, my view is that Sacks treated MCD analysis and CA as two sides of the same coin. In this chapter, my aim has been to show how many recent MCD studies have supported this treatment. For instance, as I have sought to imply, such studies appeal both to the properties of MCDs *and* to sequential features of conversation. This seems to me equally true, say, of the analysis of how pronouns or place terms take on a local meaning in Drew's (1978) discussion of the use of adjacency pairs in the context of accusations.

Additionally, although I have had little space to discuss this, many writers have taken up Sacks's example of the fruitfulness of the analysis of textual data (in both his 'navy pilot' and 'child's story' lectures). So there are recent impressive MCD studies of textual data such as newspaper stories (Lee 1984) and organizational reports (Lepper 1995).

In the face of warring camps, I prefer to take the position that no sensible person would want to rule out such data simply because it might lack some of the sequential properties of conversational turns. Equally, however, I have shown how it is completely incorrect to assume that conversation analysts simply trade off membership categories without analysing how they are locally put together. The fact is, or I at least believe it is a fact, that MCD analysis and CA need each other. In a cruel academic world, this may be true politically as well as analytically.

8

Using Conversation Analysis

With the appearance of the 'Simplest systematics' paper (Sacks, Schegloff and Jefferson 1974), conversation analysis (CA) established itself as a major, cumulative enterprise of direct relevance to most social science disciplines as well as to linguistics. From now on, there could be little doubt that CA was an important, empirically oriented research activity, grounded in a basic theory of social action and generating significant implications from its analysis of previously unnoticed interactional forms.

The specific contribution of the 'Simplest systematics' paper has been well described in a more recent paper which summarizes CA for an anthropological audience. As Goodwin and Heritage suggest (1990: 290), this earlier paper describes a system for turn-taking with three components:

1 a specification of generic turn-constructional units that provide places for possible turn-transition;
2 speaker-selection techniques, which include both self-selection by a subsequent speaker and specification of a next speaker by the current speaker;
3 a rule set that orders options for action at points of possible turn-transition.

These 'options for action' (point 3) are seen very clearly in adjacency pairs which project various second turns and can lead to 'chains' of questions and answers (see chapter 6). However, as Heritage points out, this should not lead us to an over-mechanical view of conversation: 'conversation is not an endless series of interlocking adjacency pairs in which sharply constrained options confront the next speaker' (1984: 261). Instead, the phenomenon of adjacency works according to three non-mechanistic assumptions:

1 An assumption that an utterance which is placed immediately after another one is to be understood as produced in response to or in relation to the preceding utterance.
2 Where the appropriate next action does not occur (as when a greeting is not returned) it will be treated as 'noticeably absent' and that absence 'can become the object of remedial efforts and justifiably negative inferences' (Goodwin and Heritage 1990: 287).
3 If a speaker wishes some contribution to be heard as *unrelated* to an immediately prior utterance, he or she must do something special to lift assumption 1 – for instance by the use of a prefix (like 'by the way') designed to show that what follows is unrelated to the immediately prior turn at talk.

By 1990, Goodwin and Heritage were able to argue that this kind of sequential analysis of turns-at-talk had enabled 'simultaneous understanding of (a) the organization of action and (b) understanding in interaction' (1990: 288).

In a telling phrase, Heritage argues that, in its pursuit of the fine details of the sequential organization of conversation, CA has revealed the 'architecture of intersubjectivity' (Heritage 1984: 254). In this chapter, I will show how contemporary accounts of this architecture have built upon Sacks's earlier insights. Given the constraints of space, I will begin with a simplified account of recent work on three topics dealt with at length by Sacks, namely:

1 the use of response tokens;
2 'pre-sequences';
3 preference organization.

In the second half of the chapter, I will address two further topics for which Sacks was only able to offer a sketch: the character of 'institutional talk', and the integration of talk with non-verbal elements of interaction.

Response Tokens

In chapter 6 we saw how Sacks showed that devices like story prefaces help speakers to retain the floor. Another such device, but not at the beginning of a turn, is what Schegloff refers to as 'rush throughs'. Here 'a speaker, approaching a possible completion of a turn-constructional unit, speeds up the pace of the talk, withholds a dropping pitch or the intake of breath, and phrases the talk to bridge what might otherwise be the juncture at the end of a unit' (1982: 76).

However, Sacks also shows us that such devices alone do not guarantee that speakers will retain the floor. Despite 'prefaces' and 'rush throughs', speakers minimally need utterances like 'mm' and uh huh' which serve as a signal that someone is listening, that they have identified a possible completion point but are passing their turn. Indeed, in an upgraded form ('uh <u>huh</u>?'), they may work to stake a future claim to the floor.

As Schegloff was later to put it, items like 'uh huh', except when positioned after a question, work as a 'continuer' by signalling an understanding 'that an extended unit of talk is underway by another, and that it is not yet, or may not yet be (even ought not yet be), complete. It takes the stance that the speaker of the extended unit should continue talking, and in that continued talking should continue that extended unit' (1982: 81).

As Sacks had noted, this means that if no response token is forthcoming at a possible turn-completion point, 'a speaker will attempt to find out whether the other party is listening, i.e. will attempt to get the other party to speak though perhaps only to indicate with an "Uh huh" that indeed he's listening' (*LC2*: 411–12).

A nice example of this is found in 8.1, taken from a pre-HIV test counselling interview:

8.1 [Silverman 1997a: 118]
```
1  C:  this is why we say hh if you don't know the person that
2      you're with (0.6) and you're going to have sex with them
3      hh it's important that you tell them to (0.3) use a
4      condom (0.8) or to practice safe sex that's what using a
5      condom means.
6      (1.5)
7  C:  okay?
```

8   (0.3)
9   P: uhum
10   (0.4)
11   C: has your pa:rtner ever used a condom with you?

Notice the 1.5 second pause on line 6. Since this follows a possible turn-completion point as C concludes her advice, the pause can be heard as P's pause. Moreover, C demonstrates that she monitors it this way by going in pursuit of some response token (line 7) to indicate that at least P is listening. When, after a further pause, she obtains the continuer 'uhum' (line 9), C can now continue (line 11).

However, it is also worth noting C's explanation (or gloss) which follows 'use a condom' (lines 3–4). Since that phrase could also have been heard as terminating C's advice, she seems to have inspected the 0.8 second pause that follows as representing an absent continuer and, therefore, a possible lack of understanding. So she provides her gloss in order, unsuccessfully as it turns out, to create a stronger environment in which to get a continuer.

This underlines Schegloff and Sacks's point about how speakers need such responses as continuers in order to construct multi-unit turns. But the understanding that response tokens (RTs) show is also more ambiguous than, say, laughter or 'He did?' Three such ambiguities are noted by Schegloff:

1 It is ambiguous whether an RT merely shows attention or indicates agreement (Schegloff 1982: 79). The distinction between attention and agreement can be crucial in professional–client interviews because, as in 8.1, it can leave the professional unclear as to how far the client has accepted or agreed with the advice (cf. Heritage and Sefi 1992; Silverman 1997a: 180).
2 Even when heard as an attention-marker, an RT only claims attention rather than shows (or evidences) it (Schegloff 1982: 78). For instance, where the *same* RT is used in four or five consecutive slots, its recipient may hear a lack of interest (p. 85).
3 Although RTs show no need for repair at this time and therefore appear to demonstrate 'understanding', this understanding is equivocal because 'passing one opportunity to initiate repair is compatible with initiating repair later' (Schegloff 1982: 88). Hence the recipient of a response token needs to look at the token producer's next utterance to see the analysis of their utterance that 'uh huh' is doing.

None the less, as Sacks had noted, and as 8.1 shows, despite these ambiguities, response tokens have an important role in maintaining the no gap, no overlap character of turns-at-talk by allowing present speaker to retain the floor.

Pre-sequences

As we saw in chapter 6, the requirements of recipient design mean that a speaker may try to avoid 'springing' certain kinds of first parts, like invitations and requests, upon another. Thus, before giving an invitation, they can ask a question which 'can pre-signal "invitation to come" '. So 'instead of saying "Would you like to come over to dinner tonight?" they can say "What are you doing tonight?" where the answer to that controls whether they're going to do the invitation' (*LC2*: 529). Such pre-sequences work in two ways. First, unless the right return is offered, no invitation need be offered. Second, in the case of pre-requests, you may get an offer and therefore not need to make a direct request at all (*LC1*: 685).

However, as Schegloff (1980) shows, pre-sequences extend beyond invitations and requests. More specifically, he notes a particular turn format with two features:

1 A speaker *projects* some type of action by mentioning something they will do ('let me ask you a question' or 'I wanna tell you something') or something they would like the recipient to do ('tell me something' or 'listen to this').
2 The projected turn or action does *not* occur in the same talk unit (that is, the same sentence) (p. 107).

As an instance of this second feature, Schegloff notes that 'let me ask you a question' is not usually followed by a question but by, say, information delivery. Where a question *does* follow it is usually *not* the question that has been projected. For instance it may just be a knowledge check or 'reference preparation', such as 'd'you know Queens Boulevard?'

Even where the question that follows *is* the question that has been projected, that question, Schegloff suggests, will be treated as preliminary to *further* questions, as for example:

8.2 [Schegloff 1980: 122]
1   V: lemme ask you dis question.

2   J: Yeh.
3   V: Are you getting toothaches?
4   (0.8)
5   J: No!
6   V: [(Den don't   ) –
7   J: [But I got <u>ca</u>vities!

Although in line 3, V does indeed ask the question he projected at line 1, Schegloff suggests that J's overlapping turn on line 7 shows that he understands that a possible further suggestion is coming up ('Den don't' (go to the dentist)) and *attempts to head it off* (p. 123).

Schegloff calls such action projections 'pre's'. But since, as we have seen, further preliminaries routinely follow them, they are better understood as 'pre-pre's' which work either by inserting preliminaries before the projected action or by marking the projected action 'as itself a "pre" to some contingent "next"' (p. 128).

Such 'pre-pre's' set up what Schegloff calls a 'double displacement'. This serves 'to exempt what directly follows them from being treated as "produced in its own right". They make room for and mark, what follows them as "preliminary"' (p. 112). By establishing a series of 'preliminaries', speakers also set up a series of turns. As Schegloff notes, this means that his discussion of 'pre-pre's' links up with Sacks on 'prefaces' as a way of producing a 'story' that will take more than one turn-constructional unit (pp. 146–7).

However, Schegloff observes that you can get cases where a question projection *is* followed by the question projected (that is, it was *not* a 'pre-pre'). In all the cases of such 'pre's', 'the projected question is, or is marked as, a delicate one' (p. 131). An example of this is seen in 8.3:

8.3 [Schegloff 1980: 133]
J: Uhm (0.?) Can I ask you something?
M: <u>Y</u>eah.
J: What has happened to Standard Prudential.

However, projecting an upcoming question as 'delicate' does not necessarily mean an automatic response to something that 'society' defines as delicate (in 8.3 possibly financial matters). Rather it displays that 'a question hearable as subject to delicate treatment once heard, has been so treated on this occasion, by this speaker, for this recipient' (p. 134).

A further example of the local use of a pre-sequence to construct a 'delicate' object is found in how pre-HIV test counsellors question their clients about their 'histories' (see also chapter 7). Extract 8.4 below occurs near the beginning of such an interview:

8.4 [Silverman 1997a: 49–50]

```
 1   C:   Right. hh .hhh (.) Erm: (0.5) You've come just for
 2        an HIV te:[st.
 3   P:              [uh-hum.
 4   C:   .hhh (.4) Can I just ask you briefly:: (.2) erm: one
 5        or two questions before we start. .hh Have you ever
 6        had a test before,
 7   P:   N:o.
 8   C:   No. .hhh Have you ever injected drugs:?
 9   P:   No.
10        (2.0)
11   C:   Have you ever had a homosexual relationship?
12        (.5)
13   P:   No.
14        (.5)
15   P:   And that's not really– (.5) (I mean) (.2) put me in
16        a high risk group h[as it.
17   C:                       [hnoh. No it doesn't.
```

C's question projection in line 4 sets up a pre-delicate series of questions relating to matters which can be heard to indicate that P might turn out to be HIV-positive. Note that P shows he hears these questions this way (on lines 15–16). Through these means, both speakers collaborate in identifying and managing a potentially 'delicate' topic.

Sometimes, however, the work of assigning delicacy can produce post- as well as 'pre-' sequences. For instance, look at lines 2–3 in 8.5:

8.5 [Silverman 1997a: 73]
((P has reported a phonecall from her boyfriend's ex-girlfriend saying she has been to the VD clinic and that P should go too))

```
1   C:   So: the thing is you see w– wh– what abou:t contacts
2        before your present boyfriend if I might ask about
3        (tha:[:t).
4   P:         [Well I had (.) since my: divorce in eighty-two
5        (.) I've only had two relationships.
```

6   C: Right.
7   P: And uh:m (0.2) one lasted for eight years and one
8   lasted for three year:s.

Note here how, in lines 2–3, C adds a little rider to her question ('if I might ask about (tha:[:t).'). Although, unlike question projections, this request comes after rather than before the question, it serves the same function of marking out and requesting permission for what may be heard as a delicate topic.

Preference Organization

As we saw in chapter 6, Sacks discussed preference organization in the light of the organization of agreements and disagreements. Sacks's early interest in 'agreements' was in showing how they were basic to sociality. For instance, he cites the importance of agreements in classical Greek dialogues (*LC1*: 429) and notes how, in the pre-Civil War South, slaves organized their talk so as to agree with their masters (*LC2*: 198–9; see also Libermann 1985).

However, Sacks's main interest is in how agreements are 'achieved' or 'proved', for example, by something more than a response token, such as 'I was just telling so-and-so that myself' (*LC2*: 252). In the case of 'disagreements', he suggests that by using words like 'well', speakers can provide for an upcoming disagreement and thereby tie their talk to a prior turn (*LC1*: 736).

In CA, 'preference organization' basically entails the distinction between two formats of action. Certain actions – typically actions that occur in response to other actions, such as invitations, offers or assessments – can be marked as dispreferred. Thus rejections of invitations or offers, or disagreements in response to assessments, can be performed in such a way that encodes their dispreferred status. Conversely, acceptance of an invitation or offer, or an agreement with an assessment, can be performed in a way that exhibits their status as 'preferred' activities.

Since Sacks, research has identified a number of practices through which the dispreferred status of an action can be marked. According to Heritage (1984: 265–80), these practices include:

1 the action is delayed within a turn or across a sequence of turns;

2 the action is commonly prefaced or qualified within the turn in which it occurs;
3 the action is commonly accomplished in mitigated or indirect form; and
4 the dispreferred action is commonly accounted for.

Unlike Goffman's (1959) early concept of 'face', the concept of 'preference' therefore does not refer to inner experiences of the actors about 'problems' or the lack of them involved in performing certain actions (Levinson 1983). Furthermore, the distinction between preferred and dispreferred action formats does not involve an *a priori* categorization of actions as problematic or non-problematic. Rather, the distinction provides a resource for the interactants through the use of which they can portray their actions as problematic, or alternatively as ones that do not involve problems in the interaction at hand.

In data from counselling interviews (Silverman 1997a: 134–53), I showed how such a preference organization is respected even when the advice is rejected or received equivocally. Throughout, I observed the cooperative minimization of resistance to and rejection of advice. Usually, as in 8.1 above, clients opt for unmarked acknowledgments and silences much more frequently than they choose outright advice rejections. Where they reject advice, they lead up to it through delays and mitigations, and counsellors speedily back down.

This kind of indirect resistance thus creates an environment in which all parties can seek to reaffirm social solidarity without directly acknowledging the existence of a disagreement. Equally, counsellors deploy a series of strategies for minimizing resistance, packaging their advice in questions or in an ambiguous format – as potentially information delivery rather than advice-giving (see chapter 7).

I also examined an apparently deviant case, where an advice rejection is given without delay or mitigation, to examine the kinds of local conditions which seem to threaten the displays of social solidarity observed elsewhere. This is seen in 8.6, where P has had repeated negative HIV tests:

8.6 [Silverman 1997a: 150]
1   C: so hh um (1.0) I think what you have to do is (.)
2   when you've had your clean bill of health this time
3   (0.4)

4   P: yes
5   C: is (.) ((softly)) get on with <u>living</u>
6   P: I do live my life anyway so

In line 6, note how P does not delay, preface, mitigate or account for his statement of the irrelevance of C's advice. Thus, one might suggest, P seems to be marking his statement of the irrelevance of C's advice as a preferred activity.

However, we must bear in mind that, like any human rule system, preference organization does not determine behaviour but provides a way of making behaviour accountable (see Wittgenstein 1968: 74, para. 183). Therefore, rather than ignoring preference organization, P can be heard to express an extraordinarily strong rejection of the relevance of C's advice through expressing it in the *preferred* action format. It is the very lack of delays, prefaces, mitigation or accounts that constitutes this format; and thereby, it establishes the extraordinary strength of P's rejection.

In Silverman (1997a: 150–1), I suggest that the strength of P's rejection derives from the way in which it disregards how P had, a few lines earlier, formulated his own experience in a way which denied that he felt like a hypochondriac (data not shown). Given that, as Sacks has argued, experiences are 'carefully regulated sorts of things' (*LC2*: 248), people are only entitled to have experiences that they have observed and/or that affect them directly. In this case, then, C has no warrant to build a piece of commonsensical advice which rejects P's own stated experience.

Note, moreover, how both C and P formulate their talk in terms of an appeal to a self-evident maxim ('get on with living' and 'I do live my life anyway'). As we have seen, Sacks has noted how such maxims are treated by members as patently unchallengeable (see chapter 1). So, in 8.6, P does not ignore preference organization. Instead, he uses it to mark the strong character of his disagreement based on what he has already told C about his experience. In doing so, he elegantly uses the self-same maxim device as C employed.

Context

So far, I have been freely using extracts from both casual conversation and from organizational settings. As I shall now seek to demonstrate, it is important to try to establish how far these two categories are distinct or related. To do so, we must first investigate how 'context' is approached in conversation analysis.

Contrary to some critics who accuse conversation analysts of depicting a mechanical system (see Goffman 1981: 16–17), CA takes very seriously the contexts of interaction. For instance, in the classic statement of CA by Sacks, Schegloff and Jefferson (1974), it is noted very early on that 'conversation is always "situated" – it always comes out of, and is part of, some real sets of circumstances of its participants' (p. 699). However, although such matters as place, time and the identities of the participants are undoubtedly relevant to speakers, we are reminded that we must be cautious about how we invoke them: 'it is undesirable to have to know or characterize such situations for particular conversations in order to investigate them' (p. 699).

Two decades later, this position is clearly laid out by Maynard and Clayman:

> Conversation analysts ... [are] concerned that using terms such as 'doctor's office', 'courtroom', 'police department', 'school room', and the like, to characterise settings ... can obscure much of what occurs within those settings ... For this reason, conversation analysts rarely rely on ethnographic data and instead examine if and how interactants themselves reveal an orientation to institutional or other contexts. (1991: 406–7)

This means, as Drew and Heritage point out, that while one can do 'institutional work' on a home telephone, not everything said at work is specifically 'institutional': 'Thus the institutionality of an interaction is not determined by its setting. Rather, interaction is institutional insofar as participants' institutional or professional identities are somehow made relevant to the work activities in which they are engaged' (1992: 3–4).

The question that then arises is how we demonstrate what is 'relevant'. Schegloff (1992b) has suggested that this is a basic methodological issue. It causes two problems which he calls 'relevance' and 'procedural consequentiality'.

Relevance This is the problem of 'showing from the details of the talk or other conduct in the materials that we are analyzing that those aspects of the scene are what the parties are oriented to' (Schegloff 1992b: 110). The problem arises because, as we saw in chapter 5, Sacks reveals how people can describe themselves and others in multiple ways.

This problem, Schegloff insists, is simply disregarded in social scientific accounts which rely on statistical correlations to 'demonstrate' the relevance of some such description. Instead, we need to demonstrate that participants are currently oriented to such descriptions.

Procedural consequentiality A demonstration that our descriptions of persons and settings are currently relevant for participants is not enough. We must also address the following questions:

> How does the fact that the talk is being conducted in some setting (e.g. 'the hospital') issue in any consequence for the shape, form, trajectory, content, or character of the interaction that the parties conduct? And what is the mechanism by which the context-so-understood has determinate consequences for the talk. (Schegloff 1992b: 111)

Schegloff gives two examples relevant to such 'procedural consequentiality'. First, he looks at how a particular laboratory study sought to demonstrate something about how people 'repair' mistakes in talk. He shows that in this study only the subject was allowed to talk. Hence many features which arise as to whether such repairs should be done by self or other (given that there is a preference for self-repair) were unavailable. Thus it will not do to characterize the context as a 'laboratory setting' because other features (only one person talking) can be shown to have more procedural consequentiality.

Schegloff's second example is taken from an interview between George Bush and Dan Rather in the 1988 US election campaign. The interview became famous because of the apparent 'row' or confrontation between the two men. Schegloff shows that such features were noticeable because Bush refused to cooperate in producing a central feature of 'interviews', that is, that they consist of question–answer sequences where one party asks the questions and the other holds off speaking until a recognizable question has been posed (Silverman 1973).

The implication is that we cannot describe what went on as occurring in the context of an 'interview'. Instead, interactions only become (and cease to be) 'interviews' through the cooperative activity of the participants. As Schegloff has shown in an earlier paper (1987), this may make some of the claims relating gender to interruption (Zimmerman and West 1975) somewhat premature.

These examples show that the issue of determining context is not a once-and-for-all affair because parties have to continue to work at co-producing any context. Equally, we cannot explain people's behaviour as a simple 'response' to some context when that context is actively constructed (and reconstructed).

This means that we should not assume that what we find in talk is necessarily a feature of the institutional setting or other social structural element that our intuitions tell us is relevant. Since 'not everything said in some context ... is relevantly oriented to that context' (Schegloff 1991: 62), we must not risk characterizing a conversational structure possibly found across a range of contexts as institutionally specific.

This point is made elegantly in the editors' introduction to a recent collection of studies of 'institutional talk':

> CA researchers cannot take 'context' for granted nor may they treat it as determined in advance and independent of the participants' own activities. Instead, 'context' and identity have to be treated as inherently locally produced, incrementally developed and, by extension, as transformable at any moment. Given these constraints, analysts who wish to depict the distinctively 'institutional' character of some stretch of talk cannot be satisfied with showing that institutional talk exhibits aggregates and/or distributions of actions that are distinctive from ordinary conversation. They must rather demonstrate that the participants constructed their conduct over its course – turn by responsive turn – so as progressively to constitute ... the occasion of their talk, together with their own social roles in it, as having some distinctively institutional character. (Drew and Heritage 1992: 21)

Institutionality

In chapter 5, we saw that it is illegitimate for analysts to invoke their own sense of identities. Similarly, the previous discussion has shown how, when doing CA, the analyst seeks to understand the way the participants invoke particular contexts through their use of the conversational turn-taking system which is both 'context-free and capable of extraordinary context-sensitivity' (Sacks, Schegloff and Jefferson 1974: 699). This carries two implications:

1 The turn-taking system for conversation is 'the basic form of speech-exchange system' (p. 730). As such, it is to be treated as the baseline for *any* interaction.

2 Institutionality arises through how the parties adapt or modify this system.

In his lectures, Sacks occasionally ponders such local adaptations of the turn-taking system. For instance, using Schegloff (1968), he notes how a caller has to engage in considerable work to transform the direction of a called-defined 'business call' (*LC2*: 200–1). He also implies that the absence of 'second stories' is a candidate feature of institutional talk. For instance: 'it is absolutely not the business of a psychiatrist, having had some experience reported to him, to say "My mother was just like that, too"' (*LC2*: 259).

However, in these lectures there is no systematic attention to institutional talk. This issue is first systematically addressed in his co-authored paper in *Language* (Sacks, Schegloff and Jefferson 1974). Here it is noted that 'interviews' or 'debates' are recognizable by how the length and ordering of turns are pre-specified (p. 701). This leads on to the authors' suggestion that there may be a 'linear array' of three turn-taking systems. At one extreme, all turns would be pre-allocated (for instance, certain courtroom proceedings). In the middle, we would find various mixes of pre-allocated and local-allocated turns (exemplified by meetings). At the other extreme, a purely local turn allocation would preserve one-turn-at-a-time (p. 729). Each turn-taking system would have particular functions (p. 730; cf. Peräkylä and Silverman 1991b).

Following Heritage (1984), Maynard and Clayman argue that work after Sacks's death has gone on to examine how particular sequence types found in conversation 'become specialised, simplified, reduced, or otherwise structurally adapted for institutional purposes' (1991: 407). This structural adaptation is recognized by Drew and Heritage (1992: 22–5) in their identification of three dimensions through which talk becomes institutional:

1 It is usually goal-oriented in institutionally relevant ways: thus people design their conduct to meet various institutional tasks or functions, as with emergency calls to the police, which need to be rapidly but accurately accomplished (Zimmerman 1992); alternatively, the goals of interactions can be ill-defined, creating a need for the participants to fashion a sense of what the interaction will be about (Heritage and Sefi 1992; Peräkylä and Silverman 1991b).

2 It is usually shaped by certain constraints, such as what can be done in a court of law or news interview; however, in other situations, like counselling or doctor–patient interaction, participants may negotiate or ignore such constraints.
3 It is associated with particular ways of reasoning or inference-making.

Variation in each of these three dimensions means that institutional talk spreads across a continuum of forms. At one end is strict turn and turn-type allocation of the kind found in court-rooms (Atkinson and Drew 1979). At the other end, as in some counselling settings, there is no normatively sanctionable depar-ture from conversational turn-taking, simply a mutual orientation to the tasks at hand (Peräkylä and Silverman 1991b).

There thus appears to be a range of degrees of *formality* in insti-tutional talk (Atkinson 1982). In formal settings (law, schools, news interviews), Drew and Heritage point out that we find 'specific *reductions* of the range of options and opportunities for action that are characteristic in conversation and they often involve *specializa-tions* and *respecifications* of the interactional activities that remain' (1992: 26).

In informal settings, often characterized by the lack of an over-hearing audience, there is less uniformity. Although we may find dif-ferences in the patterning of what people do (thus doctors ask questions and patients provide answers), 'these asymmetries are apparently not the products of turn-taking procedures that are norm-atively sanctionable' (1992: 28; cf. Peräkylä and Silverman 1991b). Here we detect Schegloff's 'procedural consequentiality' in such matters as 'the opening and closing of encounters ... the ways in which information is requested, delivered and received [and] with the design of referring expressions' (Drew and Heritage 1992: 28).

This analysis of the creation of contexts of 'institutionality' has led to a huge corpus of CA studies which holds out every prospect of establishing a revitalized sociology of work and occupations. In this chapter there is only space to deal with two examples. To simplify, both examples are drawn from television news interviews.

News Interviews as Institutional Talk

We discussed earlier Schegloff's (1980) argument that particular kinds of 'pre-sequences' might mark any topic as 'delicate'. Given that such 'pre-sequences' may be used in any conversational environment, how is the marking of 'delicacy' locally accomplished in a recognizably 'institutional' way?

Using the example of a telephone call from a school to the mother of an absent child, Heritage (1997) has suggested that 'expressive caution' may be a fingerprint of institutional talk. In an earlier paper, Heritage (1985) had argued that TV news interviewers proceed cautiously in order to fulfil two major professional requirements: to remain neutral and to produce talk for overhearers. As Heritage shows, this caution is seen in their avoidance of response tokens or direct comments on answers to their questions.

Following Heritage, Stephen Clayman (1992) has also characterized TV news interviewing as a site for much 'expressive caution'. Clayman uses Goffman's concept of 'footing' to show how this is achieved. Goffman (1981) suggests that people may take up various positions or 'footings' in relation to their own remarks as (1) animator, (2) author or (3) principal of what is said. Clayman analyses TV news interviews to show that interviewers typically constitute themselves as animators and, unlike a lot of ordinary conversation, deflect other identities on to some other party (although, as Clayman notes, this can happen in ordinary talk, for instance when someone uses the term 'we' or implies that they are merely reflecting some other person's view).

Clayman investigates how interviewers shift footing when they come on to relatively controversial opinion statements, as in the following extract:

8.7 [Clayman 1992: 5; Meet the Press 12/8/85] (IV = interviewer)
1   IV: Senator, (0.5) uh: President Reagan's elected thirteen
2   months ago: an enormous landslide.
3   (0.8)
4   IV: It is s::aid that his programs are in trouble

In lines 1–2, a footing is constructed whereby IV is the author of a factual statement. However, at line 4, the footing shifts to what 'it is said' – hence, here IV is no longer the author and the item is marked as possibly 'controversial'.

Footing shifts are also *renewed* during specific 'controversial' words and interviewers avoid affiliating with or disaffiliating from the statements they report. They also may comment on the authoritativeness of the source of an assertion or comment on the range of persons associated with it. However, the achievement of 'neutrality' is a locally accomplished and cooperative matter. Thus interviewees 'ordinarily refrain from treating the focal assertion as expressing the IV's personal opinion' (Clayman 1992: 180). For instance, they do this by attributing the assertion to the same third party.

As Clayman notes, his analysis of 'neutrality' as an interactional accomplishment is counter-intuitive:

> This analysis runs contrary to common-sense notions of neutrality as a trait inhering in interviewers as individuals ... From an analytic per-spective, the visibility of this journalistic 'trait' is a joint achievement of interactants acting in concert to preserve a professional posture for interviewers. In other words, neutrality is a socially organized, or more specifically, an interactionally organized phenomenon, something that the parties to an interview 'do together'. (1992: 194)

As Clayman remarks, this is unlike ordinary conversation, where it seems unlikely that speakers are expected to be neutral. As he says, minimal responses to such things as invitations or advice are *not* usually taken as evidence of the recipient's neutrality but are hearable as constituting actual or possible rejection (1992: 198, n. 5). In this way, news interviews are locally constituted as distinctly 'institutional' through using generally available conversational mechanisms in a specific way.

Like Clayman, Greatbatch (1992) notes the specific ways in which participants produce their talk as 'news interview' talk. He shows how the maintenance of an interviewer's neutrality ties in with the mutual production of the talk as aimed at an overhearing *audience*. Both parties maintain a situation in which it is not problematic that interviewees properly limit themselves to responses to the interviewer's questions. Equally, interviewers confine them-selves to asking questions and avoid a range of responsive activities which would make them a report recipient rather than just a report elicitor. So, unlike the HIV counsellor in 8.1 or storytellers in ordinary conversation, in news interviews the absence of response tokens such as mmm hm, uh huh, yes, and news receipt objects like oh, really, did you is not problematic (pp. 269–70).

In this context, 'neutrality' is not the only feature which con-trasts with talk in other settings. Greatbatch shows that 'disagree-ments' have features specific to news interview talk. In ordinary conversation: 'agreements are normally performed directly and with a minimum of delay, disagreements are commonly accom-plished in mitigated forms and delayed from early positioning within turns and/or sequences' (p. 273). As we saw earlier, this suggests that agreements, like acceptances of invitations or advice, are marked as preferred objects. However, preference organization seems to work in a different way in multi-party news interviews.

Greatbatch shows how such disagreements may arise in two ways. First, following a question repeated to the second interviewee (IE), she or he can disagree immediately with the opinion of the first IE. As Greatbatch notes, however, this disagreement is *mitigated* since it is *mediated* by the question of the interviewer (IV). As Greatbatch suggests:

> The structure of turn taking in news interviews . . . means that disagreements between IEs are ordinarily elicited by and addressed to a third party, the IV, with whom neither party disagrees. Disagreements which are produced in this manner are not systematically mitigated or forestalled by the use of the preference features that are associated with disagreement in conversation. (pp. 279–80)

Secondly, however, IEs may disagree in other turn positions, for instance following a co-interviewee's turn or during such a turn, as in 8.8:

8.8 [Greatbatch 1992: 12]
IE1: the government advertising campaign is h <u>high</u>ly
        irresponsible. h It's being given [u n d e r h ug]e
IE2:   [Utter rubbish]

This extract departs from the conversational rules of 'preference organization' which, as we saw earlier, mark disagreements as dispreferred and hence delayed objects. It also seems to clash with the normal production of a news interview format (because they are not produced as an answer to an interviewer's question).

However, Greatbatch argues, such disagreements as in 8.8 display an underlying adherence to the news interview format in two ways. In the first place, IE2 can still be heard as responding to the question that produced IE1's answer. Secondly, IE2 directs his answer to IV and *not* to IE1, and this is quite different from ordinary conversation where the person being disagreed with is also the addressee of the disagreement. Such disagreements are routinely followed (data not shown here) by the interviewer intervening to manage an exit from the disagreement without requiring the interviewees to depart from their institutional roles *as* interviewees and not, for instance, combatants, mutual insulters, etc.

Greatbatch summarizes his findings as follows:

1 In news interviews, many of the features of preference organization are rendered redundant, replaced by the interview turn-taking system.
2 Within news interviews, 'the structure of turn taking and its associated expectancies provide simultaneously for the *escalation* and *limitation* of overt disagreement' (Greatbatch 1992: 299, emphasis added). As Greatbatch suggests, this may explain why panel interviews are so common and assumed to produce 'lively' broadcasting.

Summary: Institutional Talk

The studies discussed above follow Sacks, Schegloff and Jefferson's (1974) pioneering paper on the turn-taking system. In particular, (1) they avoid invoking their own sense of the 'context' of talk; instead (2) by using the turn-taking system for ordinary conversation as a baseline, they identify what is distinctive about news interview talk.

However, this does *not* mean that such work treats institutional talk as a closed system cut off from the wider society. By contrast, without making any prior assumptions about 'context', these studies directly examine how members themselves invoke a particular context for their talk. For instance, both Clayman and Greatbatch show how TV news interviewers produce their talk as 'neutral' or 'objective', thereby displaying their attention to an overhearing audience's presumed expectations.

Elsewhere, I have argued (Silverman 1997a: 34–5) for the value of respecting CA's assertion that one's initial move should be to give close attention to how participants locally produce contexts for their interaction. By beginning with this question of 'how', we can then fruitfully move on to 'why' questions about the institutional and cultural constraints to which the parties demonstrably defer. As I argue in chapter 9, such constraints reveal the functions of apparently irrational practices and help us to understand the possibilities and limits of attempts at social reform.

Non-verbal Communication

As I remarked in chapter 4, Sacks was certainly aware of the importance of non-verbal communication. For instance, his students were given an exercise where they had to observe people exchanging glances. Sacks then showed them how you can analyse the descriptive apparatus involved in the glance (*LC1*: 88). However, he was concerned about the technical problems of working with video-recordings. For instance, he responded to a question about gaze and body movements with the assertion that, while 'it would be great to study them', there too many technical problems (like where you place the camera) (*LC2*: 26).

Since Sacks's time, many of the technical problems of recording and transcribing non-verbal communication have been resolved and some important studies have revealed the fascinating interpenetration of talk, gaze and body movements (see Heath 1986; Goodwin and Goodwin 1986; Peräkylä and Silverman 1991a). For instance, Goodwin (1981) has discussed how speakers can assess recipiency for their talk by inspecting the gaze of others. As he shows, speakers who find their addressee looking away restart their speech. This usually solicits the orientation of a recipient to a newly initiated complete turn.

However, people attend to other objects in their environment than just co-conversationalists. For instance, as I noted in chapter 7, place and location can be an important topic for members. Equally, as I show below, mechanical objects, such as computer screens and photocopiers, are routinely made the focus of joint attention.

In this part of the chapter, I will not attempt to provide a summary of such studies (for a valuable discussion, see Heath 1997). Instead, I will review just two studies: Don Zimmerman's (1992) work on emergency calls and Lucy Suchman's (1987) study of how photocopiers are used. Both these studies show how video data can be used in CA. They also bear on two themes discussed above: the character of 'institutionality' and the relevance of CA studies for practical organizational problems.

Calls to Emergency Services

Zimmerman (1992) is concerned with the interactional organization of the talk occurring in calls to 9–1–1 emergency telephone numbers operated by the US emergency services. His research was based on data from three centres (one in the Mid-West, two on the West Coast).

The study focuses on calls to two of the centres which have a computer-assisted dispatch system (CAD). This follows the following pattern: requests for police, fire and medical assistance are taken by call-takers (CTs); CTs enter information received from callers (Cs) into a computer terminal; and this information is transmitted to dispatchers (Ds) who further process it and forward it to appropriate field units.

Zimmerman argues that this pattern means that we need to look at each call in terms of the *functions* it fulfils in relation to organizational and callers' concerns. This often involves complicated management in order to align callers to the needs of call-takers.

The work of call-takers responds to a number of organizational constraints, including:

1 obtaining *accurate* locations, for example, Mid-West centre's CAD will reject intersections it does not recognize;
2 establishing the nature of the problem;
3 in the case of criminal activity, obtaining 'full' descriptions of suspects;
4 obtaining the name and location of the caller; and
5 fitting all of the above speedily into a 'dispatch package' entered into the available CAD codes which, among other things, characterize the 'problem' (so 'pergun' means person with a gun and 'p1' means priority 1).

Zimmerman shows that these constraints shape the character of C–CT talk in the following ways. First, CTs have to cut off long-winded or 'hysterical' Cs. They attempt to do this by issuing directives ('stop shouting', 'answer my questions') or offering reassurance ('help is on the way'). Second, by contrast, CTs simultaneously have to ensure that Cs don't hang up before the relevant information has been given. However, 'help is on the way' may be heard as a closing invitation. So, typically, it is combined with a 'stay on the line' request as in 8.9:

8.9 [Zimmerman 1992: 8]
CT: We have units on the way, okay just stay on the phone with me
C: Okay

Finally, at all times, CTs have to attend to Cs' talk in terms of what is reportable via the CAD codes. This means that response tokens from the CT are often replaced by the sound of the computer keyboard, as in 8.10:

8.10 [Zimmerman 1992: 4] ([kb = sound of keyboard being used)
```
1   C:   hhh Uh there's uh (0.2) oh I think it's uh (.) white jeep
2        (.) hh jeepster tha[t pulled up here uh in front.
3                           [kb----------------
4   C:   =An there's about (0.1)] five Nihgro guys tha' got out, I
5        --------------- ]
6        heard=um tal[kin about (0.1) hh going (.) to thee] next
7                    [---------------------]
8        apartment building uh fur uh fight (0.2) [hh a]n I jus'
9                                                 [---]
10       am going down tuh check it out
```

As Zimmerman notes about this extract:

> At the possible conclusion of C's account of the trouble . . . (on line 8) CT says nothing while she continues her keyboard activity. After a pause of 0.2 second, C initiates [an] elaboration . . . which, in the absence of a receipt of acknowledgment from CT, may be oriented to the possibility of some problem with his narrative. (1992: 427)

This absence of response tokens, one expected feature of hearers' activities when not taking a turn at any given possible turn-transition point in ordinary conversation, thus has observable consequences in these calls. As Zimmerman suggests, the absence of such a response token may be heard by C as indicating a trouble in the report. Thus it can lead to hedges and downgrades (for example, less than ten lines after the part of the extract given above, C hedges, stating that 'it might not be anything').

CTs must also orient both to what Cs are saying and to what they are *about* to say. Hence they may defer initiating inquiries if their monitoring of the C's talk suggests the upcoming delivery of a piece of pertinent information. Some of these kinds of organizational 'solutions' are oriented to by Cs. So here, unlike other telephone calls, the opening sequence does not routinely contain a greeting or a 'how are you' sequence. Both parties typically seek to reach the 'reason for the call' sequence as soon as possible.

However, some callers may be particularly responsive to what CTs require. For instance, organizations routinely in contact with the emergency services offer ordered tellings of problems, oriented to the organizational needs of CTs. This is seen in 8.11, where C is a caller from the staff of a hospital ('General'):

8.11 [Zimmerman 1992: 56]
CT: Emergency
C: Hi hh General, there's been an overdose. (.) Twenty three twenty three hh
    I[daho: hh
CT: [(keyboard) O:kay
C: Upstairs apartment num:ber two: hh
CT: Thank you=
C: =Umhm bye

In 8.11, C's two turns convey all the information that CT needs. Hence her 'thank you' is closing implicative and heard as such by C.

However, in the case of non-institutional callers, there is often an intractable problem in aligning Cs' and CTs' perspectives. For CTs, calls have to be made as routine as possible – hence 'emergencies' have to be transformed into ordinary, predictable events. Conversely, for Cs 'emergencies' are, by definition, non-routine and must be displayed as such.

Communicating with a Photocopier

Like Zimmerman, Lucy Suchman (1987) is concerned with the interaction between people and machines. However, in this case, the communication is not mediated through a caller or client. Instead, she takes the example of a computer-based system attached to a photocopier and intended to instruct the user in the photocopier's operation.

Suchman focuses on how rules function in human–computer interaction. She draws upon Gladwin's (1964) account of the navigation methods of a South East Asian tribe, the Trukese, with no 'rational' Western theory of navigation. Instead, the Trukese navigate by various ad hoc methods (responding to wind, waves, stars, clouds, etc.). Suchman asks how real is the contrast between Western and Trukese methods of navigation? Theories and plans do not *determine* the actions of either Western or Trukese navigators. Rather Western navigators *invoke* a plan when asked to account for their navigation which itself, inevitably, depends on ad hoc methods (accounting, for example, for disasters like the Exxon Valdez oil spill off Alaska).

This creates a problem in artificial intelligence systems which are 'built on a *planning model* of human action. The model treats a plan as something located in the actor's head, which directs his or her behaviour' (1987: 3). As Suchman notes, plans neither determine action nor fully reconstruct it. Thus she argues that 'artifacts built on the planning model confuse *plans* with *situated actions*,' and she proposes 'a view of plans as formulations of antecedent conditions and consequences that account for actions in a plausible way' (p. 3).

Conversely, Suchman suggests, the successful navigation of the Trukese shows that 'the coherence of situated action is tied in essential ways not to . . . conventional rules but to local interactions contingent on the actor's particular circumstances' (pp. 27–8). This implies that, in the design of computers that can interact with humans, the system of communication 'must incorporate both a sensitivity to local circumstances and resources for the remedy of troubles in understanding that inevitably arise' (p. 28). This will mean that 'instead of looking for a structure that is invariant across situations, we look for the processes whereby particular, uniquely constituted circumstances are systematically interpreted so as to render meaning shared and action accountably rational' (p. 67).

There is a methodological basis behind Suchman's focus on processes of systematic interpretation that is worth noting. Although we have not reproduced her data here, her analysis, like that of Zimmerman, is concerned with the sequential organization of verbal and non-verbal interaction. Suchman's data derive from videos of four sessions, each of more than an hour, involving first-time users of this 'expert system'. In each session, two novices worked together in pairs. She is particularly concerned with how interactional 'troubles' arise and are resolved.

In Suchman's study the computer used in the photocopier 'project[s] the course of the user's actions as the enactment of a *plan* for doing the job, and then use[s] the presumed plan as the relevant context for the action's interpretation' (p. 99, emphasis added). However, the problem is that 'plans' have a different status for computers and users: 'While the [design] plan directly *determines* the system's behaviour, the user is required to *find* the plan, as the prescriptive and descriptive significance of a series of procedural instructions' (p. 101, emphasis added).

This is shown in Suchman's model of how the computer is

The basic interactional sequence between machine and user

1 MACHINE PRESENTS INSTRUCTION
User reads instruction,
locates referents
and interprets action descriptions

2 USER TAKES ACTION
Design assumes that the action means that the user has
understood the instruction

3 MACHINE PRESENTS NEXT INSTRUCTION

Source: Based on Suchman 1987: 107.

---

supposed to 'instruct' a user, set out in the box. Despite this rational model, much of the user's behaviour is unavailable to the system, for instance, 'the actual work of locating referents and interpreting action descriptions' (p. 107). This means that if an instruction is *misunderstood* by the user, the error will go unnoticed.

Predictably, Suchman's study reveals many conflicts between the design assumptions (DA) built into the machine and user assumptions (UA). Some examples of this are set out in the second box overleaf. As it shows, a faulted action can go unnoticed at the point where it occurs. This is because 'what is available to the system is only the action's effect and that effect satisfies the requirements for the next instruction' (p. 167).

As a consequence, while, from the point of view of the design, users have achieved precisely what they want, this is not how users actually perceive their situation. Because of these kinds of conflicts between the assumptions of designers and users, Suchman concludes that users often fail to get what they want from the photocopier: 'Due to the constraints on the machine's access to the situation of the user's inquiry, breaches in understanding that for face-to-face interaction would be trivial in terms of detection and repair become "fatal" for human–machine communication' (p. 170).

Like many studies concerned with the mechanics of organizational interaction, Suchman's findings are both analytically and practically rich. Among the practical implications of her study, we may note that, first, it reveals the character of practical decision-making in a way relevant to the design of expert systems.

Design assumptions (DA) and user assumptions (UA)

DA: treat the question 'what next?' as a request for the next ste p – attended to by presentation of the next instruction.
UA: can ask 'what next' sometimes in order to know how to abort or repair an activity (for instance, where only one photocopy obtained instead of the five desired).

DA: repeat instructions either (a) where task needs to be repeated or (b) where user's action in response to the instruction is in error such as to return the system to a state prior to the instruction being given (a loop).
UA: in the case of repeated instructions, (b) does *not* occur in human interaction. Instead, the repetition of an instruction indicates that the action taken in response to the instruction in some way fails to satisfy the intent of the instruction, and needs to be remedied.

DA: users will follow instructions; where they do not, this will be detected by the machine.
UA: can sometimes ignore instructions because of preconceptions about what is appropriate, based on prior experience.

Source: Based on Suchman 1987: 148–67.

Secondly, it suggests the constructive role of users' troubles in system design, that is, troubles arise not by departing from a plan but in the situated contingencies of action. She notes how such systems may not seek to eliminate user errors but 'to make them accessible to the student, and therefore instructive' (p. 184).

Returning to the theme of institutional talk, Suchman's work is important because of its focus on the precise mechanics of institutional interaction. In particular, Suchman begins by using everyday interaction as a baseline and then seeing how far human–computer interaction departs from it. This means that she avoids beginning with the commonsense assumption that there is a stable organizational or institutional order separate from everyday interaction.

Concluding Remarks

In this chapter, we have seen how many topics foreshadowed in Sacks's lectures and in Sacks, Schegloff and Jefferson (1974) have since been developed. As I have suggested, these developments, most notably in studies of human–computer interaction and of institutional talk, have delivered substantial analytical development of basic concepts and raised central issues for the practical functioning of organizations and occupations.

As in chapter 7, I hope to have demonstrated that twenty or so years after Sacks's untimely death, the vitality of his contribution lives on. In my final chapter, I underline this point by assessing Sacks's legacy not as a museum exhibit of past thought but as a continuing inspiration for addressing central issues in contemporary social science.

9
Sacks's Legacy

> If what I do lives to have an epitaph,
> I won't write it.
>
> **Harvey Sacks**

Sacks's remarks on his epitaph, in a lecture given in 1967 (*LC1*: 621), show contemporary readers that they cannot escape from their responsibility to find meaning and relevance in Sacks's work. We do not need to fall back on fashionable theories of the 'death of the author' (Barthes 1977) to recognize that we necessarily (and rightly) produce our own contemporary readings of Sacks.

One consequence, as Schegloff notes, is that there is little point in trying to follow Sacks's projects *literally* since such projects depended on what influenced him and the trajectory of his own work. Instead, what is needed is:

> a continuous re-energizing of inquiry by the example of his own work and the possibilities which it revealed ... Not mechanical imitation or extrapolation but the best possible effort to advance the undertaking in original ways will constitute the most appropriate and enduring celebration of Sacks' contribution. (Schegloff in *LC2*: xlix–l)

As I shall shortly argue (and as Schegloff was aware), the exact nature of Sacks's 'undertaking' and its 'possibilities' are fiercely contested more than twenty years after his death. However, I have no doubt that Schegloff is right to call for 'a continuous re-energizing of inquiry' as the best way to celebrate Sacks's example. As with other important thinkers, we keep his work vital by treating it as an inspiration or, more prosaically, as a toolbox. Indeed, this volume will have more than served its purpose if my readers are sufficiently stimulated to turn to Sacks's own writings to locate his legacy for themselves.

In chapters 7 and 8 of this book, I have specifically addressed Sacks's direct legacy for contemporary work in both categorization and conversation analysis. In this short concluding chapter, for reasons that will become apparent, I want to broaden the perspective to look at Sacks's more indirect legacy for social science as a whole. Before I do this, however, I want to consider Sacks's achievement by 1975 – particularly in relation to the direction suggested by Garfinkel (1967).

The Achievement

Sacks began his public contribution with his first published paper in 1963. Goodwin and Heritage (1990: 284–5) have described the unpromising situation for any detailed account of social interaction at that time. True, sociology had been bequeathed by Max Weber (1949) a methodology of 'interpretive understanding'. However, while this appeared to get at participants' orientations, in fact it offered decontextualized 'ideal-types' with, as Weber himself acknowledged, very unclear research imperatives.

A more solid base for the study of social interaction appeared to be present in anthropology's concept of 'culture'. However, as Goodwin and Heritage note, in the hands of the social theories of Talcott Parsons (1937), culture was reduced to a set of internalized norms which shaped personality.

Language, largely unaddressed by Parsons, was handed over to linguistics and philosophy. But, as Goodwin and Heritage show, Chomsky's (1965) interest in generative structures and Saussure's (1974) lack of interest in talk meant that they were of limited relevance to students of social interaction. Finally, although the 'ordinary language' philosophers like Austin (1962) and Searle (1969) had much to say about talk, their analysis was based on invented examples. Thus it was that by 1960, as Goodwin and Heritage put it, the study of talk-in-interaction had fallen between disciplinary boundaries.

Before Sacks's death in 1975 there were, however, some more helpful developments in the social sciences. In sociolinguistics and cognitive anthropology, systematic attention was starting to be paid to everyday descriptive categories (see Giglioli 1972; Gumperz and Hymes 1972). In sociology, in his own idiosyncratic way, Erving Goffman was at least making the study of face-to-face interaction a semi-respectable research topic.

Ultimately, however, as Goodwin and Heritage (1990) point out, none of these developments could constitute a decisive breakthrough for the understanding of talk-in-interaction. Cognitive anthropology could not resolve the distinction it proposed between categories which belong to members ('emic') and those which belong to analysts ('etic'). At the same time, as we saw in chapter 2, from Sacks's point of view Goffman's unwillingness to work with detailed transcripts of naturally occurring data meant that his contribution could be treated as anecdotal.

In this intellectual context, Sacks's achievement was to show us that conversation is not, in the words of the novelist Milan Kundera, 'a pastime': 'on the contrary, conversation is what organizes time, governs it, and imposes its own laws, which must be respected' (Kundera 1996: 28). Put more directly, Sacks revealed the existence and the analysability of a new domain: talk-in-interaction. By recording, transcribing and analysing data from this domain, Sacks showed that conversation was locally organized and independent of traditional social science 'face-sheet' variables like gender or class. As Sacks puts it: 'it's not particularly a feature of, e.g., male conversation or female conversation or female–male conversation that one party talks at a time and speaker change recurs. They hold also across types of conversations – argument, business talks, whatever else' (*LC2*: 34).

Of course, the obvious contemporary person to share Sacks's achievement was Harold Garfinkel. As I suggested in chapter 2, Garfinkel's insistence on the need to create a distinct approach focused on members' methods for producing social order constituted a distinct breakthrough in the 1960s. Moreover, as an established scholar, Garfinkel was able to create a secure intellectual environment for Sacks at UCLA in the mid-1960s – a debt which Sacks repeatedly acknowledged in his early publications. Indeed, even though Garfinkel's name is not mentioned in Sacks's lectures, his (and ethnomethodology's) presence is obvious to the informed reader, in the lectures on measurement systems (*LC1*: 435–40), 'relevancy constraints' (*LC1*: 739–47) and doing 'being ordinary' (*LC2*: 215–21).

What, then, were the relative achievements of Sacks and Garfinkel? It turns out that there are widely differing views on this question. As I noted in chapter 2, Schegloff, when listing writers concerned with 'other processes' (than Sacks was concerned with), includes not only Bales but Schutz (concerned with 'interpretive strategies') *and* Garfinkel (commonsense methods) (*LC1*: xviii). So, for Schegloff, Sacks's project needs to be separated from ethno-methodology's philosophical ancestor and its founding father.

At the other end of the spectrum, some contemporary ethno-methodologists have used Garfinkel's position to develop a strong *critique* of Sacks's later work, most notably Sacks, Schegloff and Jefferson's (1974) explication of conversation analysis in *Language*. Thus Lynch and Bogen (1994) react against what they call this paper's 'strikingly formalist and foundationalist rhetoric' (p. 76).

Lynch and Bogen's response derives from their reading of Garfinkel's insistence that the reflexivity of any account means that ethnomethodology cannot develop into another systematic or cumulative science. For Lynch and Bogen, if accounts of members' methods 'are part and parcel of the concerted practices that enable them to be descriptive and instructive' (p. 89), then the hopes of Sacks and his colleagues of building systematic knowledge of talk-in-interaction were doomed to ironic failure. Indeed, the only interest of these accounts is as possible *data* on which ethno-methodologists can do their own analyses. As Lynch and Bogen put it: 'While Sacks and his colleagues sought to build a natural observational science of human behavior ... Garfinkel [and others] began to investigate natural scientists' and mathematicians' practices' (p. 84).

For Lynch and Bogen, then, Sacks's (and CA's) attempt to develop an analytical understanding of members' vernacular understanding 'indicates the extent to which conversation analysis has become a professionalized analytic endeavor' (p. 81) in which 'the adequacy of such accounts no longer depends upon their effective use as instructions for reproducing the practices described' (p. 83).

The import of this argument is stark and unrelenting. For Lynch and Bogen, Sacks ultimately takes us down a wrong turning which disastrously assimilates Garfinkel's radical position to that of other social sciences. There is only one solution: to drop 'science' with its baggage of 'data', 'concepts' and 'cumulative knowledge'. Instead, as they suggest, 'Garfinkel invited [us] ... to embark upon a voyage in a "boat without a bottom"' (p. 84).

Did Sacks and CA 'sell out' ethnomethodology, as Lynch and Bogen imply? Or did Sacks rescue Garfinkel's focus on members' 'interpretive procedures' from leading to a directionless recurring series of ironic 'demonstrations' of reflexivity (as Schegloff appears to imply)?

Clearly, I would not have written this book unless I believed that Sacks (and CA) do have a great deal to offer. At the same time, there are two reasons why I am cautious about choosing a 'side' in this debate. First, I would not dispute that contemporary wearers of Garfinkel's mantle continue to provide fascinating analyses of members' activities (see Lynch 1984; Livingston 1986). Second, I do not see why these two traditions cannot live side by side without making globalistic claims or sniping at one another – indeed this was precisely the import of my argument in chapter 7.

Frankly, having seen at first hand the destructive internal fights in the early years of ethnomethodology, I believe that the next generation should have learned enough to do better. Moreover, the continuing marginal status of both 'sides' in most departments of sociology should give pause for thought.

As I argue below, in assessing Sacks's achievement, such political issues cannot, unfortunately, be excluded. But internal rivalries are only part of the issue. As I go on to suggest, aesthetic judgements cannot be left out of account either. Not everybody will be tempted by Lynch and Bogen's voyage in a 'boat without a bottom', while others may recoil at the prospect of the sober, cumulative enterprise that is CA.

For, as we saw in chapter 2, there is no doubt that, unlike Garfinkel, Sacks aimed for a cumulative science of conversation. For subsequent generations of scholars, this opened up the exciting prospect of empirical examinations of how members somehow made sense together in talk-in-interaction. But, of course, this excitement can be seen as both aesthetic and political.

Bearing this in mind, the rest of this chapter deals, as briefly as possible, with the following four topics:

1 The politics of reading Sacks – in particular, how to preserve Sacks's work for a variety of audiences.
2 Sacks as the inspiration for an aesthetic of social research.
3 Sacks's relevance beyond conversation analysis – particularly for anthropology and ethnography and for psychology and discourse analysis.
4 Sacks's relevance for other users – particularly social science students and people concerned with 'social problems'.

The Politics of Readings

In his introductions to the two volumes of Sacks's lectures, Schegloff makes it clear that he understands that 'political' issues are important in how we read Sacks. Writing about how the 'textual adjustments' made by Gail Jefferson in her editing of the tapes of the lectures may have created a political impression of Sacks's position, Schegloff explains: 'By "political" I mean, in this context, a relative positioning by Sacks of himself, his undertakings, his colleagues, the established contours of the disciplines etc.' (Schegloff in *LC1*: xi).

As I have just suggested, to answer the question of whether Sacks was 'undoing' Garfinkel's inspiration or turning it in a 'properly' empirical direction, we must take such a political position. In turn, our answers may have consequences for more than mere intellectual positions – for instance, in the hiring and firing of teachers and researchers.

Elsewhere (Silverman 1993a: 205–6), I have used Mary Douglas's work on 'anomaly' to discuss a way in which we can put such academic rivalries into context. Douglas (1975) shows how a central African tribe, the Lele, are an exception to a general tendency to reject apparently 'anomalous' entities. This suggests to Douglas that there may be no *universal* propensity to frown upon anomaly. If there is variability from community to community, then this must say something about their social organization.

Sure enough, there is something special about the Lele's social life. Their experience of relations with other tribes has been very successful. They exchange goods with them and have little experience of war. In relating well with other tribes, the Lele have successfully crossed a frontier or boundary exactly as do anomalous entities. Douglas takes the view that the Lele's response to anomaly derives from experiences grounded in their social organization. They perceive anomalous entities favourably because they cut across boundaries just as the Lele do in their cross-tribal trade. Conversely, since the Old Testament reads as a series of disastrous exchanges between the Israelites and other tribes, we should not be surprised that the ancient Israelites regarded anomalies unfavourably.

It seems to me that Douglas's account of the relation between responses to anomaly and experiences of boundary-crossing can also be applied to other settings (see Silverman 1993a: 206). Few can doubt that ethnomethodologists and conversation analysts have had bad experiences of exchanges with other groups. Certainly, this would also offer an anecdotal 'explanation' of the apparent desire of some contemporary writers to erect strong boundaries between Garfinkel and Sacks and to divide themselves between warring camps (so shunning anomaly).

In my reading, however, Sacks was not a 'strong boundaries' person. He showed that in his ability to draw inspiration from a wide variety of data (ranging from biblical scripture to novels and newspaper headlines) and technical approaches (including anthropology, linguistics and philosophy). Of course, it might be argued that we should not read too much into Sacks's openness. After all, this was the sixties, in which people were generally more laid back about such apparent audacity. And, in any event, if we believe Thomas Kuhn (1970), innovators usually give birth to a more sober and specialized 'normal science'.

However, I believe that we can still learn something from Sacks's example of challenging boundaries. It shows that conversation analysts need not be an 'armed camp', pulling together their wagons because of their fears of external threats. Indeed, just one part of Sacks's achievement was to show us how lateral thinking can be relevant to even the most specialized discipline.

Sacks's Aesthetic for Social Research

As I have already implied, even 'lateral thinking' can be a matter of taste. Consonant with my philosophy of 'inclusiveness', it seems to me that Sacks offers us a distinct aesthetic that inspires a range of contemporary social science extending beyond conversation analysis.

Elsewhere, I have set out some aspects of a contemporary aesthetic for qualitative research (Silverman 1997b). Here I want to emphasize those parts of that aesthetic which, I believe, we owe to Harvey Sacks.

1 Smallness

'Pursue truth, not rarity. The atypical can fend for itself ... And very often, when we are looking over several common truths, holding them next to one another in an effort to feel again what makes them true, rarities will mysteriously germinate in the charged space between them' (Baker 1996: 24). For Sacks, like the essayist Nicholson Baker, rarity was never the point. The mysterious germination of rarities out of the familiar to which Baker refers is matched by Schegloff's observation that in Sacks's work 'previously unsuspected details were critical resources in [seeing] what was getting done in and by the talk' (*LC1*: xviii).

As we saw in chapter 4, Sacks rejected 'the notion that you could tell right off whether something was important' (*LC1*: 28). He uses the case of biology to show how the study of an apparently minor object ('one bacterium') can revolutionize our knowledge. Why assume, for instance, you need to look at states and revolutions, when 'it's possible that some object, for example proverbs, may give an enormous understanding of the way humans do things and the kinds of objects they use to construct and order their affairs' (*LC1*: 28).

Like Sacks, Baker refuses to accept the prevailing version of the 'big' question. Baker's (1996) essays on apparently tiny topics from the history of punctuation to the aesthetics of nail-clippings and old library index cards may infuriate some readers. However, behind such seeming trivia lies what I take to be a serious intent – to seek clarity and insight by closely examining apparently 'small' objects. No reader of Sacks's lectures can doubt that, thirty years earlier, social scientists had been invited to walk down this very path, eschewing empty accounts of 'big' issues in favour of elegant analyses which make a lot out of a little.

2 *Slowness*

'The degree of speed is directly proportional to the intensity of forgetting' (Kundera 1996: 114). Milan Kundera's novels remind us of a world which demands immediate gratification in the form of simple narratives containing exciting 'incidents'. It has no time to gaze around, no desire to take pleasure in the unremarkable, no ability to view without background sounds or to listen without distracting images. Speed is all.

Like Kundera, Sacks speaks to us today about the pleasures of slowness. He adopts what he calls 'a counter-strategy' of choosing specifically *uninteresting* data (*LC1*: 293). In this way, he set out to try to make the unremarkable remarkable by 'picking up things which are so overwhelmingly true that if we are to understand that sector of the world, they are something we will have to come to terms with' (Sacks 1987: 56).

But none of this required indecent haste or over-rapid elaboration of large claims. As he said about one topic he set as a classroom exercise: 'the sort of things I'm trying to do are not particularly to develop anything like a comprehensive analysis of what actually happened, but to begin to set minimal constraints on what an explanation or a description of talking or doing things together would look like' (*LC2*: 26).

3 Clarity

'He felt as if he were seasick. He felt he was on a ship rolling in heavy seas' (Kafka 1953: 83). Kafka is describing, in *The Trial*, the emotions of Joseph K after an unsuccessful attempt to confront the court that has inexplicably arrested him. As he tries to work out the underlying rationality of his situation, he finds himself going round in circles and feels 'seasick'.

Perhaps it is only a small leap from Joseph K's ship to Garfinkel's 'boat without a bottom'. In any event, judging by Garfinkel's less than crystal-clear prose, his passengers might well feel seasick too. But if we are obsessed by the reflexivity of our own accounts, it seems that we have little choice but to circle around the limits of language, where our every proposition can only be an ironic demonstration of what makes it possible.

One response to this reflexive turn is found in the many texts of the 1980s that invited us to peer behind the curtain of social science narratives or even set out to construct new literary forms (Woolgar 1988; Mulkay 1985). However, such experimental writers need to be reminded of Kafka's caution about the modernist experiments in which he himself participated in the early years of the twentieth century (see Silverman and Torode 1980: 69–93; Silverman 1997b).

Kafka's (1961) wonderful short story 'Investigations of a dog' creates a marvellous image of 'Airdogs' (*Lufthunde*) who, like many European intellectuals, then as now, get above themselves. By contrast, as Greenberg (1971) notes, Kafka adopted a classically plain style, using German that avoided the verbal excesses of his late-Habsburg contemporaries.

Now, if we simply judge Sacks by his published writings, the phrase 'classical plainness' hardly comes to mind. Indeed, Sacks's tendency to write entirely in numbered points can make readers feel that they are confronting a text filled with some impenetrable logic. However, we need to bear in mind that Sacks often wrote in this way because of his desire to get things exactly 'right'. So, although the product appears difficult to the untutored eye, once we become familiar with Sacks's approach to his topic, it is easy to discern clear and testable propositions.

So at least Sacks wrote with the *aim* of clarity. And his lectures are as clear and as fresh as when they were given. Faced with the (post)modern reflexive turn celebrated by Garfinkel and his contemporary followers, Sacks and CA have undoubtedly elected the Enlightenment aesthetic of clarity. Whether readers – like Lynch and Bogen – see this as a cause for reproach seems to me ultimately an aesthetic judgement.

4 Non-Romantic

'The chief contribution of the romanticists to the prevailing concept of the person was their rhetorical creation of *the deep interior* ... the existence of a repository of capacities or characteristics lying deeply within human consciousness' (Gergen 1992: 208–9). Romantic accounts assume, as the psychologist Kenneth Gergen suggests, that 'human consciousness' has a 'deep interior'. Of course, as we learn from modernism, Romanticists adopt a style of writing which, through valorizing tropes like 'emotion' and 'authenticity', rhetorically constitute such a 'person'.

Although Gergen takes this argument in a postmodernist direction, we could use it to support Sacks's and ethnomethodology's focus on the properties of actual language use (as in members' descriptions). Indeed, this is implied in Gergen's discussion of 'representation as a communal artifact' (1992: 214).

Gergen's battle is against 'humanistic' psychologists who favour Romantic representations. As we saw in chapter 3, Sacks fought a similar battle against Romantic sociologists concerned with 'authentic' presentations of 'experience' (cf. Silverman 1989; 1993b). For Sacks, 'experience' exists through a powerful descriptive apparatus (see chapter 5). In his very first transcribed lecture, he warns his students against worrying about the speed with which people do things:

> Don't worry about how fast they're thinking. First of all, don't worry about whether they're 'thinking'. Just try to come to terms with how it

is that the thing comes off. Because you'll find that they can do these things. Just take any other area of natural science and see, for example, how fast molecules do things. And they don't have very good brains. So just let the materials fall as they may. (*LC1*: 11)

Sacks's preparedness to celebrate the study of molecules in the natural sciences as a model for social science still has the power to shock contemporary Romanticists – perhaps in the same way as beginning sociology students are even today shocked by Émile Durkheim's (1982) nineteenth-century injunction to treat 'social facts' as 'things'. In both cases, I believe, the sense of shock derives from the profoundly Romantic turn of contemporary cultural representations.

Milan Kundera has attempted to unpick the modern world's version of 'authentic' experience in the stirring parades of Soviet Eastern Europe and the 'revealing' biography or chat-show interview of the contemporary media. For Kundera, East and West offer two versions of kitsch dressed up in different clothes (see Atkinson and Silverman 1997).

The kitsch world of the chat show (and the Romantic sociologist) depends on the valorization of 'personal experience'. In this context, Sacks's observation that experiences are 'carefully regulated sorts of things' (*LC2*: 248) comes as a shock. But, as Sacks shows, you are indeed only entitled to have certain 'experiences'. For instance, on being told about someone's good experience, you can be 'pleased for her' but there are sharp limits on how good you can feel about it and even sharper limits on the good feeling you can give to a third party with the story (*LC2*: 244).

Sacks was able to show us these things because, as Schegloff comments, he was prepared to examine talk 'as an object in its own right, and not merely as a screen on which are projected other processes' (Schegloff in *LC1*: xviii). But this conceptual preference also expressed, I believe, a profoundly anti-Romantic aesthetic preference. When wedded to slow (and careful) pursuit of (apparently) small objects, described with clarity, I suggest that Sacks offers an inspiring path for any contemporary social science which is prepared to take a step away from the powerful messages provided by the prevailing representations of our time. In this sense, it is not just CA specialists who should (and do) still read Sacks.

Beyond Conversation Analysis

Goodwin and Heritage (1990: 301) refer to 'the great debate between cognitive anthropology and cultural materialists on the status of emic analysis'. The debate turns on the relative reliability of native and analysts' understandings of culture. However, as both Garfinkel and Sacks show, commonsense and analytic under-standings are in no way *competitive*. Instead, the point is to see how members produce the sense that they do without confusing commonsense interpretations with social science explanations.

These imperatives have been taken on board in two major ethnographies by anthropologists (Moerman 1988 and Goodwin 1990). As Goodwin and Heritage argue, these writers do not appeal to natives' accounts, but instead rely upon the actions of participants themselves as they interactively and sequentially make sense. In terms of my argument above, we might call such studies examples of non-Romantic ethnography. As I noted earlier, they also serve to reopen a debate between ethnography and Durkheim (see also Gubrium 1988).

As an instance of this, the reader might try to guess the author of the following observation: 'Folk beliefs have honorable status but they are not the same intellectual object as a scientific analysis.' If you guessed that the author was Émile Durkheim you were wrong but also right in the sense that the observation could be seen as true to Durkheim's dictum to treat 'social facts' as 'things'. Its actual author was the anthropologist (and Sacks's colleague) Michael Moerman (1974: 55).

Of course, unlike Durkheim, ethnographers can take from Sacks a concern with understanding the 'apparatus' through which members' descriptions are properly (that is, locally) produced. And this message has been taken on board by sociological ethno-graphers like Gubrium (1988; 1989), who are centrally concerned with the descriptive process.

In a series of ethnographies, Gubrium has shown how, in local environments, descriptions are cooperatively assembled. For instance in a support group for patients suffering from Alzheimer's disease, one caregiver could be variously described as an exemplary devoted wife or as a 'second victim' who showed the bad effects of 'over-devotion' (1988: 100–1). In a residential treat-ment centre for emotionally disturbed children, 'disturbance' tended to be framed as a 'therapeutic' problem during the day shift and as a problem of 'patient management' at night (pp. 103–6). Equally, at a physical rehabilitation hospital, 'progress' was defined in 'educational' terms to patients who were told they could only get better through their own efforts. However, for insurance companies, who were paying the bill for these patients, progress was related to medical interventions. Finally, for families of patients at this hospital, successful progress was related to medical interventions; lack of progress to lack of patient motivation (p. 107).

Gubrium does not set out to do MCD analysis or still less CA. This is seen clearly in the way his analysis appeals to non-sequential matters and involves more conventional ethnographic concepts (like 'frame'). However, although Gubrium's work is clearly *not* conversation analysis, he does write ethnographies concerned with how descriptions are locally accomplished. Acknowledging his debt to Sacks, Gubrium shows how participants use time, space and audience to produce 'sensible' accounts.

If a case can be made out for Sacks's influence on (some) ethnography, it would appear at first sight difficult to make the same case for psychology. After all, Sacks's analysis of the sequential organization of conversation clearly reveals the inadequacies of any analyst's attempt to treat any utterance as an expression of someone's thoughts or, indeed, of any other apparently 'psychological' categories.

By contrast, in hearing how what they have just said is heard, speakers discover what they meant *after they have spoken* (for examples of this, drawn from AIDS counselling interviews, see Silverman 1997a: 78–84, 100–6). The critical implications of this for any psychology of, say, 'motive' are effectively underlined by Heritage (1974: 278–9), who reveals the inadequacies of any social psychology which tacitly treats common sense as both a resource and a topic.

More recently, however, Derek Edwards, while reiterating Heritage's critique, has called for a psychology able 'to follow Sacks and look at how people use categories interactively' (1995: 582). Accepting that 'talk is action not communication', Edwards argues for a psychology which draws from Sacks and CA the assumption that there is 'no hearable level of detail that may not be significant, or treated as significant by conversational participants' (p. 580).

The direction in which Edwards wants to take psychology clearly leads towards what has become called discourse analysis or DA (see Billig 1992; Edwards and Potter 1992; Gilbert and Mulkay 1984;

Potter and Wetherell 1987; Potter 1997). A straightforward version of DA has recently been offered by one of its leading exponents:

> DA is characterised by a meta-theoretical emphasis on anti-realism and constructionism. That is, DA emphasises the way versions of the world, of society, events, and inner psychological worlds are produced in discourse. On the one hand, this leads to a concern with participants' constructions and how they are accomplished and undermined; and, on the other, it leads to a recognition of the constructed and contingent nature of researchers' own versions of the world. (Potter 1997: 146)

At first glance, as Edwards implies, this seems to represent a fairly accurate reading of Sacks's programme. However, as Schegloff points out, in practice DA has not always been responsive to the relevance of all aspects of talk to the local production of sense. For instance, DA may treat particles like 'mm', and 'uh huh' as 'conversational "detritus" apparently lacking semantic content, and not contributing to the substance of what the discourse ends up having said' (Schegloff 1982: 74). For Schegloff, then, DA ignores a basic aspect of CA by treating talk:

> as the product of a single speaker and a single mind; the conversation-analytic angle of inquiry does not let go of the fact that speech-exchange systems are involved, in which more than one co-participant is present and relevant to the talk, even when only one does the talking. (p. 72)

It is for the reader to judge whether, given the time that has passed since Schegloff wrote, DA is still susceptible to Schegloff's criticisms. Certainly, there is some evidence in recent work (such as Potter 1997) that at least some DA researchers pay considerable attention to the turn-by-turn organization of talk. Of course, if this is so, we may end up in a pointless debate about whether such work is DA or CA! Indeed, in some cases, this distinction has more to do with whether the author pays his or her disciplinary dues to, respectively, psychology or sociology.

In any event, writers who use the term DA have undoubtedly succeeded in showing the unlikely legacy that Sacks has given psychology. In a more obvious way, as we have seen, Sacks's contemporary influence also extends beyond conversation analysis and into ethnography, whether located in departments of anthropology, sociology or even education (see Watson 1992).

Other Potential 'Users'

Having shown how ethnographers and psychologists have learned from Sacks, I now want to touch briefly on Sacks's potential relevance for two other groups of people so far largely untouched by his example. I refer to social science students and people concerned with 'social problems'.

I suspect that the work of Harvey Sacks is often not even a minor component in contemporary social science courses. In part, no doubt, this reflects the unavailability of Sacks's lectures in published form until 1992. However, I suspect that it also reflects either plain ignorance in the social science community or straightforward prejudice against 'another of those ethnos'.

Perhaps one way to make teaching Sacks more inviting to social scientists is to suggest that it might be a successful way to introduce more life into certain tired courses. Personally, I have never wanted to teach courses in social theory which, in my prejudiced way, I assume often contain empty syntheses, deadening critiques and the latest fashions in jargon. Certainly, the consumers of such courses respond as if this is what they have been taught.

How invigorating then to introduce some of Sacks's examples on to such courses, such as 'the baby cried', the Vietnam pilot, and so on. Talking through such examples with students must surely convey a little of the liveliness of social theory and its potential to deal with the world around them. Even more obviously, it is difficult to see how a course on research methodology could not gain by using material from Sacks. In this sense, I would demand that Sacks's writings should be *basic* reading on introductory classes in social theory and method.

On the face of it, teachers of social problems and, even more so, caring professionals, would seem to be a very unlikely audience to appreciate Sacks's work. As I noted earlier in this book, Sacks refused to respond to suggestions that social science must justify itself by its contribution to 'society', as this question and answer session with a student shows:

Q: Will it ever have any possible relevance to the people who were involved in producing it?
A: It needn't have any relevance ... I take it that there's an enormous amount of studies that are not intended to be relevant. For example, studies of how cancer does cancer is not intended to build better cancer ... (LC1: 470)

In this answer, Sacks closely follows what Garfinkel terms 'ethno-methodological indifference' to questions of how things (whether cancer, social problems or, indeed, social science itself) *should be*. As I have already noted, his answer depends on a degree of sophistry – presumably the student did not intend that research should help cancer!

However, we do not have to judge Sacks's potential contribution to social problems by this answer. In particular, recent applied work using methods that ultimately derive from Sacks has, in my view, undoubtedly contributed to the solution of several practical issues, most notably in the field of organizational interaction (see Drew and Heritage 1992; Peräkylä 1995; Silverman 1997a).

The practical relevance of such 'applied' conversation analysis shows 'why language and interaction matter to the sociology of social problems' (Maynard 1988: 312). As Maynard points out, CA (and Sacks) can be useful precisely because it avoids any 'abstract formulation' of interaction (for instance, in terms of social science concepts like 'role', 'label', 'deviance'). So, if 'labelling' and 'societal reactions' set careers of deviance in motion, such motion depends upon 'the ordered activities of telling troubles and proposing problems' (1988: 325). Such ordered activities can be made visible because, as Maynard puts it, CA demands the 'observation and scrutiny of the details of actual talk and interaction' (p. 320).

Maynard concludes that CA is able to make a basic contribution to the study of fundamental social processes and problems. As he argues:

> To the extent that we have learned about such interactional phenomena as diversity, conflict, domination, troubles and problems, the institutional processing of deviance, and mediated versions of social problems, it is because we have propositions about systems of vernacular talk, turn-taking, troubles-telling, commonsense knowledge, conversational sequencing, rhetoric and so on. (p. 326)

Moreover, it is not just what Sacks said about turn-taking that is relevant to contemporary studies of social problems. Sacks's work on 'description' has inspired a generation of ethnographers who have studied topics as diverse as mental illness hearings (Holstein 1988), schemes to get the unemployed into work (Miller 1993), family therapy (Miller 1987; Gubrium 1992) and care of the elderly (Gubrium 1980).

Conclusion

In many respects, Schegloff sums up the four most crucial things which Sacks left us:

1 *A methodology* 'A most remarkable inventive and productive account of how to study human sociality' (*LC1*: xii).
2 *A topic* 'the distinctive and utterly critical recognition ... that ... talk can be examined in its own right, and not merely as a screen on which are projected other processes' (*LC1*:xviii).
3 *A discipline* 'whether or not the efforts of others succeed in establishing a discipline with satisfactory payoffs and sustainable continuity, we shall not have the discipline, or the understanding, which we would have had with him' (*LC2*: xlix).
4 *An inspiration* 'what is needed is a continuous re-energizing of inquiry by the example of his work and the possibilities which it revealed' (*LC2*: xlix).

However, Sacks's endeavour ultimately resists any formulation which either Schegloff or myself might offer. As Sacks himself put it:

> I can tell you something, but you have to be careful what you make of it ... The upshot of what I've said is this: I make no commitment to what kind of placing anyone makes of what it is that I do, nor to whatever recommendations anyone might provide me, which turn on such a treatment. (*LC1*: 621)

As with Wittgenstein and Saussure, Sacks's work is largely available to us in notebooks and lectures published posthumously. Like these other two great thinkers, Sacks will continue to exert an influence on many subsequent generations. However, although Sacks can inspire, he cannot tell us all that we have to do. Following Wittgenstein's (1971) analogy of the 'ladder', we can use Sacks's work to climb up higher, but we have to proceed carefully and thoughtfully. To repeat Sacks's words: 'I can tell you something, but you have to be careful what you make of it.'

Appendix 1
Simplified Transcription Symbols and Selected Abbreviations

Transcription Symbols

[	A: B:	quite a [while [yea	Left brackets indicate the point at which a current speaker's talk is overlapped by another's talk.
//	A:	Hi, Jim // c'mon in	Overlapping talk (now replaced in CA notation by square brackets, i.e. []).
=	A: B:	that I'm aware of = =Yes. Would you confirm that?	Equals signs, one at the end of a line and one at the beginning, indicate no gap between the two lines.
(.4)		Yes (.2) yeah	Numbers in parentheses indicate elapsed time in silence in tenths of a second.
(.)		to get (.) treatment	A dot in parentheses indicates a tiny gap, probably no more than one-tenth of a second.
_____		What's <u>up</u>?	Underscoring indicates some form of stress, via pitch and/or amplitude.
::		O:<u>kay</u>?	Colons indicate prolongation of the immediately prior sound. The length of the row

		of colons indicates the length of the prolongation.
WORD	I've got ENOUGH TO WORRY ABOUT	Capitals, except at the beginnings of lines, indicate especially loud sounds relative to the surrounding talk.
.hhhh	I feel that (.2) .hhh	A row of h's prefixed by a dot indicates an inbreath; without a dot, an outbreath. The length of the row of h's indicates the length of the in- or outbreath.
( )	future risks and ( ) and life ( )	Empty parentheses indicate the transcriber's inability to hear what was said.
(word)	Would you see (there) anything positive	Parenthesized words are possible hearings.
(( ))	confirm that ((continues))	Double parentheses contain author's descriptions rather than transcriptions.
> <	>an'ibody<	Greater than and less than symbols enclose talk that is noticeably faster than surrounding talk.
° °	° or (0.7) um°	Enclose speech softer than surrounding talk.
?	What do you think?	Indicates rising intonation.
.	That's all.	Falling intonation.
,	First,	Flat or slightly rising intonation.

Abbreviations

AIS	Advice-as-Information-Sequence
CA	Conversation analysis
CBA	Category-bound activity
DA	Discourse analysis
MCD	Membership categorization device
POTS	Proposal of the situation
RT	Response token
SRP	Standardized relational pair

Appendix 2
Sacks's Lectures: Some Key References

Membership Categorization

An initial formulation LC1: 40–8, lecture 6, fall 1964–spring 1965.
Category-bound activities LC1: 179–181, lecture 8, fall 1965; LC1: 301–2, lecture 4, spring 1966; LC1: 333–40, lecture 8, spring 1966; LC1: 568–96, lectures 11–14, spring 1967.
The consistency rule LC1: 326–7, lecture 7, spring 1966.
The hotrodders example LC1: 169–74, lecture 7, fall 1965; LC1: 396–403, lecture 18, spring 1966.
The navy pilot example LC1: 205–22, research notes, fall 1965; LC1: 306–7, lecture 5, spring 1966.
The child's story LC1: 223–31, appendices A and B, fall 1965; LC1: 236–66, lectures 1–2(R), spring 1966.
On inferring LC1: 113–25, lecture 14, fall 1964–spring 1965.
'Identification reformulation' LC2: 126–31, lecture 8, winter 1969.
Doing 'being ordinary' LC2: 215–21, lecture 1, spring 1970.
A 'defensively designed' story LC2: 453–7, lecture 6, fall 1971.

Conversation Analysis

The limits of linguistics LC1: 95; LC1: 647.
Rules of sequencing in conversation LC1: 95–103, fall 1964–spring 1965; LC2: 32–43, lecture 3, fall 1968; LC2: 223–6, lecture 2, spring 1970.

Adjacency pairs LC2: 188–96, lecture 4, winter 1970; LC2: 533–6, lecture 2, spring 1972; LC2: 554–60, lecture 4, spring 1972.

Insertion sequences LC2: 528–9, lecture 1, spring 1972.

Greeting sequences LC1: 96–9, lecture 12, fall 1964–spring 1965; LC1: 306–11, lecture 6, spring 1966.

The 'chaining rule' LC1: 49–56, lecture 7, fall 1964–spring 1965; LC1: 102–3, lecture 12, fall 1964–spring 1965.

Speaker transition LC1: 527, March 2, winter 1967; LC1: 665–7, lecture 6, fall 1967.

Telephone calls LC1: 1–11, lecture 1, fall 1964–spring 1965; LC1: 624–32, lecture 1, fall 1967; LC2: 157–74, lecture 1, winter 1970; LC2: 360–6, April 19, spring 1971.

Storytelling LC1: 681–4, lecture 7, fall 1967; LC2: 3–16, lecture 1, fall 1968; LC2: 303–17, March 4, winter 1971.

Story prefaces LC2: 226–8, lecture 2, spring 1970; LC2: 256–65, lecture 5, spring 1970.

Tying rules LC1: 370–5, lecture 14, spring 1966; LC2: 6–8, lecture 1, fall 1968; LC2: 352, April 9, spring 1971; LC2: 554–60, lecture 4, spring 1972.

'Next' position and repairs LC2: 554–60, lecture 4, spring 1972.

Response tokens LC1: 746–7, lecture 14, fall 1967; LC2: 410–12, May 24, spring 1971.

Pre-sequences LC1: 304–5, lecture 5, spring 1966; LC1: 685–92, lecture 8, fall 1967.

Preference organization LC2: 414, May 24, spring 1971.

Laughter LC2: 275, lecture 7, spring 1970; LC2: 395, May 10, spring 1971.

Appendix 3
Summaries of Sacks's
Major Published Papers

Harvey Sacks, **'Sociological description'** *Berkeley Journal of Sociology*, 8 (1963), 1–16.

- Notes his indebtedness to Garfinkel for his funding (from a US Air Force grant) and for 'the stimulus for these thoughts'. Indeed, in this paper, Sacks acknowledges his use of Garfinkel's concepts of 'the commonsense perspective', 'practical theorizing', the 'etcetera principle' (p. 10) and the topic/resource distinction (p. 16). But adds that Garfinkel 'is far from agreeing with all that I have to say' (p. 1n).
- Based on his reading of Durkheim (*Suicide*) and Weber's methodological writings: aim 'to make current sociology strange' because 'the stance it adopts towards its subject matter seems so peculiar to me' (p. 1).
- How does this arise?
  1 Sociology seeks to be a science;
  2 science seeks a 'literal' description of its subject matter;
  3 but uses concepts ('a descriptive apparatus') based on unexplicated assumptions (p. 2).
- 'The essential "message" of this paper is: even if it can be said that persons produce descriptions of the social world, the task of sociology is not to clarify these, or to "get them on the record" or to criticize them, but to describe them' (p. 7).
- Uses the example of 'a machine which the layman might describe in the following terms': 'It has two parts; one part is engaged in doing some job, and the other part synchronically

narrates what the first part does. For the commonsense perspective the machine might be called a "commentator machine", its parts "the doing" and "the saying" parts' (p. 5).

- For a native speaking sociologist, the 'saying' part of the machine is to be analysed as a good, poor or ironical description of the actual working of the machine (pp. 5–6).

- But this trades off two kinds of unexplicated knowledge: 'a. knowing in common with the machine the language it emits and b. knowing in some language what the machine is doing' (p. 6).

- Trades off a set of commonsense assumptions: relation between 'facts' and 'fancy' using everyday language.

- So: 'that persons describe social life ... is a happening' which 'poses the job of sociology' (p. 7) i.e. to describe 'practical theories' rather than tacitly to use them.

- Problem with Durkheim: 'The crucial problem with Durkheim's *Suicide* is not that he employs official statistics, but that he adopts the problem of practical theory. "Suicide" is a category of the natural language. It leads to a variety of practical problems, such as, for example, explaining particular suicides or explaining the variety of suicide rates. To say that Durkheim's error was to use official records rather than for example studying the variation in the reporting of suicides is to suppose that it is obvious that events occur which sociologists should consider "really suicide" ... An investigation of how it is that a decision that a suicide occurred is assembled, and an investigation of how an object must be conceived in order to talk of it as "committing suicide", these are the preliminary problems for sociology. Till we have described the category, suicide, i.e. produced a description of the procedure employed for assembling cases of the class, the category is not even potentially part of the sociological apparatus' (p. 8, n. 8).

- Shows how Sacks's version of sociology is radically different from interactionist or subjectivist sociologies which, in Sacks's and Garfinkel's view, take for granted some social 'reality' to which people respond or describe a process (e.g. 'labelling') identified on the basis of tacit commonsense reasoning. Returning to 'suicide': 'To employ an undescribed category is to write descriptions such as appear in children's books. Interspersed with series of words there are pictures of objects' (p. 8, n. 8).

- Notes that most sociology proceeds on the basis simply of pointing at familiar objects (what philosophers call 'ostensive' definition). Able to claim that they are offering a 'literal' description by invoking 'what everybody knows' about how things are in society to cover 'neglect [of] some undetermined set of their features' (p. 13) (the 'etcetera principle').

• It is no solution simply to seek agreement among sociologists (e.g. intercoder agreement as a basis for claiming that one's descriptions are reliable) because such agreement would depend upon the 'etcetera' principle.

• How can we build a sociology that does more? 'Sociology must free itself from the common-sense perspective' (pp. 10–11). How? By treating commonsense categories 'as features of social life which sociology must treat as subject matter' rather than 'as sociological resources' (p. 16).

Michael Moerman and Harvey Sacks, **'On understanding in conversation'** unpublished paper, 70th annual meeting, American Anthropological Association, New York City, 20 November 1971.

• Why do people understand one another? Anthropology appeals to 'culture', linguistics to the linguistic organization that allows speakers to understand novel sentences. But what about *social* organization? 'What forms of social organization secure the recurrence of understanding among parties to conversation, the central institution of language use?' (MS 3).

• Ethnomethodology/reflexivity: 'What forms of social organization get participants to occasions of talk to do the work of understanding the talk of others in the very ways and at the same times as they do that work?' (MS 3).

• CA: Similarities between Thai and American English speakers. That one speaker talks at a time with no gaps or overlaps is accomplished by:
  –speakers noticing and correcting violations;
  –collaboratively locating transition points;
  –collaboratively locating next speaker;
  –co-participants listening for completions, turn transitions, insults, etc.
  'Participants must continually, there and then – without recourse to follow-up tests, mutual examination of memoirs, surprise quizzes and other ways of checking on understanding – demonstrate to one another that they understood or failed to understand the talk they are party to' (MS 10).

- 'The instant availability of elaborate rules of grammar shows that our naive notion of how little the human brain can do quickly is wrong' (MS 11).

Harvey Sacks, **'Notes on police assessment of moral character'** in D. Sudnow (ed.), *Studies in Social Interaction* (New York: Free Press, 1972), pp. 280–93.

- Using Adam and Eve as the example, Sacks notes that 'to be observable is to be embarrassable' (p. 281). Problem: how we infer moral character from appearances (cf. Goffman).
- How police 'learn to treat their beat as a territory of normal appearances' (p. 284). Now can treat slight variations as incongruities worthy of investigation, working with the assumption of 'normal' crimes (cf. Sudnow).
- Looks like Goffman – indeed Sacks notes that the paper was originally written when he was a student on one of Goffman's courses (p. 280n). But unlike Goffman:
  –Numbered points (cf. Wittgenstein).
  –Sacks also notes that he is 'much indebted' to Garfinkel (p. 280n). This is seen in Sacks's insistence that there is no definitive set of features that constitutes an investigable incongruity (this means that members must use 'ad hoc' understandings).

Harvey Sacks, **'On the analyzability of stories by children'** in J. Gumperz and D. Hymes (eds), *Directions in Sociolinguistics* (New York: Holt, Rinehart and Winston, 1972), pp. 325–45.

- MCD: 'any collection of membership categories, containing at least a category, which may be applied to some population containing at least a member, so as to provide, by the use of some rules of application, for the pairing of at least a population member and a categorization device member. A device is then a collection plus rules of application' (p. 332).
- The economy rule: 'a single category from any MCD can be referentially adequate' (p. 333).
- Duplicative organization: The device 'family' is one of a series that can be heard as constituting a 'team'. Duplicative organization means that we treat any 'set of categories as defining a unit,

and place members of the population into cases of the unit. If a population is so treated and is then counted, one counts not numbers of daddies, numbers of mommies, and numbers of babies but numbers of families – numbers of "whole families", numbers of "families without fathers", etc.' (p. 334).

Harvey Sacks, **'An initial investigation of the usability of conversational data for doing sociology'** in D. Sudnow (ed.), *Studies in Social Interaction* (New York: Free Press, 1972), pp. 31–74.

- Sacks acknowledges Garfinkel's 'pervasive impact on me' (p. 32n).
- 'For any population there are at least two categorization devices available to Members' (p. 32).
- '*Consistency Rule*. If some population of persons is being categorized, and if some category from a device's collection has been used to categorize a first Member of the population, then that category or other categories of the same collection *may* be used to categorize further members of the population' (p. 33).
- MCDs, especially the economy rule, as a way of addressing children's socialization: learning how single categories fit into collections; learning various combinatorial tasks – but they have already learned 'what in principle adequate reference consists of' (p. 35).
- Collection R: a collection of paired relational categories (standardized relational pairs – SRPs) 'that constitutes a locus for a set of rights and obligations concerning the activity of giving help' (p. 37) e.g. husband–wife, parent–child, neighbour–neighbour, boyfriend–girlfriend, etc.
- Device R provides members with a search procedure (e.g. search for help with suicidal people; being suicidal as a result of an analysis; 'I have no one to turn to') (pp. 53–5).
- Programmatic relevance: 'if R is relevant, then the non-incumbency of any of its pair positions is an observable, i.e. can be proposedly a fact' (p. 38), e.g. missing players in a sporting team (some non-incumbencies as being a criterion of suicidalness, e.g. a widow).
- Collection K: 'a collection constructed by reference to special distributions of knowledge existing about how to deal with some trouble' (p. 37), e.g. suicidalness and professionals and their clients.

Emanuel A. Schegloff and Harvey Sacks, **'Opening up Closings'** in R. Turner (ed.), *Ethnomethodology* (Harmondsworth: Penguin, 1974), pp. 233–64.

- Seek to achieve: 'a naturalistic observational discipline that could deal with the details of social action(s) rigorously, empirically and formally' (p. 233).
- Orderliness for members: 'insofar as the materials we worked with exhibited orderliness, they did so not only to us, indeed not in the first place for us, but for the co-participants who had produced them' (p. 234). Problems have to be problems for members in order to be interesting for analysts (p. 234).
- Culture: Rejection of Dell Hymes's suggestion that they might characterize their findings as relating to 'conversation rules in American English' (p. 235) – depends on appeal to national and language identification but cite Moerman to the contrary.
- Closings: How to arrive at a point 'where one speaker's completion will not occasion another speaker's talk, and that will not be heard as some speaker's silence' (p. 237). Examples:
  –an exchange of 'good-byes' where completion of the pair demonstrates that last speaker has understood what the prior term was aimed at and goes along with it (p. 240);
  –preceded by a 'closing section' (p. 242), later termed 'pre-closing' (p. 246), e.g. 'okay.' or 'we-ell' or in telephone calls by referring to the interests of the called party, e.g. 'well I'll letchu go', or to the caller, e.g. 'This is costing you a lot of money', or by reference to previous activities cited by called party (watching TV, eating, having people over) (p. 250).

Harvey Sacks, Emanuel A. Schegloff and Gail Jefferson, **'A simplest systematics for the organization of turn-taking in conversation'** *Language*, 50.4 (1974), pp. 696–735.

- An economy (cf. Saussure on synchronic disciplines): 'For socially organized activities, the presence of "turns" suggests an economy, with turns for something being valued – and with means for allocating them, which affect their relative distribution, as in economies' (p. 696).
- Context: e.g. places, times and identities of the participants: 'conversation is always "situated" – always comes out of, and is part of, some real sets of circumstances of its participants'

(p. 699). But 'it is undesirable to have to know or characterize such situations for particular conversations in order to investigate them' (p. 699).

- 'Turn-taking organization for conversation ... [as] context-free and capable of extraordinary context-sensitivity' (p. 699). Context-free: 'major aspects of the organization of turn-taking are insensitive to such parameters of context' (p. 699n). Context-sensitivity: 'it is the context-free structure which defines how and where context-sensitivity can be displayed' (p. 699n).
- Conversation as 'the basic form of speech-exchange system' (p. 730), e.g. length and ordering of turns pre-specified in interviews or debates (p. 701); 'linear array' of turn-taking systems:
  –local allocation to preserve one-turn-at-a-time;
  –pre-allocation of all turns;
  –medial types (exemplified by meetings) involve various mixes of pre-allocational and local-allocational means (p. 729).
- Looking at functions of each turn-taking system (p. 730).
- Sequences: 'Turns display gross organizational features that reflect their occurrence in a series. They regularly have a three-part structure: one which addresses the relation of a turn to a prior, one involved with what is occupying the turn, and one which addresses the relation of the turn to a succeeding one' (p. 722), e.g. repair mechanisms:
  –who is to speak? (Who me? Or stopping an interruption when first speaker continues.)
  –repairs of utterances done within a turn (p. 724).

Harvey Sacks, **'Everyone has to lie'** in M. Sanches and B. G. Blount (eds), *Sociocultural Dimensions of Language Use* (New York: Academic Press, 1975), pp. 57–79.

- 'Everyone has to lie' not as something to be sad about but something to be grateful for, e.g. greeting sequences don't usually call for a 'true' response to 'how are you' (pp. 71, 78); bores are people who tell us how they really feel.
- 'Everyone' might refer only to a relatively small group (among people we know, everyone who is anyone) (p. 63) – what 'everyone' means 'turns on the [complete] utterance and the occasion on which it was used' (p. 64).
- We often hear assertions regarding the qualities of certain classes of people, e.g. lawyers, males, women. But do members

of such classes who don't fit the bill *disprove* the assertion? No: for instance, his failure to conform to the assertion may simply reflect on 'his status as a proper member of that class' (p. 60) (e.g. not 'really' a man etc.).

Harvey Sacks, **'Hotrodder: a revolutionary category'** in G. Psathas (ed.), *Everyday Language: Studies in Ethnomethodology* (New York: Irvington, 1979), pp. 7–14.

- 'Teenager' part of a category system that adults administer. 'Hotrodder' as a counter-category not enforced by ruling groups, hence these groups no longer able to 'recognize whether somebody is a member of [the] category and what that membership takes' (p. 11).
- Categories implicated in systems of social control: 'any person who is a case of a category is seen as a member of a category, and what's known about that category is known about them, and the fate of each is bound up in the fate of the other [so] if a member does something like rape a white woman, commit economic fraud, race on the street, etc., then that thing will be seen as what a member of some applicable category does, not what some named person did. And the rest of them will have to pay for it' (p. 13).
- By implication, 'social order' can be seen as sets of categories + rules of application. Social change = shifts in the properties of categories and in their rules of application (p. 14).

Harvey Sacks, **'Notes on methodology'** in J. M. Atkinson and J. Heritage (eds), *Structures of Social Action: Studies in Conversation Analysis* (Cambridge: Cambridge University Press, 1984), pp. 21–7 (based on transcripts of several lectures).

- Ethnomethodology and CA have established a unique domain which 'seeks to describe methods persons use in doing social life' (p. 21).
- Explanations in terms of social structures are avoided in favour of description of members' practices: 'whatever humans do can be examined to discover some way they do it' (p. 22).
- 'There is order at all points' (p. 22): so infants experience a small part of that order, yet 'come out in many ways much like

everybody else' and 'research might employ the same resources. Tap into whomsoever, wheresoever and we get much the same things' (p. 22). 'Given the possibility that there is overwhelming order, it would be extremely hard *not* to find it, no matter how or where we looked' (p. 23).

- Observation is used as a basis for theorizing. 'Thus we can start with things that are not currently imaginable, by showing that they happened' (p. 25). Therefore 'the kind of phenomena I deal with are always transcriptions of actual occurrences in their actual sequence' (p. 25).
- Tape-recorded conversations are used because they can be replayed, 'not from any large interest in language' (p. 26).
- The interest is not in any particular conversation but in transforming 'our view of "what happened" from a matter of a particular interaction done by particular people, to a matter of interactions as products of a machinery' (p. 26).
- 'We are trying to find the machinery. In order to do so we have to get access to its products' (pp. 26–7).
- Problems are not to be brought to the data but instead 'make a bunch of observations and see where they will go' (p. 27); 'an 'unmotivated examination' of data (p. 27).

Harvey Sacks, **'On doing "being ordinary"'** in J. M. Atkinson and J. Heritage (eds), *Structures of Social Action: Studies in Conversation Analysis* (Cambridge: Cambridge University Press, 1984), pp. 513–29.

- Initial reports of President Kennedy's assassination were of hearing a car backfiring – people work at producing banal explanations as their first thoughts.

Harvey Sacks, **'On the preferences for agreement and contiguity in sequences in conversation'** in G. Button and J. R. E. Lee, *Talk and Social Organization* (Clevedon, Pa.: Multilingual Matters, 1987), pp. 54–69 (from a 1970 lecture, edited by E. Schegloff).

- Sequential analysis of conversation: rough meaning 'that the parts which are occurring one after the other, or are in some before and after relationship, have some organization as between them' (p. 54).

- Generality: 'omnipresence and ready observability need not imply *banality*, and, therefore, silence. Nor should they only set off a search for exceptions or variation. Rather, we need to see that with some such mundane occurrences we are picking up things which are so overwhelmingly true that if we are to understand that sector of the world, they are something we will have to come to terms with' (p. 56, emphasis added).
- Apparatus: On preference for agreement, 'it is not that "people try to do it" ... [rather] there is an *apparatus* that has them being able to do that' (p. 65).
- Preference organization: 'If a question is built in such a way as to exhibit a preference as between "yes" and "no" ... then the answerers will pick that choice' (p. 57) and will delay any other elements. Yes-like preference:

A: And it– apparently left her quite permanently damaged (I suppose).
B: Apparently. Uh he is still hopeful. (p. 57)

No-like preference:

A: Well is this really whatchu wanted?
B: Uh ... not originally? <u>No</u>. But it's uh ... promotion? en it's <u>very</u> interesting. (p. 57)

'well' prefaces, warrants and 'excepts' as well as delays in dispreferred turns:

A: Yuh coming down early?
B: Well, I got a lot of things to do before gettin cleared up tomorrow. I don't know. I w–probably won't be too early. (p. 58)

A: 'N they haven't heard a <u>word</u> huh?
B: Not a word, <u>uh</u>–uh. Not– Not a word. Not at all. <u>Except</u> – Neville's mother got a call. (p. 63)

Cooperative: where questioners monitor an upcoming disagreement, they reformulate their question in the direction of possible agreement (p. 65).

References

Albert, E. (1964) Rhetoric, logic, and poetics in Burundi: cultural patterning of speech behavior. *American Anthropologist*, 66(6), part 2, 33–54.

Atkinson, J. M. (1982) Understanding formality. *British Journal of Sociology*, 33(1), 86–117.

Atkinson, J. M. and Drew, P. (1979) *Order in Court: The Organization of Verbal Interaction in Judicial Settings*. London: Macmillan.

Atkinson, J. M. and Heritage, J. (eds) (1984) *Structures of Social Action: Studies in Conversation Analysis*. Cambridge: Cambridge University Press.

Atkinson, P. and Silverman, D. (1997) Kundera's *Immortality*: the interview society and the invention of self. *Qualitative Inquiry*, 3(3), 304–25.

Austin, J. L. (1962) *How to Do Things with Words*. Oxford: Clarendon Press.

Baker, C. D. (1982) Adolescent–adult talk as a practical interpretive problem. In G. Payne and E. Cuff (eds), *Doing Teaching: The Practical Management of Classrooms*, London: Batsford, 104-25.

Baker, C. D. (1984) The search for adultness: membership work in adolescent–adult talk. *Human Studies*, 7, 301–23.

Baker, N. (1996) *The Size of Thoughts*. London: Chatto.

Bales, R. F. (1950) *Interaction Process Analysis*. Cambridge: Addison-Wesley.

Barthes, R. (1977) *Image, Music, Text*. London: Fontana.

Billig, M. (1992) *Talking of the Royal Family*. London: Routledge.

Blumer, H. (1969) On the methodological status of symbolic interaction. In H. Blumer, *Symbolic Interactionism*, Englewood Cliffs: Prentice Hall, 1–60.

Boden, D. and Zimmerman, D. (eds) (1991) *Talk and Social Structure*. Cambridge: Polity Press.

Button, G. (1992) Answers as interactional products: two sequential practices used in job interviews. In Drew and Heritage 1992.

Chomsky, N. (1965) *Aspects of the Theory of Syntax*. Cambridge: MIT Press.

Clavarino, A., Najman, J. and Silverman, D. (1995) Assessing the quality of qualitative data. *Qualitative Inquiry*, 1(2), 223–42.

Clayman, S. C. (1992) Footing in the achievement of neutrality: the case of news-interview discourse. In Drew and Heritage 1992, 163–98.

Cuff, E. C. (1980) Some issues in studying the problem of versions in everyday life. *Manchester Sociology Occasional Papers*, no. 3, Manchester University.

Cuff, E. C. and Payne, G. C. (eds) (1979) *Perspectives in Sociology*. London: Allen and Unwin.

Douglas, M. (1975) Self-evidence. In M. Douglas, *Implicit Meanings*, London: Routledge.

Drew, P. (1978) Accusations: the occasioned use of members' knowledge of 'religious geography' in describing events. *Sociology*, 12, 1–22.

Drew, P. and Heritage, J. C. (eds) (1992) *Talk at Work*. Cambridge: Cambridge University Press.

Drew, P. and Holt, E. (1988) Complainable matters: the use of idiomatic expressions in making complaints. *Social Problems*, 35(4), 398–417.

Durkheim, É. (1952) *Suicide: A Study in Sociology*, trans. J. A. Spaulding and G. Simpson. London: Routledge.

Durkheim, É. (1982) *The Rules of Sociological Method*, trans. W. D. Halls. London: Macmillan.

Edwards, D. (1995) Sacks and psychology. *Theory and Psychology*, 5(3), 579–96.

Edwards, D. and Potter, J. (1992) *Discursive Psychology*. London: Sage.

Eglin, P. and Hester, S. (1992) Category, predicate and task: the pragmatics of practical action. *Semiotica*, 88(3–4), 243–68.

Evans-Pritchard, E. E. (1937) *Witchcraft, Oracles and Magic among the Azande*. Oxford: Oxford University Press.

Filmer, P., Phillipson, M., Silverman, D. and Walsh, D. (1972) *New Directions in Sociological Theory*. London: Collier-Macmillan.

Garfinkel, E. (1967) *Studies in Ethnomethodology*, Englewood Cliffs: Prentice Hall.

Gellner, E. (1975) Ethnomethodology: the re-enchantment industry or a Californian way of subjectivity. *Philosophy of the Social Sciences*, 5(4), 431–50.

Gergen, K. (1992) Organization theory in the postmodern era. In M. Reed and M. Hughes (eds), *Rethinking Organization: Directions in Organization Theory and Analysis*, London: Sage, 207–26.

Giglioli, P.-P. (ed.) (1972) *Language and Social Context*. Harmondsworth: Penguin.

Gilbert, G. N. and Mulkay, M. (1984) *Opening Pandora's Box: A Sociological Analysis of Scientists' Discourse*. Cambridge: Cambridge University Press.

Gladwin, T. (1964) Culture and logical process. In W. Goodenough (ed.), *Explorations in Cultural Anthropology*, New York: McGraw-Hill.

Goffman, E. (1959) *The Presentation of Self in Everyday Life*. New York: Doubleday Anchor.

Goffman, E. (1961) *Asylums*. New York: Doubleday Anchor.

Goffman, E. (1964) *Stigma: Notes on the Management of Spoiled Identity*. Englewood Cliffs: Prentice Hall.

Goffman, E. (1974) *Frame Analysis*. New York: Harper and Row.

Goffman, E. (1981) *Forms of Talk*. Oxford: Blackwell.

Goodwin, C. (1981) *Conversational Organization: Interaction between Speakers and Hearers*. New York: Academic Press.

Goodwin, C. and Heritage, J. (1990) Conversation analysis. *Annual Review of Anthropology*, 19, 283–307.

Goodwin, M. H. (1990) *He-Said-She-Said: Talk as Social Organization among Black Children*. Bloomington: Indiana University Press.

Goodwin, M. H. and Goodwin, C. (1986) Gesture and co-participation in the activity of searching for a word. *Semiotica*, 62(1–2), 51–75.

Greatbatch, D. (1992) On the management of disagreement among news interviewers. In Drew and Heritage 1992, 268–301.

Greenberg, M. (1971) *The Terror of Art: Kafka and Modern Literature*. London: Deutsch.

Gubrium, J. (1980) Patient exclusion in geriatric settings. *Sociological Quarterly*, 21, 335–48.

Gubrium, J. (1988) *Analyzing Field Reality*, Qualitative Research Methods Series, 8. Newbury Park: Sage.

Gubrium, J. (1989) Local cultures and service policy. In Gubrium and Silverman (eds), *The Politics of Field Research: Sociology beyond Enlightenment*, London: Sage, 94–112.

Gubrium, J. (1992) *Out of Control*. Newbury Park: Sage.

Gumperz, J. and Hymes, D. (eds) (1972) *Directions in Sociolinguistics*. New York: Holt, Rinehart and Winston.

Hammersley, M. (1989) *The Dilemma of Qualitative Method: Herbert Blumer and the Chicago Tradition*. Routledge: London.

Heath, C. C. (1986) *Body Movement and Speech in Medical Interaction*. Cambridge: Cambridge University Press.

Heath, C. C. (1997) Using video: analysing activities in face to face interaction. In Silverman 1997b, 183–200.

Heath, C. C. and Luff. P. (1992) Collaboration and control: crisis management and multimedia technology in London underground line control rooms. *Journal of Computer Supported Cooperative Work*, 1(1–2), 69–94.

Heritage, J. (1974) Assessing people. In N. Armistead (ed.), *Reconstructing Social Psychology*, Harmondsworth: Penguin, 260–81.

Heritage, J. (1984) *Garfinkel and Ethnomethodology*. Cambridge: Polity Press.

Heritage, J. (1985) Analyzing news interviews: aspects of the production of talk for an overhearing audience. In T. Van Dijk (ed.), *Handbook of Discourse Analysis*, vol. 3, London: Academic Press, 95–117.

Heritage, J. (1997) Conversation analysis and institutional talk: analyzing data. In Silverman 1997b.

Heritage, J. and Sefi, S. (1992) Dilemmas of advice: aspects of the delivery and reception of advice in interactions between health visitors and first time mothers. In Drew and Heritage 1992, 359–417.

Hester, S. and Eglin, P. (eds) (1996) *Membership Categorization*. Lanham: University Press of America.

Holstein, J. (1988) Court ordered incompetence: conversational organization in involuntary commitment hearings. *Social Problems*, 35(4), 458–73.

Homans, G. C. (1961) *Social Behaviour: Its Elementary Forms*. New York: Harcourt Brace.

Jayyusi, L. (1984) *Categorization and the Moral Order*. London: Routledge.

Kafka, F. (1953) *The Trial*. Harmondsworth: Penguin.

Kafka, F. (1961) Investigations of a dog. In F. Kafka, *Metamorphosis and Other Stories*, Harmondsworth: Penguin.

Kinnell, A. M. and Maynard, D. W. (1996) The delivery and receipt of safer sex advice in pre-test counseling sessions for HIV and AIDS. *Journal of Contemporary Ethnography*, 24(4), 405–37.

Kuhn, T. S. (1970) *The Structure of Scientific Revolutions*, 2nd edn. Chicago: University of Chicago Press.

Kundera, M. (1996) *Slowness*, trans. Linda Asher. London: Faber.

Lee, J. R. E. (1984) Innocent victims and evil doers. *Women's Studies: International Forum*, 7, 69–73.

Lepper, G. (1995) Making trouble: the uses of 'formal organization' as an institutional resource. *Studies in Cultures, Organizations and Societies*, 1, 189–207.

Levinson, S. C. (1983) *Pragmatics*. Cambridge: Cambridge University Press.

Libermann, K. (1985) *Understanding Interaction in Central Australia: An Ethnomethodological Study of Australian Aboriginal People*. London: Routledge.

Livingston, E. (1986) *The Ethnomethodological Foundations of Mathematics*. London: Routledge and Kegan Paul.

Lynch, M. (1984) *Art and Artifact in Laboratory Science*. London: Routledge.

Lynch, M. and Bogen, D. (1994) Harvey Sacks's primitive natural science. *Theory, Culture and Society*, 11, 65–104.

McHoul, A. (1982) *Telling HowTexts Talk: Essays on Reading and Ethnomethodology*. London: Routledge.

McHoul, A. and Watson, D. R. (1984) Two axes for the analysis of 'commonsense' and 'formal' geographical knowledge in classroom talk. *British Journal of the Sociology of Education*, 5(3), 281–302.

Maynard, D. W. (1988) Language, interaction and social problems. *Social Problems*, 35(4), 311–34.

Maynard, D. W. and Clayman, S. E. (1991) The diversity of ethnomethodology. *Annual Review of Sociology*, 17, 385–418.

Mead, G. H. (1934) *Mind, Self and Society*. Chicago: University of Chicago Press.

Mehan, H. (1979) *Learning Lessons: Social Organization in the Classroom*. Cambridge: Harvard University Press.

Miller, G. (1987) Producing family problems: organization and uses of the family perspective and rhetoric in family therapy. *Symbolic Interaction*, 10, 245–65.

Miller, G. (1993) *Enforcing the Work Ethic*. Albany, N.Y.: SUNY Press.

Mitchell, J. C. (1983) Case and situational analysis. *Sociological Review*, 31(2), 187–211.

Moerman, M. (1974) Accomplishing ethnicity. In R. Turner (ed.), *Ethnomethodology*, Harmondsworth: Penguin, 54–68.

Moerman, M. (1988) *Talking Culture: Ethnography and Conversation Analysis*. Philadelphia: University of Pennsylvania Press.

Moerman, M. and Sacks, H. (1971) On Understanding in Conversation. Unpublished paper, 70th annual meeting, American Anthropological Association, New York City, 20 Nov. 1971.

Molotch, H. and Boden, D. (1985) Talking social structure: discourse, domination and the Watergate hearings. *American Sociological Review*, 50(3), 273–88.

Mulkay, M. (1985) *The Word and the World*. London: Allen and Unwin.

Opie, I. and Opie, P. (1959) *The Lore and Language of Schoolchildren*. Oxford: Clarendon Press.

Parsons, T. (1937) *The Structure of Social Action*. New York: McGraw-Hill.

Peräkylä, A. (1995) *AIDS Counselling*. Cambridge: Cambridge University Press.

Peräkylä, A. and Silverman, D. (1991a) Owning experience: describing the experience of other persons. *Text*, 11(3), 441–80.

Peräkylä, A. and Silverman, D. (1991b) Reinterpreting speech-exchange systems: communication formats in AIDS counselling. *Sociology*, 25(4), 627–51.

Peyrot, M. (1987) Circumspection in psychotherapy: structures and strategies of counselor–client interaction. *Semiotica*, 65, 249–68.

Pollner, M. (1987) *Mundane Reason: Reality in Everyday and Sociological Discourse*. Cambridge: Cambridge University Press.

Pomerantz, A. M. (1984) Agreeing and disagreeing with assessments. In Atkinson and Heritage 1984, 57–101.

Potter, J. (1997) Discourse analysis as a way of analysing naturally-occurring talk. In Silverman 1997b, 144–60.

Potter, J. and Wetherell, M. (1987) *Discourse and Social Psychology: Beyond Attitudes and Behaviour*. London: Sage.

Richards, T. J. and Richards, L. (1994) Using computers in qualitative research. In N. K. Denzin and Y. S. Lincoln (eds), *Handbook of Qualitative Research*, London: Sage, 445–62.

Sacks, H. (1963) Sociological description. *Berkeley Journal of Sociology*, 8, 1–16.

Sacks, H. (1972a) An initial investigation of the usability of conversational data for doing sociology. In Sudnow 1972, 31–74.

Sacks, H. (1972b) Notes on police assessment of moral character. In Sudnow 1972, 280–93.

Sacks, H. (1972c) On the analyzability of stories by children. In Gumperz and Hymes 1972, 325–45.

Sacks, H. (1975) Everyone has to lie. In M. Sanches and B. G. Blount (eds), *Sociocultural Dimensions of Language Use*, New York: Academic Press, 57–79.

Sacks, H. (1979) Hotrodder: a revolutionary category. In G. Psathas (ed.), *Everyday Language: Studies in Ethnomethodology*, New York: Irvington, 7–14.

Sacks, H. (1984a) Notes on methodology. In Atkinson and Heritage 1984, 21–7. Based on transcripts of several lectures.

Sacks, H. (1984b) On doing 'being ordinary'. In Atkinson and Heritage 1984, 513–29.

Sacks, H. (1987) On the preferences for agreement and contiguity in sequences in conversation. In G. Button and J. R. E. Lee, *Talk and Social Organization*, Clevedon: Multilingual Matters, 54–69. From a lecture by H. Sacks in 1970, edited by E. Schegloff.

Sacks, H. (1992) *Lectures on Conversation*, ed. by Gail Jefferson, introduction by Emanuel Schegloff. 2 vols, Oxford: Blackwell. Abbreviated as *LC* in the text. Combined in one paperback vol. 1995.

Sacks, H., Schegloff, E. A. and Jefferson, G. (1974) A simplest systematics for the organization of turn-taking in conversation. *Language*, 50(4), 696–735.

Saussure, F. de (1974) *Course in General Linguistics*. London: Fontana.

Schegloff, E. A. (1968) Sequencings in conversational openings. *American Anthropologist*, 70, 1075–95. Repr. in Gumperz and Hymes 1972, 346–80.

Schegloff, E. A. (1972) Notes on a conversational practice: formulating place. In Sudnow 1972, 75–119.

Schegloff, E. A. (1980) Preliminaries to preliminaries: 'Can I ask you a question?' *Sociological Inquiry*, 50(3–4), 104–52.

Schegloff, E. A. (1982) Discourse as an interactional accomplishment: some uses of 'uh huh' and other things that come between sentences. In D. Tannen (ed.), *Georgetown University Round Table on Language and Linguistics: Analyzing Discourse: Text and Talk*, Washington, D.C.: Georgetown University Press, 71–93.

Schegloff, E. A. (1987) Between macro and micro: contexts and other connections. In J. Alexander, B. Giesen, R. Munch and N. Smelser (eds), *The Micro-Macro Link*, Berkeley: University of California Press, 207–34.

Schegloff, E. A. (1991) *Reflections on Talk and Social Structure*. In D. Boden and D. Zimmerman (eds), *Talk and Social Structure: Studies in Ethnomethodology and Conversation Analysis*, Cambridge: Polity Press, 44–70.

Schegloff, E. A. (1992a) Introduction. In Sacks, 1992, vol. 1, ix–lxii; vol. 2, ix–lii.

Schegloff, E. A. (1992b) On talk and its institutional occasions. In Drew and Heritage 1992, 101–36.

Schegloff, E. and Sacks, H. (1974) Opening up closings. In R. Turner (ed.), *Ethnomethodology*, Harmondsworth: Penguin, 233–64.

Schutz, A. (1962) *Collected Papers*, vol. 1. The Hague: Martinus Nijhoff.

Searle, J. (1969) *Speech Acts*. Cambridge: Cambridge University Press.

Sharrock, W. W. (1974) On owning knowledge. In R. Turner (ed.), *Ethnomethodology*, Harmondsworth: Penguin, 45–53.

Sharrock, W. and Anderson, B. (1986) *The Ethnomethodologists*. London: Tavistock.

Silverman, D. (1973) Interview talk: bringing off a research instrument. *Sociology*, 7(1), 31–48.

Silverman, D. (1989) Six rules of qualitative research: a post-Romantic argument. *Symbolic Interaction*, 12(2), 215–30.

Silverman, D. (1993a) *Interpreting Qualitative Data: Strategies for Analysing Talk, Text and Interaction*. London: Sage.

Silverman, D. (1993b) The machinery of interaction: Sacks' *Lectures on Conversation*. *Sociological Review*, 41(4), 731–52.

Silverman, D. (1997a) *Discourses of Counselling: HIV Counselling as Social Interaction*. London: Sage.

Silverman, D. (ed.) (1997b) *Qualitative Research: Theory, Method and Practice*. London: Sage.

Silverman, D. and Gubrium, J. (1994) Competing strategies for analyzing the contexts of social interaction. *Sociological Inquiry*, 64(2), 179–98.

Silverman, D. and Peräkylä, A. (1990) AIDS counselling: the interactional organization of talk about 'delicate' issues._*Sociology of Health and Illness*, 12(3), 293–318.

Silverman, D. and Torode, B. (1980) *The Material Word: Some Theories of Language and its Limits*. London: Routledge and Kegan Paul.

Smith, D. E. (1978) K is mentally ill: the anatomy of a factual account. *Sociology*, 12, 23–55.

Suchman, L. (1987) *Plans and Situated Actions: The Problem of Human–Machine Communication*. Cambridge: Cambridge University Press.

Sudnow, D. (1965) Normal crimes: sociological features of the penal code in a public defender's office. *Social Problems*, 12, 255–76.

Sudnow, D. (ed.) (1972) *Studies in Social Interaction*. New York: Free Press.

Watson, D. R. (1978) Categorizations, authorization and blame-negotiation in conversation. *Sociology*, 12, 105–13.

Watson, D. R. (1987) Interdisciplinary considerations in the analysis of pro-terms. In G. Button and J. Lee (eds), *Talk and Social Organization*, Clevedon: Multilingual Matters, 261–89.

Watson, D. R. (1992) Ethnomethodology, conversation analysis and education: an overview. *International Review of Education*, 38(3), 257–74.

Watson, R. (1996) Some general reflections on 'categorization' and 'sequence' in the analysis of conversation. In S. Hester and P. Eglin (eds), *Culture in Action: Studies in Membership Categorization Analysis*, Lanham: University Press of America.

Watson, R. (n.d.) Categorization and the later work of Harvey Sacks. Paper prepared for a special issue of *Raisons Pratiques*.

Weber, M. (1949) *Methodology of the Social Sciences*. New York: Free Press.

Wittgenstein, L. (1968) *Philosophical Investigations*, Oxford: Basil Blackwell.

Wittgenstein, L. (1971) *Tractatus Logico-Philosophicus*. London: Routledge.

Woolgar, S. (ed.) (1988) *Knowledge and Reflexivity*. London: Sage.

Zimmerman, D. (1992) The interactional organization of calls for emergency assistance. In Drew and Heritage 1992, 418–69.

Zimmerman, D. and West, C. (1975) Sex roles, interruptions and silences in conversations. In B. Thorne and N. Henley (eds), *Language and Sex*, Rowley: Newbury House, 105–29.

Name Index

Subject Index